Core

MODERN WORLD HISTORY

for OCR specification 1937

Nigel Kelly • Greg Lacey

Heinemann

Heinemann Educational Publishers
Halley Court, Jordan Hill, Oxford, OX2 8EJ
a division of Reed Educational and Professional Publishing Ltd

Heinemann is a registered trademark of
Reed Educational and Professional Publishing Ltd

OXFORD MELBOURNE AUCKLAND JOHANNESBURG BLANTYRE GABORONE IBADAN PORTSMOUTH NH (USA) CHICAGO

First published 2001

ISBN 0 435 30830 0

03 02
10 9 8 7 6 5 4 3
This publication is a revised and updated version of *OCR Modern World History* for Syllabus 1607, published in 1999.

Photographic acknowledgements
The author and publisher would like to thank the following for permission to reproduce photographs:

A Krause/The Guardian: 255L; AKG: 58F, 80O, 108C, 113H, 116D, 121A, 124D, 129K, 227M; Bridgeman: 152L; British Library of Economics: 132A; Cartoons UKC/Solo Syndication: 63A; Cartoons UKC/Telegraph Group Ltd: 244T; Centre for the Study of Cartoon and Caricature: 229A, 236H, 245A; Christies Images: 106K; Corbis: 143B, 145D, 155C, 158F, 159H, 169J, 239J, 241M, 251G, 252H, 254K; David King: 92O, 177C, 179E, 180F, 185M, 191D, 192E, 195H, 198L, 200B, 201C, 205G, 208B, 211E, 212B, 240L; Hulton Getty: 51B, 51C, 83D, 98B, 99C, 105I, 117F, 172A, 173C, 181G, 183I, 189B, 190C, 193F, 232B, 247B, 248C, 249E; Hulton/Archive: 6A, 7B, 17J, 36B, 43G, 44H; Imperial War Museum: 28B, 29C, 34B, 38B, 40D; Low/Solo Syndication: 67B, 78K, 96A, 128J, 216A, 220E; Magnum: 250F, 258F; Mary Evans Picture Library: 10E, 19C, 22E, 26A, 42A, 45B, 46E; Museum of London: 24J; Peter Newark: 50A, 138B, 140D, 141E, 142A, 146E, 147F, 148H, 149I, 162D, 168I, 170L, 243P; Popperfoto: 88H, 95Q, 156D, 176B, 184L, 186N, 196I, 221G; Private Collection/Bridgeman Art Library: 39B; Punch: 8C, 13A, 43F: 62K; Scarfe/Sunday Times, 1980: 253I; Topham Picturepoint: 46F; Topham: 72D, 144C, 167H, 243Q

Cover photograph: © Hutton Getty

Designed and typeset by Visual Image, Taunton

Illustrated by Paul Bale and Jane Watkins

Printed and bound in Italy by Printer Trento s.r.l.

Index compiled by Indexing Specialists

The publishers have made every effort to trace copyright holders of material in this book. Any omissions will be rectified in subsequent printings if notice is given to the publisher.

The publisher would like to thank Dr Keir Thorpe for his comments on the original manuscript.

Contents

1 How was British society changed, 1906–18?

In the first twenty years of the twentieth century, British society underwent profound changes. There was a growing awareness that more would have to be done to protect the weakest and poorest members of society – the old and the young, the sick, the unemployed and the low-paid. Previously the fate of these people was not regarded as the responsibility of government, but the Liberal government that came to power in 1906 took a different view. A series of laws was passed which attempted to deal with the problem of poverty. The state set out to guarantee a basic minimum standard of living for all its citizens. The foundations of what became known as the 'welfare state' were laid.

In 1900 Britain was still not a democratic country. Well over half of all adults, including all women, were not allowed to vote in parliamentary elections. The women's movement was about to challenge this. A campaign for women's suffrage (the right to vote) was launched, which reached its peak in the years immediately before the First World War (1914-18) with the violent activities of the Suffragettes. War broke out before the Suffragettes achieved their goal, but the work done by women in helping the war effort finally persuaded even their strongest opponents that they could no longer be excluded from the vote. An Act of 1918 gave many women over the age of 30 the vote. Finally women could play a full part in national political life.

Few aspects of British life were untouched by the First World War. Millions of young men were recruited into the armed forces, of whom nearly a million were killed in the fighting. Their jobs at home were filled by women, many of whom had never been in paid employment before. Society discovered that women were capable of a whole range of tasks once regarded exclusively as men's work. The government was forced to interfere more and more in people's lives. It took over industries, controlled prices, introduced rationing, and finally introduced conscription (compulsory military service). Everything was focused on the war effort, and everyone was expected to make a contribution.

This topic is examined in Paper 2 of the examination. Paper 2-type exercises are included at the end of the chapter. Mark schemes, sample answers and comments can be found in the accompanying Teacher's Resource Pack.

How was British society changed, 1906–18?

Why did the liberal governments introduce reforms to help the young, old and unemployed?

The General Election of 1906 brought a Liberal government to power. Over the next five years, the Liberals passed a series of important social reforms that created the foundations of a 'welfare state' in Britain. From now on the State would look after those too poor to help themselves, but to do this would be expensive. Taxes had to be raised so that money could be spent on giving the poor the help they needed.

This idea of raising money by taxes to help the poor was not universally popular. Many rich people objected to the idea that they would have to pay for the government's reforms. They claimed that helping the poor would just encourage them to be lazy, and make them less likely to help themselves. However, by 1906, fewer and fewer people shared this attitude. Most people had come to recognise that in a civilised society government could not ignore the plight of the poorest members of the community. Why was it, in the early years of the twentieth century, that attitudes became more sympathetic towards the poor?

Working class housing in the East End of London, 1909.

SOURCE A

Reasons for the Liberal reforms

The political background

In the second half of the nineteenth century, Britain began to move towards democracy. At first only the better-off men in society were allowed to vote, but Reform Acts in 1867 and 1884 extended the franchise (the vote) to significant numbers of working-class people. By 1900 about seven times as many men were allowed to vote compared with fifty years earlier, and by this time about half of the electorate came from the working class.

These changes had the effect of focusing national politics on issues which were of interest and concern to working people, though at first they did not really have a political party to represent them. The Liberals and the Tories, the two main parties, both realised how important it would be to appeal to the new electorate, but it was difficult for them both to do this and to represent the interests of their existing middle and upper-class supporters.

It was the trade unions who did most to bring a new political party for the workers into existence. The unions saw that they might achieve their aims of better pay and working conditions through Parliament, In 1900 they helped to set up the Labour Representation Committee, which was to help 'Labour' candidates to stand in Parliamentary elections. The Liberals were keen to co-operate with this new organisation, and in 1903 they reached a secret agreement not to oppose Labour candidates in certain areas of the country. Because of this, 53 Labour MPs were elected in 1906. It is no surprise, then, that the Liberal government formed in that year put a high priority on helping working-class people.

QUESTION

Study Source B.

a What was the cartoonist saying about the relationship between Labour and the Liberal Party?

b Do you think Keir Hardie would have agreed with the cartoonist? Explain your answer.

SOURCE B

A cartoon of 1903 commenting on the relationship between Labour and the Liberal Party. It shows Keir Hardie, one of Labour's early leaders.

Social and economic changes

Due to the Industrial Revolution, Britain was transformed during the nineteenth century. Factories and towns developed where previously there had only been countryside. This change brought many problems. Conditions in the new industrial towns were often terrible. Housing for the workers was poor, cramped and dirty, often with no proper sanitation. Epidemic diseases, such as cholera, spread easily. Working conditions in the factories were dangerous and unhealthy. Eventually governments were forced to deal with these problems, and Factory Acts, Education Acts and Public Health Acts followed.

At the start of the nineteenth century governments interfered very little in most people's lives, but by 1900 the idea that only the government was powerful enough to deal with society's most serious problems was well established. The Liberals after 1906 took this idea an important step further by accepting that governments should not only protect the population from harm, but that they should also try to guarantee a good, basic minimum standard of living for everyone, even if the only way to do this was to take money from the rich to help the poor.

Political personalities

The Liberal governments after 1906 included a number of outstanding personalities. The determination and vision of these men was sufficient to carry out a sweeping programme of reforms, sometimes in the face of violent opposition. Amongst these were two who stood out because of their radical, reformist beliefs, and who, between them, were responsible for many of the Liberals' most important reforms.

David Lloyd George, who was Chancellor of the Exchequer after 1908, came from a humble Welsh background. He was well-known for his fiery speeches and his willingness to whip up the feelings of the poor against the rich and privileged. He

QUESTION

Look at Source C.

a Explain the message of the cartoon.

b Do you think the cartoonist approved of the 'People's Budget'? Explain your answer.

SOURCE C

PUNCH, OR THE LONDON CHARIVARI.—APRIL 28, 1909.
BERNARD PARTRIDGE.
RICH FARE.
THE GIANT LLOYD-GORGIBUSTER: "FEE, FI, FO, FAT,
I SMELL THE BLOOD OF A PLUTOCRAT;
BE HE ALIVE OR BE HE DEAD,
I'LL GRIND HIS BONES TO MAKE MY BREAD."

A cartoon showing Lloyd George, and commenting on the 'People's Budget' of 1909.

was mistrusted by his colleagues because of his obvious talent and ambition. It was his 'People's Budget' of 1909 which increased taxes to pay for the government's reforms, and provoked a political crisis when the House of Lords refused to accept it. He was also the mastermind behind the National Insurance scheme. Winston Churchill joined the Cabinet in 1908, and was responsible for the system of unemployment insurance set up in 1911. Both these men later became Prime Minister – Lloyd George in the First World War, and Churchill in the Second.

Poverty in 1906

Perhaps the most important reason of all for the reforms of the Liberal governments after 1906 was the growing public awareness of the problem of poverty. Britain was one of the richest countries in the world, yet millions of its citizens lived below the poverty line.

Many people in the nineteenth century thought that it was the poor who were responsible for their own poverty; that they were lazy, or wasted money on alcohol, tobacco and other non-essential goods. Although there was help for the poor, this help was very limited and based on principles set down in the Poor Law of 1834. The most important feature of this Law was that any able-bodied person wanting help would have to agree to go into a workhouse. These were set up all over the country and paid for out of the rates (money collected from householders by the parish). Conditions in workhouses were deliberately made so hard that only the most desperate would want to enter. The food and clothing provided were very basic. Men, women and children were separated and were forced to work for long hours at hard and boring tasks. Above all there was a great sense of shame at having to depend on the workhouse for charity.

In fact, the 1834 Poor Law never worked totally as intended. In some industrial areas in times of economic hardship, so many people needed help that they could not possibly all be found places in

SOURCE D

When we entered the workhouse in 1895, my mother was shown to the women's ward, and my brother and I went in another direction into the children's ward. Once a week we were allowed to meet. How well I remember that first visiting day, the shock of seeing mother garbed in workhouse clothes. How forlorn and embarrassed she looked. In one week she had aged and grown thin.

From the autobiography of Charlie Chaplin, the famous comedian.

QUESTIONS

1 What social and economic changes were occurring in nineteenth-century Britain?

2 How did these changes affect Britain's political life?

3 What was new about the attitudes of the Liberal governments after 1906 to social problems?

workhouses. In these cases, the authorities gave *outdoor relief* – in other words they gave handouts of money or food, which is exactly what the Law was supposed to avoid. The most serious problem, however, was that the Poor Law was not really intended to solve the problem of poverty, but rather to reduce the amount spent on the poor. It was reasonably effective in achieving this, and Poor Law Unions in many parts of the country worked well in providing not just poor relief but also some basic education and medical care for the poor. However, by the end of the nineteenth century it was becoming ever clearer that poverty remained one of society's greatest problems.

- *Helping the sick*
  Those who were sick could not work. Even in the nineteenth century the link between illness and poverty was recognised, and outdoor relief was available to those in need. By the end of the century Poor Law hospitals offering free treatment had been built throughout the country, providing the basis for a national hospital system.

- *Helping the unemployed*
  By the end of the nineteenth century, the attitude of the Poor Law authorities to the unemployed had softened a little. From 1886 local authorities were allowed to provide work for the unemployed, and the Unemployed Workmen Act of 1905 allowed them to raise money specifically for this purpose.

QUESTIONS

1 What arrangements did the Poor Law of 1834 make for dealing with the able-bodied poor?

2 By the end of the nineteenth century, what help was available to poor people who were not able-bodied?

3 Look at Source E. What can you tell about life in a workhouse from this source?

4 What were the weaknesses in the system of dealing with the poor?

SOURCE E

Women in the St Pancras workhouse eating a meal, 1901.

- *Helping the old*
  The old were also entitled to outdoor relief, but many had to be admitted to workhouses in order to be looked after. Old age was probably the single most important cause of poverty. Estimates put the proportion of old people receiving relief at around 30-40 per cent. Their treatment in the workhouse improved as the century progressed. Eventually couples were not split up, they were allowed visitors, and given allowances for 'luxuries' like tea and tobacco.

- *Helping the young*
  Pauper (poor) children had to be admitted to the workhouse along with their parents, but attitudes towards them tended to be slightly kinder, since they could not really be blamed for being poor. Many Poor Law Unions attempted to remove children from the workhouses by sending them to live with local families. Schooling was also provided.

QUESTION

Look at Source F.

a Was this a good or a bad diet? Explain your answer.

b Do you think that the labourer's family were poor? Explain your answer.

SOURCE F

A week's menus for the labourer's family

Menu of meals provided during week ending June 21, 1901

	Breakfast.	Dinner.	Tea.	Supper.
Friday	Bread, butter, tea.	Bread, bacon.	Bread, butter, lettuce, tea.	
Saturday	Bread, butter, tea.	Meat, potatoes, Yorkshire pudding.	Bread, butter, tea, onions.	Fish, bread.
Sunday	Fish, bread, tea.	Beef, cabbage, potatoes, rhubarb pie (1).	Bread, butter, tea-cake, tea.	Bread, butter, tea-cake.
Monday	Bread, butter, tea-cake.	Cold meat, potatoes, pie.	Bread, butter, tea-cake, custard.	Bread, butter, pie.
Tuesday	Bread, bacon-fat, tea.	Cold meat, potatoes, pie.	Bread, meat, dripping.	Bread, cheese.
Wednesday	Bread, butter, tea, bacon.	Hashed cabbage, meat, bread.	Bread, butter, tea, lettuce.	
Thursday	Bread, butter, tea.	Liver, bread, bread pudding.	Bread, butter, tea.	Bread, butter.

(1) Rhubarb and cabbage given.

A typical week's menu for a labouring family in York.

Thus although the working of the Poor Law became more flexible towards the end of the nineteenth century, it was only concerned with coping with the worst *effects*, rather than dealing with the *causes*, of poverty. Before the causes could be tackled, detailed studies of the lives of the poor would be needed, so that the nature, extent and causes of poverty could be identified.

Studies in poverty: Charles Booth and Seebohm Rowntree

Towards the end of the nineteenth century many books were published about poverty. These did much to make the general public more sympathetic towards the poor. Two of the most influential studies were carried out by Charles Booth and Seebohm Rowntree.

Booth studied the lives of the poor in London, and Rowntree concentrated on York.

Between 1886 and 1903 Booth published a series of volumes called *Life and Labour of the People in London*. Using evidence from house-to-house enquiries, school records, census returns, and interviews with doctors and clergy who worked in these areas, he described in great detail what it was like to be poor. He defined poverty as an income of less than £1 a week for a family of five, and calculated that around 30 per cent of the population of these areas lived below this 'poverty line'. He demonstrated the link between poverty and a high death rate. He identified the main causes of poverty: sickness, old age, unemployment, large families, low wages. Above all, he demonstrated that the great majority of the poor were not responsible for their own poverty, and that they were forced into poverty by factors beyond their control.

In case anyone should imagine that these conditions were only to be found in London, the publication of Rowntree's *Poverty: a Study of Town Life* in 1901 demonstrated that the situation was just as bad even in a medium-sized provincial city like York. Rowntree's findings were similar to those of Booth. He, too, found around 30 per cent of the population living in poverty, with an income of around £1 a week or less. Above all, both studies demonstrated that the existing Poor Law was totally inadequate for dealing with the problem of poverty.

After the publication of these studies there was no longer any excuse for a lack of action. When the Boer War broke out in 1899, 40 per cent of all recruits were found to be unfit for military service because of the effects of poverty, and the government had to set up a committee to enquire into the 'Physical Deterioration of the People'. This was followed in 1905 by the appointment of a Royal Commission to review the Poor Law. Although this Commission did not report until 1909, and its members disagreed over what improvements to recommend, its appointment showed that the problem of poverty had become one of the major issues of the time.

SOURCE G

There are ten millions in this country enduring year after year the torture of living while lacking a sufficiency of the bare necessities of life...Shame on rich Britain that she should tolerate so much poverty among her people...There is plenty of wealth in this country. What is wanted is a fairer distribution.

Lloyd George writing in 1906.

QUESTIONS

1 What did Booth and Rowntree find out about poverty in Britain?

2 Why was the work of Booth and Rowntree important?

3 Read Source G. Do you think most people in Britain at that time would have agreed with Lloyd George? Explain your answer.

How effective were the Liberal reforms?

Children

- The School Meals Act of 1906 allowed local authorities to provide free school meals for the poor. By 1914 around 150, 000 free meals a day were being served.

- Free school medical inspections were introduced from 1907. All children were to be inspected by a doctor or nurse at least once a year. At first, any necessary treatment was not free, but this too was provided from 1912.

- A collection of measures in 1908 became known as the 'Children's Charter'. These dealt with a wide range of issues affecting children. Child Care committees were set up to try and support families where children were obviously suffering from the effects of poverty or neglect. Young offenders were dealt with in special courts, and the probation system was set up, whereby offenders were released as long as they then behaved, and were placed under the supervision of a probation officer. For those cases where it was necessary to keep young people in custody, borstals (reforming houses for young people) were established so that they would not have to be sent to the same jails as adults. It was made illegal to sell tobacco, alcohol or fireworks to young people under the age of 16. The working hours for children were strictly limited, and it was made illegal for children to do certain types of unsuitable work.

QUESTION

Look at Source A.

a Why did the cartoonist refer to Old Age Pensions as a 'gift'?

b Do you think the cartoonist approved of Old Age Pensions? Explain your answer, using details of the cartoon.

SOURCE A

PUNCH, OR THE LONDON CHARIVARI.—JANUARY 6, 1909.

THE NEW YEAR'S GIFT.

A cartoon about the introduction of old age pensions, first paid in 1909.

Old age pensions

The Old Age Pensions Act was passed in 1908. This established a system to give the poorest people over the age of 70 (who were those with an income of less than £21 a year), a pension of 5s a week which they could collect at their local Post Office. Smaller pensions were paid to those who were slightly better-off. The fact that the pension was paid outright as a 'present', with no contribution to it from the old themselves, was a complete novelty, and was much criticised by opponents of the government. They claimed it would discourage old people in future from saving for their own retirement, and would rob them of their independence by making them dependent on government handouts.

The pensions were paid for out of taxes collected from the richer people, and the government felt that national finances would be able to afford it. Actually, they seriously underestimated the numbers of old people who would qualify for a pension. It was expected that the scheme would cover about half a million people, but by 1913 nearly double this number were receiving pensions. In some areas of the country as many as four out of every five old people qualified for the pension.

QUESTIONS

1 How did the Liberal reforms improve life for children?

2 What did the Liberals do to help the unemployed and the low paid?

Reactions to the introduction of old age pensions

SOURCE B

There were one or two poorer couples, just holding on to their homes, but in daily fear of the workhouse. The Poor Law authorities allowed people too old to work a small weekly sum as outdoor relief; but it was not enough to live on. Unless they had very successful children to help support them, there came a time when the home had to be broken up. When twenty years later, the old age pensions began, life was transformed for such aged cottagers. They no longer worried. They were suddenly rich. Independent for life!

At first, when some of them went to the Post Office to draw their pension, tears of gratitude would run down their faces, and they would say as they picked up their money, 'God bless that Lord George', for they could not believe one so powerful and munificent could be a plain Mr.

Remembered by Flora Thompson, in her account of rural daily life in the 1890s, Lark Rise to Candleford.

SOURCE C

We've often thought it would be best for us to die, and sometimes I've almost prayed to be taken, for we were just a burden to our children who kept us. They were good and wouldn't let us go into the workhouse if they could help it. But now we want to go on living for ever, because we give them our ten shillings a week, and it pays them to have us with them.

The husband of a couple aged over 90 talking to a journalist about the introduction of old age pensions.

SOURCE D

How can any sensible man regard the situation (the introduction of pensions) without dismay? The strength of this kingdom has been its great reserve of wealth and the sturdy independent character of its people. The Bill which is being pushed through the House of Commons with haste and enthusiasm will destroy both these strengths. The money from unjust taxation will be distributed in small hand outs and will weaken the character of the people by teaching them to rely, not on their own hard work and savings, but on the state.

A letter to *The Times* (1908) about the Old Age Pensions Bill.

Labour Exchanges

The idea of labour exchanges was put forward in an important report on unemployment published in 1909 by the economist, William Beveridge. He saw the problem of unemployment as being caused largely by inefficiency. Too many men were employed in casual work, from which they would be frequently laid off. Then they would face the problem of finding more work. Beveridge felt they should be given help to find good, permanent employment. The Labour Exchanges Act of 1909 was intended to help them do this.

Labour Exchanges were set up throughout the country and the unemployed were expected to register with them. Local employers looking for workers would notify the Labour Exchange of vacancies, and unemployed workers would then be put in touch with these employers. This was a convenient arrangement which was efficient and meant that the unemployed no longer had to go around looking for work for themselves. The first Labour Exchanges were set up in 1910, and by 1914 there was a national network of around 400 exchanges, filling a million vacancies a year.

Low pay was also an important cause of poverty. The Trade Boards Act of 1909 tried to do something about problems of low pay and poor conditions in what were known as the 'sweated industries', small-scale industries not covered by the rules of the various Factory Acts. The Act meant that minimum rates of pay could be established for these trades.

National Insurance

Even reasonably well-off workers could be plunged into poverty if they lost their jobs. Many already paid into private insurance schemes, and some unions also arranged benefits for their members. Roughly 50 per cent of the working population had taken out some kind of insurance against sickness, but a much lower proportion, around 10 per cent, were covered against the effects of unemployment. Lloyd George was aware of health insurance schemes already operating nationally in other countries, and he chose the German system as the one to copy.

SOURCE E

The first person to draw an old age pension, 1909.

The National Insurance Act of 1911 was in two parts. The first dealt with health insurance, and the second with unemployment insurance.

QUESTIONS

1. Read Sources B, C and D. Which two of these sources are the most similar? Explain your answer.
2. What were the arguments for and against the introduction of old age pensions?

Health insurance

This scheme was compulsory, and covered all workers earning £160 a year or less. In 1911, £160 a year was a good wage, and the insurance therefore covered much of the working population – around 16 million people in total. Out of their wages, people had to pay 4d a week (17s a year) into an insurance fund. Employers had to add 3d to this, and the government 2d, making a total of 9d a week (nearly £2 a year) for each worker.

Employers were responsible for running the scheme; they collected contributions from their workers' wages, and stamped each worker's national insurance card as evidence that payments had been received. The insurance cover itself was not provided by the government, but instead was in the hands of large insurance companies and 'Friendly Societies'. The scheme gave workers free medical care from a doctor, although workers still had to pay for their own medicines. After at first opposing the plan, doctors soon changed their minds when they realised that it would guarantee them much more work than they had ever had before. When ill, or unable to work, workers could claim payment of 10s a week for 26 weeks. The scheme also included a maternity benefit payment of 30s on the birth of a child, but apart from this families of insured workers were not covered.

SOURCE F

Taffy was a Welshman.
Taffy was a thief.

A chant directed against Lloyd George by workers who objected to having to pay national insurance contributions.

QUESTION

Read Source F. Do you think it was fair to call Lloyd George a thief? Explain your answer.

Unemployment insurance

This part of the National Insurance Act was the work of Winston Churchill. Unlike health insurance, which was provided in several countries before Britain, unemployment insurance was available nowhere else.

This scheme did not include all workers. It was intended to protect men in industries particularly affected by seasonal unemployment, such as building, shipbuilding and engineering. It covered about two and a half million workers. Contributions to the fund were 2.5d a week from the worker and 2.5d from the employer. When unemployed, workers in the scheme could claim 7s a week for up to 15 weeks, not enough to live on, but enough to help them cope until they found another job. Benefits were paid out at a Labour Exchange, and to receive the money unemployed men had therefore to be registered with the Labour Exchange to be looking for alternative work.

The significance of the Liberal reforms

Consider Sources G–J, and decide for yourself how significant the reforms of the Liberals were.

SOURCE G

The 1911 Act (the National Insurance Act) was not really part of a programme towards a socialist state; in fact, it was quite the opposite. By insisting upon the insurance principle, the government was making the point that it was the efforts of *individuals* that paid for the benefits they received. The Liberal governments of 1906-14 did not lay the foundations of the welfare state; they created a social service state in which everyone was expected to contribute towards the benefits they received in times of need.

Quoted from a recent British history book.

SOURCE H

The years between 1906 and 1914 saw the building of the foundations of the welfare state of today. The Liberals were prepared to go further than the Victorians by allowing the state to take an active part in people's lives. By 1914 they had improved on the work of their predecessors, enlarged the field of direct state aid, and pointed the way to the future. They had not produced a social revolution as their opponents predicted...Their proposals were not very extreme; for all the fuss, there was virtually no redistribution of income (when money is taken from the rich to be distributed to others).

From a British history book published in 1971.

SOURCE I

By this Act (the National Insurance Act of 1911), Lloyd George introduced into Great Britain the scheme of paying for social reform mainly out of the pockets of the poor. Instead of taxation falling chiefly on the richer classes, he successfully introduced a different sort of 'sideways' redistribution, whereby the healthy and employed workers were made to contribute towards the needs of the sick and the workless.

From *A History of The Common People* published in 1938.

SOURCE J

CRESCENDO;
OR, THE TUNE THE OLD COW'S LIKELY TO DIE OF.
THE COW. "STOP! STOP! THIS ISN'T MILKING; IT'S MURDER!"

A British cartoon of 1914, showing Lloyd George, then Chancellor of the Exchequer.

QUESTIONS

1. Look at Source J. How accurate is the impression this cartoon gives of the impact of the Liberal reforms?
2. Why does Source J give a different impression of the impact of the reforms from the other three sources?
3. How far do Sources G, H and I agree about the significance of the Liberal reforms? Explain your answer.
4. Which of these four sources do you think gives the fairest judgement on the Liberal reforms? Explain your answer.

What were the arguments for and against women's suffrage?

In nineteenth-century Britain, men and women were not equal. Economically women were dependent on men, socially they were expected to be obedient to men, and legally they had fewer rights than men. The range of employment open to them was very limited, and in any case, married women were not expected to work. As late as 1911, barely 10 per cent of married women were in paid employment.

However, by 1900, attitudes were beginning to change. It was becoming easier for women to gain a proper education, and to train for certain professions, mainly teaching. Indeed, by 1914, more girls were staying in education after the age of 16 than boys. Inventions such as the telephone and typewriter brought women into offices, and the development of shops and department stores opened up new job opportunities for women as shop assistants. Young, unmarried, middle-class women, in particular, benefited from these opportunities, and could lead more independent lives. It was just as well that they could: Britain's population was unbalanced, with well over a million more women than men. Out of these social changes, a women's movement, campaigning for women's rights, began to develop. By the turn of the century, this movement focused on one issue in particular – women's suffrage (the right to vote).

QUESTIONS

1 Why was a campaign for women's suffrage beginning by the end of the nineteenth century?

2 Why did some people think it would be a bad idea for women to have the vote?

3 Read Source B. Do you think Prime Minister Asquith wanted women to have the vote? Explain your answer.

SOURCE A

The inclusion of women in politics would harm the number, character and strength of our future race. It would limit women's ability and inclination for motherhood, and would lead to their unwillingness to manage the home, and home is the first and lasting strength of social life in all countries.

From a speech given in February 1912 by Charles Hobhouse, a member of the Liberal government.

SOURCE B

There are very few issues in politics which arouse such exaggerated language both from one side and the other. I am sometimes tempted to think, when I listen to the arguments of the supporters of women's suffrage, that there is nothing to be said for it. And sometimes I am tempted to think, when I listen to the arguments of opponents of women's suffrage, that there is nothing to be said against it.

Prime Minister Asquith, speaking in the House of Commons, May 1913.

Arguments for and against women's suffrage

Against

- It was claimed by some men that politics was an unsuitable activity for women. They said that women had no interest in politics, and would not understand difficult political issues.
- Many women, including Queen Victoria, were against the idea of giving women the vote.
- There were many more important social issues to be fighting for, which would affect the lives of large numbers of women, rather than the vote, which was only really of interest to a small number of middle-class women.
- Not all men had the vote at this time, so why should women have it?

SOURCE C

SHE. IT IS TIME I GOT OUT OF THIS PLACE. WHERE SHALL I FIND THE KEY?
CONVICTS AND LUNATICS HAVE NO VOTE FOR PARLIAMENT
Should all Women be classed with these?
Emily J. Harding Andrews

A British cartoon published in 1910.

QUESTIONS

Look at Source C.

1. What is the message of this cartoon?
2. Was the cartoon drawn by an opponent or a supporter of women's rights? Explain your answer.

- Almost nobody, even male supporters of women's suffrage, thought you could give the vote to all women. But giving the vote to some women (the wealthiest, or the most educated) might give an advantage to one political party (probably the Conservatives) over the other (the Liberals).

- Opponents of women's suffrage claimed that the violent tactics of some of the campaigners proved women did not deserve the vote.

- Women should not be able to vote because they would take no part in protecting the country in time of war (an argument used more and more as war approached).

For

- Women had as much right to the vote as men.

- Votes for women had already been introduced in other parts of the world, such as New Zealand, and parts of the USA and Australia.

- Some women (since 1888) already had the right to vote in local elections. Why not in parliamentary elections too?

- Modern women were more independent and educated than women used to be.

- It would be democratic to give women the vote. Through the nineteenth century the right to vote had been given to more and more men – now was the time to include women.

SOURCE D

Suppose, for instance, the great majority of men were in favour of a war against Russia, and the women were against it, or even that the women were in favour and the men against it. In either case it would be felt that as the men supply by far the greater part of the blood and the money which would be spent in a war, and are in a far better position to judge the effect of such a war on the honour, welfare and commerce of the country, the final decision must rest with them.

From an article in *The Girl's Own Paper*, May 1896.

QUESTIONS

1 Some of the arguments against women's suffrage seem strange to us now. Why, then, were these arguments used at that time?

2 Do you think that all men would have opposed women's rights, and all women supported the campaign for the vote? Explain your answer.

3 Read Source D. Why do you think this article was published?

How effective were the activities of the Suffragists and the Suffragettes?

The Suffragists

By the end of the nineteenth century, the campaign for women's rights was well under way. In 1897 Millicent Fawcett formed the NUWSS (National Union of Women's Suffrage Societies) which united most of the existing campaign groups into a single, national organisation. The NUWSS was orderly, moderate and believed in using peaceful, persuasive tactics. Its members were known as Suffragists. Their campaign was quite successful in getting the issue of votes for women into the public eye, and they won a good deal of support for their cause. Their slow but sure approach would probably have succeeded eventually, but some women did not want to wait that long.

The Women's Social and Political Union (WSPU) – the Suffragettes

In 1903 a group of Suffragists, frustrated by the lack of progress made by the NUWSS, broke away and formed their own organisation, the WSPU (Women's Social and Political Union). This group was led by Emmeline Pankhurst, and her daughter, Christabel. Another Pankhurst daughter, Sylvia, was also a leading figure in the movement, but her priorities were rather different. She worked in the East End of London, trying to help improve conditions for poor women in that area. This led to quarrels with her mother and sister, and eventually Sylvia formed her own organisation, the Women's Suffrage Federation, in protest against her mother's support for the First World War.

What action did the Suffragettes take?

Members of the WSPU were determined to use direct, and if necessary violent, actions to achieve their aims. The organisation was largely middle-class in nature, which made their noisy, awkward and 'unladylike' behaviour totally mystifying to their opponents. They soon became known as the 'Suffragettes'. At first their campaign consisted of demonstrations and minor acts of public disorder, such as chaining themselves to the railings outside Buckingham Palace, or disturbing the meetings of political opponents. However, their frustration increased as, time and again, Parliament discussed, but refused to agree, proposals for women's suffrage. They turned to violent, illegal methods, such as smashing windows, arson, and assaults on leading politicians.

SOURCE A

Our heckling campaign made women's suffrage a matter of news – it had never been that before. Now the newspapers were full of us. We woke up the old suffrage associations. We had defied the police, we were awake at last. We were prepared to do something that women had never done before – to fight for themselves, for their own human rights.

From Emmeline Pankhurst's autobiography.

SOURCE B

Be very careful not to open suspicious parcels arriving by post. On the other hand do not leave them lying unopened in the house. They should be dealt with carefully and promptly. These harpies (i.e. the Suffragettes) are quite capable of trying to burn us out.

A letter from Winston Churchill to his wife, written in February 1913.

SOURCE C

From every part of the crowded and brilliantly lit streets came the crash of splintered glass. Suddenly there was another crash in front of them; on the other side of the street; behind – everywhere. Scared shop assistants came running out on the pavements; traffic stopped; policemen sprang this way and that; five minutes later the streets were a procession of excited groups, each surrounding a woman wrecker being led into custody at the nearest police station. Meanwhile the shopping quarter of London had plunged itself into a sudden twilight. Shutters were hurriedly fitted, the rattle of iron curtains being drawn came from every side. Guards of commissionaires and shop-men were quickly mounted, and any unaccompanied lady in sight, especially if she carried a handbag, became an object of threatening suspicion.

The *Daily Mail*, 2 March 1912, reporting on the Suffragettes' window-smashing demonstration.

QUESTIONS

1 What were the differences between the Suffragists and the Suffragettes?

2 Look at Source C.
What tactics did the Suffragettes use to bring the cause of votes for woman to the notice of the public?

SOURCE D

In 1913 the Suffragettes found their first martyr when Miss Emily Davison, after having laid a wreath before Joan of Arc's statue, flung herself to her death under the hoofs of the King's horse at the Derby.

From a history book written in 1960.

SOURCE E

Emily Davison is knocked to the ground by the King's horse at the 1913 Derby.

The Suffragette campaign reached a new peak of violence in 1913 when yet again Parliament failed to grant women the vote. There was a renewed outburst of window smashing, cutting telegraph wires, and burning empty buildings. Politicians lived in dread of receiving letter bombs. Charles Hobhouse, the well-known Liberal opponent of women's suffrage, frequently received letters full of grass seed and pepper from local suffragettes who knew he suffered from hay fever. More seriously, there was an arson attack on his home which, fortunately, only succeeded in setting his back door on fire.

The 1913 Derby

Events at the famous horse race, the Derby, brought the situation to a climax. During the race, a suffragette, Emily Davison, walked out in front of the horses. She tried to grab hold of one of them, which happened to be the King's horse, Anmer, but in the collision she was knocked to the ground and fatally injured. She died in hospital four days later. It is clear that her actions were a deliberate protest, probably an attempt to draw attention to the Suffragette cause by stopping or disrupting the race. Many people have assumed that she committed suicide in order to be a martyr to the women's cause. Certainly her death was treated that way by the Suffragettes. There is, though, as you will see from the sources, considerable doubt about this interpretation of what happened.

QUESTIONS

1 Did Emily Davison deliberately kill herself?

2 Did she aim to involve the King's horse in her protest?

3 Was her death important?

SOURCE F

The desperate act of the woman who rushed from the rails onto the course as the horses swept around Tattenham Corner, apparently from some mad notion that she could spoil the race, will not impress the general public. She did not interfere with the race, but she nearly killed a jockey as well as herself, and she brought down a valuable horse.

A deed of this kind, we need hardly say, is not likely to increase the popularity of the cause with the public. Reckless fanaticism is not regarded by them as a qualification for the franchise. Persons who wantonly destroy property and endanger lives must be either desperately wicked or entirely unbalanced.

From *The Times*, 5 June 1913.

SOURCE G

In 1988 historians found and examined the contents of Emily Davison's handbag, and discovered she had bought a return ticket that day, and that her diary included a number of appointments in the days immediately after the Derby.

From a recent history book.

SOURCE H

The cause needs a martyr.

Emily Davison.

SOURCE I

The coroner, in summing up, said he did not think that Miss Davison aimed at the King's horse in particular, but that her intention was to upset the race. The jury would probably dismiss from their minds the idea that she intended to take her own life.

A report on the inquest into Emily Davison's death, published in *The Suffragette* newspaper, 13 June 1913.

The reactions of the authorities

At first many men did not take the Suffragettes seriously. Then they became exasperated as they realised that the Suffragettes were serious and were not going to give up. But above all, the authorities were rather confused about how to deal with them. The problem was that decent, well brought up young ladies were not supposed to behave like the Suffragettes. The fact that most Suffragettes came from middle-class backgrounds, were educated and apparently had quite comfortable lives, made it even harder for men to understand what they were complaining about. The frustration and hostility this caused led to many Suffragettes being very roughly treated by men who objected to their activities, and tried to break up their demonstrations.

QUESTIONS

1 Look at Source J. Explain what is happening in this picture.

2 What techniques did the artist who painted the poster use to turn people's opinions against the government? Use details from the poster to explain your answer.

SOURCE J

An election poster using the issue of force-feeding to attack the government.

The tactics of the Suffragettes forced the authorities to take action against them. More and more were sent to jail as punishment for their protests. The Suffragettes responded by going on hunger strike. Scared of the consequences of women starving themselves to death, the prison authorities felt they had no choice but to force-feed the hunger strikers, which caused a public outcry and led to widespread criticism. Finally, in 1913, parliament passed what was known as the 'Cat and Mouse' Act. This allowed prisons to release hunger-strikers whose health was deteriorating, but once the women had recovered they could be arrested again and taken back to prison to continue their sentence. After her arrest in February 1913 Emmeline Pankhurst went on hunger strike. During the rest of the year she was released and re-arrested on six occasions as she repeatedly went back on hunger strike.

QUESTIONS

1 'By 1914 the Suffragettes had not succeeded in winning votes for women. This means their campaign was a failure.' Explain whether or not you agree with the statement.

2 Do you think the Suffragists would have done better without the Suffragettes? Explain your answer.

Conclusion: Did the Suffragettes help the women's cause?

Historians are undecided whether or not the Suffragettes' campaign was effective. They certainly caught the public's attention. The problem was that their violent tactics lost them much support which they might otherwise have gained through the justice of their cause. Despite several votes in parliament on the issue, by the time the First World War broke out in the summer of 1914, women's suffrage still had not been achieved. The Suffragettes abandoned their campaign and supported the war effort. As matters turned out, this was the most effective way of achieving their aims. In the end it was not violent protests and demonstrations that won women the vote, but the contribution they made to winning the war.

SOURCE K

Emmeline Pankhurst being arrested at a Suffragette demonstration in 1914.

How did women contribute to the war effort?

Women in employment during the First World War

When the war broke out in August 1914, the women's movement immediately abandoned the struggle for the vote, and leading suffragists and suffragettes promised that their followers would devote themselves to the struggle of winning the war. In the first rush of enthusiasm which greeted the outbreak of war, as men flocked to join the armed forces, women prepared to take the places at work that men left behind. However, to start with, things did not work out quite that way. Only in March 1915 did the government get round to creating a register of women willing to do war work, but even then it failed to find enough work for all the volunteers to do.

However, by this time individual women had begun to find work for themselves as drivers, bus conductors, police, railway staff – all traditionally men's work – but there was no official blessing for their efforts. In July 1915, as a result of growing frustration at how little was being done, the Suffragettes organised a huge demonstration in London demanding the 'Right to Serve'. It seemed to do the trick; from this point on, numbers of women entering vital war work of various kinds increased rapidly.

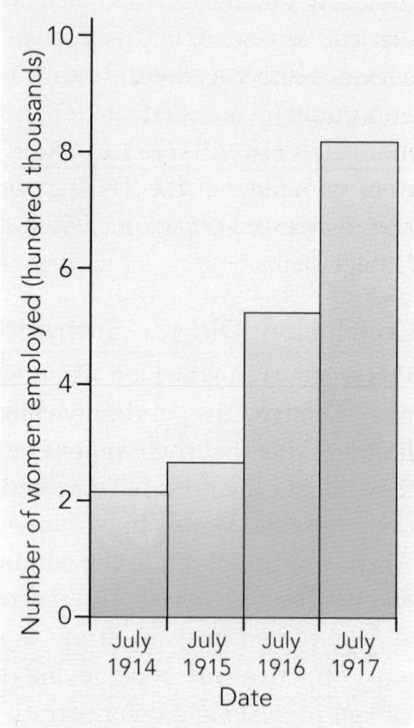

Employment of women in the munitions industry.

QUESTIONS

1 Why were women needed to help the war effort?

2 What kind of work did women do in the war?

3 How did the experience of war work change women's lives?

SOURCE A

Women working in an engineering factory in 1917.

The demand for female labour increased even more after the introduction of conscription (compulsory military service for men) in 1916. During the war a total of around five million men joined the armed forces. To keep British industry going, it was vital that their places at work were filled. Women worked in factories, steel mills, driving buses, building ships, or working in agriculture in the 'Land Army'. Perhaps most importantly, they worked in huge numbers in the munitions factories, making bullets and shells. Some women went to the war zones to help out, and did valuable work in the Voluntary Aid Detachment, Women's Auxiliary Army Corps, and Women's Royal Naval Service.

	Number of women employed	
Type of work	1914	1918
Industrial work	2,200,000	3,000,000
Transport	15,000	117,000
Commerce (office work)	505,000	934,000
Government (inc. teachers)	262,000	460,000

The increase in women's employment, 1914–18.

For large numbers of middle-class women, employment during the war was the first time they had received their own wage packet and been financially independent from their husbands. For many working-class women, of course, working was nothing new, but the war gave all women a much greater sense of their value to society. Although many lost their jobs once the war was over and the men returned home, attitudes had changed permanently, and there were never again such clear divisions between men's and women's work.

SOURCE B

I was working filling the bullets. You sat there with boxes of empty bullets, and you filled them with powder from a big thing like a dispenser. Then we put them into trays, and a couple of men came to take them away. There were people there working with liddite and cordite. Their faces went all yellow from the yellow stuff. You wouldn't sit near them, because if your clothes touched them, all the yellow stuff would come out. They had to have a place apart from us. One day some flames started to come along the line towards us, and two men in the shop got hold of us and threw us outside onto the grass. It was raining like the dickens. They knew something was going to happen. The alarm was going and Queenie, our supervisor, had to go back for her watch. She was blown to pieces.

Interview in 1984 with a woman who was describing her experiences as a munitions worker in the First World War.

SOURCE C

The wartime business girl is to be seen any night dining out alone or with a friend, in the moderate priced restaurants in London. Formerly she would never have had her meal in town unless in the company of a man friend. But now with money and without men she is more and more beginning to dine out.

From the *Daily Mail*, April 1916.

SOURCE D

They appear more alert, more critical of the conditions under which they work, more ready to make a stand against injustice than their pre-war selves. They have a keener appetite for experience and pleasure, and a tendency quite new to their class to protest against wrongs even before they become intolerable.

Comments about women workers, from the Report of the Chief Factory Inspector, 1916.

How were civilians affected by the war?

Recruiting

At the start of the war, volunteers rushed to join the armed forces. Lord Kitchener, the Minister for War, was in charge of raising an army. There was a genuine surge of patriotism, encouraged by the belief that Britain was right to go to war against the brutal aggression of Germany. There was also a widespread misunderstanding of what the war would be like. People had a romantic idea of war as an exciting adventure that would, in any case, be over before Christmas. Over half a million men joined up in the first six weeks of the war, many of them worried that if they waited, they might miss the 'fun'.

QUESTION

Study Sources A, B, C. Explain the various ways in which the authorities ensured enough men joined the armed forces.

SOURCE A

'Name please.'
'Austin J Heraty, 15 Bailey Street, Newcastle.'
'Age?'
'18, sir.'
The sergeant looked at me and said, 'Did you say 18, Mr Heraty? I am very sorry, but I'll tell you what you can do. You can walk around the town, but if you come back into this room tonight, you must be 19 years of age.'
Only then did the penny drop. I walked around the town and in 60 seconds was back in the room. Soon I had signed up.

A soldier describes how he signed up for the war.

SOURCE B

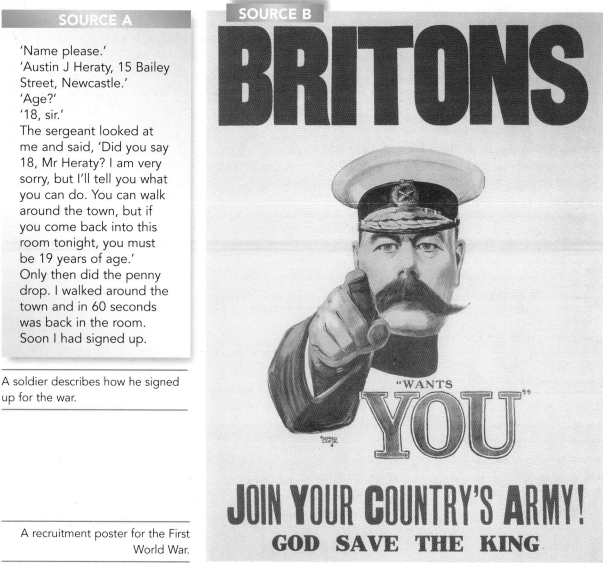

BRITONS
"WANTS
YOU"
JOIN YOUR COUNTRY'S ARMY!
GOD SAVE THE KING

A recruitment poster for the First World War.

By the end of November 1914, Parliament had authorised the recruitment of two million men.

It took some time for the early enthusiasm to fade, and for an awareness of the reality of war to sink in. By 1915 casualties were mounting fast, and a massive propaganda effort was made to try and keep up the numbers prepared to enlist. There were posters everywhere urging men to join up.

New government powers and their impact on civilian life

The First World War had a greater impact on civilian life than any previous war. This was clearly shown by the passing of the Defence of the Realm Acts in 1914. These acts, known as 'DORA', gave the government powers to intervene in people's lives to a degree that had never been known before. This even included the introduction of British Summer Time (to allow more daylight hours to work in) and the right to water down beer in pubs (to reduce drunkenness and improve productivity).

DORA gave the Government control over the newspapers and other mass communications, like the radio. All news had to be approved by the government's press office, and newspapers were not allowed to tell people the truth about the casualties on the Western Front. Instead they told stories about heroic deeds and victories.

The Government also had the power to force workers to stay in jobs that were considered vital, and to take over control of mines and railways. This became particularly important in 1916 when a 'munitions crisis' left soldiers short of equipment.

Conscription

Many of the soldiers who joined up at the start of the war were soon killed or wounded. Long periods of stalemate in the fighting were interrupted by attacks on the enemy's trenches in which thousands of casualties occurred in a single day. The longer it went on, the more men were needed to fight.

SOURCE C

REMEMBER SCARBOROUGH!
The Germans who brag of their "CULTURE" have shown what it is made of by murdering defenceless women and children at SCARBOROUGH.
But this only strengthens
GREAT BRITAIN'S
resolve to crush the
GERMAN BARBARIANS
ENLIST NOW!

A recruitment poster. The reference to Scarborough relates to German naval attacks on several East Coast towns in December 1914 in which over 100 people were killed.

QUESTIONS

1 What was DORA?

2 What was conscription?

3 Why do you think the Government did not introduce conscription at the start of the war?

By 1915 the British Government was beginning to consider conscription (making military service compulsory) but it was reluctant to introduce this. It had never been done before, and they were worried about how controversial it might be. As a first step, a National Register was made of all men and women between the ages of 15 and 65, giving details such as age and occupation. Now at least it was possible to identify all those who might be eligible for national service.

This was followed by the 'Derby Scheme', which invited men to promise that they would join up if they were asked to do so. They were told that those who had a good reason not to join up would not be called up, and that no married men would be taken before all the unmarried ones had gone. Needless to say, the scheme did not work too well, with less than half of those of military age being prepared to make the promise! From the government's point of view, however, it was not a waste of time, because they had now demonstrated that a voluntary approach would not work. They were now in a much stronger position to introduce conscription.

The Military Service Acts

In 1916, two acts brought in conscription, first for unmarried men, and then, in May, for all men of military age (between 18 and 41). This did not, of course, mean that all men had to join up. Those in 'reserved occupations' doing vital war work, such as miners, could be exempted. There was also a small number, who, because of their anti-war beliefs, refused to fight. These were known as conscientious objectors. In all there were about 16,000 'conchies', most of whom were prepared to accept other kinds of war work, such as driving ambulances. However, about 1500 refused to co-operate in any way, and were imprisoned.

The introduction of conscription ensured that there was a hardly a family in the country who was not affected by the war. Of the five million who served in the British armed forces during the war, around 750,000 were killed and two million injured. Families left at home lived in constant fear of hearing that a husband, brother or son had been killed. Everyone knew someone who had lost a loved one.

SOURCE D

5 Questions to those who employ male servants

1. HAVE you a Butler, Groom, Chauffeur, Gardener, or Gamekeeper serving you who at this moment should be serving your King and Country?
2. Have you a man serving at your table who should be serving a gun?
3. Have you a man digging your garden who should be digging trenches?
4. Have you a man driving your car who should be driving a transport wagon?
5. Have you a man preserving your game who should be helping to preserve your Country?

A great responsibility rests on you. Will you sacrifice your personal convenience for your Country's need?

Ask your men to enlist TO-DAY.

The address of the nearest Recruiting Office can be obtained at any Post Office.

God Save the King.

An advertisement from December 1914.

SOURCE E

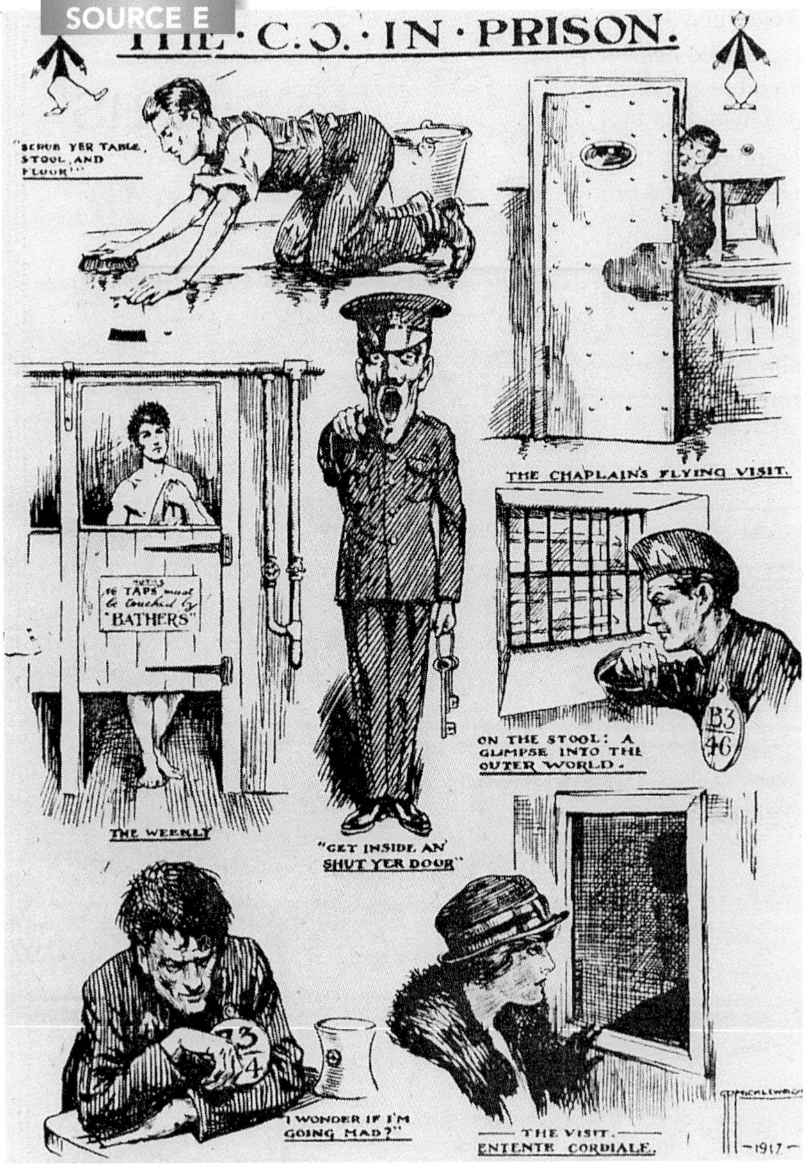

C.O. · IN · PRISON.
"SCRUB YER TABLE, STOOL, AND FLOOR!"
THE CHAPLAIN'S FLYING VISIT.
No TAPS must be touched by "BATHERS"
THE WEEKLY
"GET INSIDE AN' SHUT YER DOOR"
ON THE STOOL: A GLIMPSE INTO THE OUTER WORLD.
B3 46
"I WONDER IF I'M GOING MAD?"
THE VISIT. ENTENTE CORDIALE.
1917

A postcard published in 1917, showing the treatment of conscientious objectors.

QUESTIONS

1 Look at Source E. What can you learn from this source about the treatment of conscientious objectors?

2 Why were they treated this way?

Rationing

DORA allowed the government to take over land in order to grow crops for food. It also set up the 'Land Army'. In 1914 much of Britain's food came from abroad, but German submarines had begun sinking the ships that carried the food. So more food had to be grown in Britain – and less eaten.

By 1917, under the pressure of an intensified German U-boat campaign, food was certainly in much shorter supply. In some areas of the country it became necessary to queue for coal, sugar, potatoes and margarine. The royal family announced that it would cut its food consumption by a quarter. The government tried a scheme of voluntary rationing, and when this did not work, a system of 'meatless days', which was equally useless. Eventually, individual shopkeepers and local councils began to introduce their own rationing schemes to make sure that available goods were shared around fairly. By the end of the year a national system of sugar rationing had been set up, with each household sent a rationing card which entitled the holder to half a pound of sugar a week.

As goods became scarcer, so prices rose. The government began to subsidise the price of bread and potatoes. During 1918 rationing was extended to other goods: meat in April, with the ration fixed at three-quarters of a pound per week. Tea and butter followed. Ration cards, from which shopkeepers would clip 'coupons' as they were used, were issued by the government.

These measures were enough to ensure that the British people did not suffer too much during the war. In fact, for many, and particularly for the less well-off, rising wages during the war actually meant they were able to afford an improved diet.

SOURCE F

Our records indicate that the families of unskilled workmen were slightly better fed at the later date (1918), in spite of the rise in the price of food. From London it is officially reported, after inspection of all the children entering school, that the percentage of children found in a poorly nourished state is considerably less than half the percentage of 1913. A similar improvement is shown by the figures furnished by Birmingham, Bolton, Bristol, Bradford, Glasgow and Nottingham. It is only in very exceptional circumstances that education authorities are reporting anything like as many (free) meals as before the war.

From the *Report of the Working Classes Cost of Living Committee*, 1918.

SOURCE G

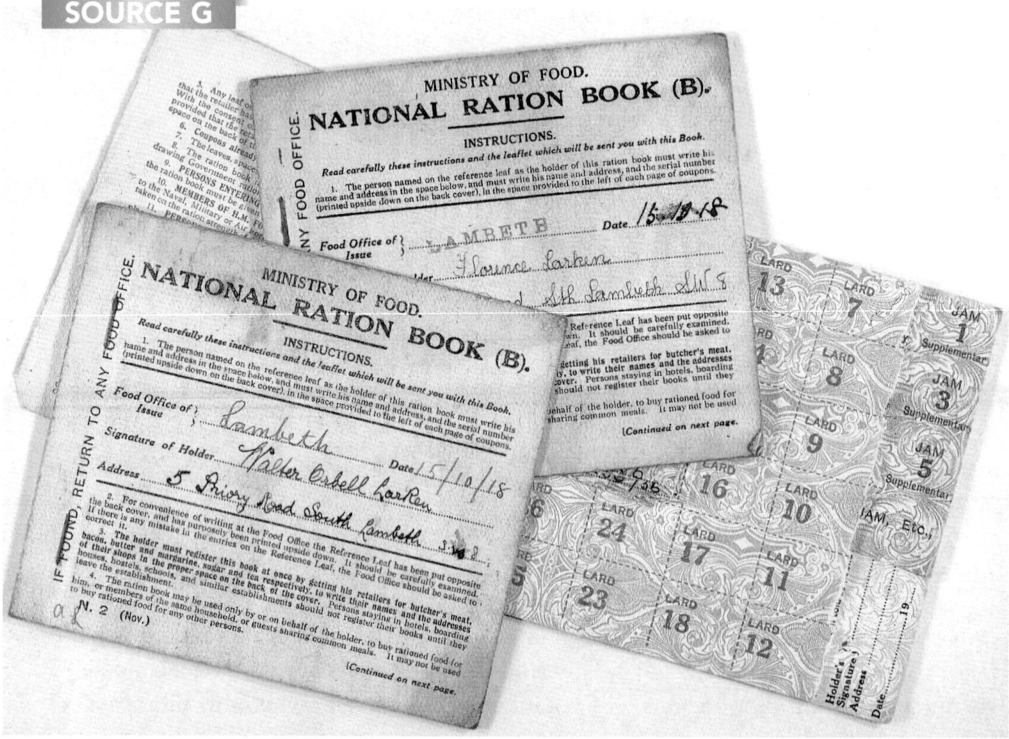

First World War ration cards.

QUESTIONS

1 How did the government make sure that everyone had enough to to eat during the war?

2 Would you say that the civilian population of Britain suffered hardship during the First World War? Explain your answer.

How effective was government propaganda during the war?

During the First World War, the government used propaganda to try and ensure that the attitudes of the people remained positive towards the war effort. In order to win a major war, a nation needs the unswerving support of its people. Without such support it cannot rely on its workers to make extra efforts to produce vital war equipment. Nor can it rely on its citizens to go without everyday necessities which can no longer be provided. So it was essential that the British people felt that they were fighting a 'just war' and the Germans were evil and had to be stopped. It was for this reason that the government encouraged people to think that they were fighting a war to help 'brave little Belgium'. They also did nothing to stop the extraordinary stories that German soldiers were carrying out acts of atrocity such as bayoneting babies.

As the war went on soldiers saw the realities of war. At home people realised that it was not some glorious game that 'would be all over by Christmas'. But even though disillusionment increased as losses mounted, and there seemed no prospect of an end to the fighting, there is no evidence that the British people ever lost their basic determination to see the war through to a successful end. In fact, in the early stages of the war, the general population was so positive in its attitudes that an official propaganda effort was hardly needed – the media were in any case full of pro-war messages. Almost everyone shared the same patriotic, anti-German feelings, whipped up by flood of stories about the terrible behaviour of the Germans during the invasion of Belgium.

Some of the most famous propaganda stories developed by exaggeration as they passed, almost like 'Chinese whispers', from one newspaper to the next. A famous example was given by the poet Robert Graves, in his book about the war, 'Goodbye to All That'. He showed how a false story about atrocities in Belgium emerged from a simple report in a German newspaper, as the story was passed from one country (including Britain) to the next (see page 40).

QUESTIONS

1 What is propaganda?

2 Why do governments use propaganda in war time?

3 Read Source A. Do you think this story was probably true? Explain your answer.

SOURCE A

I saw eight German soldiers and they were drunk. They were singing and making a lot of noise and dancing about. As they came along the street, I saw a small child, whether boy or girl I could not see, come out of a house. The child was very young and came into the middle of the street so as to be in the way of the soldiers. The soldiers were walking in twos. The first line of two passed the child; one of the second line, the man on the left, stepped aside and drove his bayonet with both hands into the child's stomach, lifting the child into the air and carrying it away on his bayonet, he and his comrades still singing. The child screamed when the soldier struck it with the bayonet, but not afterwards.

An account of a German atrocity in Belgium included in the British Report of 1915.

DORA made sure that what the press printed was approved by the government, but most newspaper editors were only too happy to print what the government wanted. Even private companies, notably the London Electric Railways Company, joined in the recruitment drive, printing and displaying their own propaganda posters. The government's propaganda efforts, then, could afford to concentrate on specific campaigns like saving food, buying savings bonds or recruitment into certain industries.

However, early in the war, the Government established a secret War Propaganda Bureau. One of its first efforts was to appoint a committee to see whether some of the German atrocities had happened. A report published in 1915 concluded (on remarkably little evidence), that many of the atrocities had indeed occurred.

QUESTION

Study Source B.

a What is the message of this poster?

b Explain how the poster tries to persuade the viewer to accept its message.

Later in the war, Lloyd George set up a Department of Information, which co-ordinated propaganda efforts. It had four main functions: providing propaganda material to shape opinion at home and abroad, supervising propaganda material for use in cinemas, gathering political intelligence from abroad, and controlling war news released to the newspapers. In March 1918 it became the Ministry of Information under the leadership of Lord Beaverbrook, owner of the *Daily Express* newspaper.

It is impossible to judge how effective the government's propaganda efforts were. The anti-German propaganda, however widely believed, could not have done any more than reinforce existing opinions held by the British people. The stories may, however, have been more important in persuading neutral countries, particularly the USA, to support the Allied side in the war. Most propaganda, though, does not consist of outright lies and distortions. British society came under unprecedented government control during the war, and most propaganda was simply information that the government wanted presented in the most favourable way.

SOURCE B

A British propaganda poster to raise funds for the war.

Why were some women given the vote in 1918?

The 1918 Representation of the People Act

It was women's contribution to the war effort by working on the land, in factories, in all sorts of jobs at home and with the troops that made certain they would be granted the vote. Though, before the war, the majority of British women had not actively supported the campaign for the vote, the experience of war work changed attitudes in many important ways. Women felt more independent, and aware that they were capable of making a much more important contribution to society than men had previously allowed. They were beginning to feel equal to men.

Women had shared the burdens and dangers of winning the war – why should they not have the same rights as men? But men's attitudes began to change as well. The sight of women doing all kinds of 'men's work' had challenged traditional ideas and stereotypes about women. This made it much harder for the opponents of women's suffrage to argue that they were not capable of voting responsibly.

The fact that the wartime government became a coalition of all the political parties also helped the women's cause. The arguments which had been used to deny them the vote before the war were now put to one side, especially once Lloyd George, a prominent supporter of women's rights, became Prime Minister in December 1916. At last there was recognition that, when the time came to deal again with the issue of the franchise, women would have to be included.

As the war went on, it became obvious that the franchise would, as a matter of urgency, have to be reviewed. Under the 1867 and 1884 Reform Acts, the vote was give to male householders who could prove they had lived in the same place for twelve months at the time the electoral register was drawn up. Technically, then, all the soldiers serving overseas had, by 1916, lost the right to vote! The second problem was that not all men possessed the vote, yet it was widely accepted that, since all soldiers had faced together the slaughter and sacrifice of the war, they should all have the vote after the war.

If, then, Parliament would have to review the male franchise, there would also be the chance of introducing votes for women. This is exactly what happened. Proposals for extending the franchise were agreed, though Parliament still could not bring itself to grant women the vote on the same basis as men. By the terms of the Representation of the People Act (1918) all adult males over the age of 21 were given the vote.

QUESTIONS

1 Explain how the First World War helped women to win the right to vote.

2 What changes did the Representation of the People Act (1918) make to the franchise?

SOURCE A

In the midst of this time of terrible anxiety and grief, it is some little comfort to think that our large organisation, which has been completely built up during past years to promote women's suffrage, can be used now to help our country through the period of strain and sorrow.

Mrs Fawcett, leader of the Suffragists, writing in August 1914.

SOURCE B

Women voters going to the polls.

However, only those women over the age of 30, who were householders or the wives of householders were allowed to vote.

Though the Act still discriminated against women, most supporters of the campaign for women's rights were prepared to accept it, on the grounds that it was obvious that votes for all women could not be long delayed. In fact, it took ten years; universal suffrage for women was achieved in 1928.

QUESTION

Read Source C. Why do you think Asquith changed his mind about votes for women?

SOURCE C

How could we have carried on the war without women? Short of actually bearing arms in the field, there is hardly a service in which women have not been at least as active and efficient as men. But what I confess moves me still more is the problem of reconstruction when the war is over. The questions which will then necessarily arise with regard to women's labour and women's functions in the new order of things are questions in which I find it impossible to withhold from women the power and the right of making their voices directly heard.

Asquith, the former Prime Minister and opponent of women's rights, speaking in Parliament in favour of votes for women in 1917.

What was the attitude of the British people at the end of the war towards Germany and the Paris Peace Conference?

The mood of the British people at the end of the war

Having spent over four years fighting the Germans, when the end of the war finally came in November 1918 the British people were not inclined to forgive and forget. Although, unlike France, Britain had suffered relatively little damage during the war, the casualty rate amongst the armed forces was horrifying. Almost every family had been touched by bereavement. Germany was blamed for starting the war, and there was a strong desire for revenge.

Much of the propaganda of the war had portrayed the Germans as brutes and barbarians. There was little pity or sympathy in Britain for the Germans, even though there had been far more German than British casualties, and civilians in Germany had suffered much more than in Britain from shortages of food and other vital supplies. There was an almost universal desire, stirred up by the popular press, to make Germany pay. Headlines like 'Hang the Kaiser!' summed up the popular mood.

QUESTIONS

1 What was the attitude of the British people towards the Germans at the end of the war?

2 Read Source A. Did Winston Churchill approve of popular attitudes towards the Germans?

The fact that there was a General Election in Britain at the end of 1918 made matters worse, as politicians vied with each other to promise ever harsher treatment for Germany. Even Lloyd George, the Prime Minister, who well understood the dangers of treating Germany too harshly, was swept along on the wave of anti-German feeling and promised at a meeting in Bristol that 'Germany must pay to the uttermost farthing, and we shall search their pockets for it'. After the election, as preparations for the Paris Peace Conference began, he would come to regret having encouraged the British public's thirst for revenge.

SOURCE A

The Prime Minister and his principal colleagues were astonished by the passions they encountered in the constituencies, The brave people whom nothing had daunted had suffered too much. Their feelings were lashed by the popular press into fury. The crippled and mutilated soldiers darkened the streets. Every cottage had its empty chair. Hatred of the beaten foe, thirst for his just punishment, rushed up from the heart of deeply injured millions...In my own constituency of Dundee, respectable, orthodox, life-long Liberals demanded the sternest punishment for the broken enemy. All over the country the most bitter were the women, of whom seven millions were for the first time to vote. In this turmoil, state policy and national dignity were speedily engulfed.

Winston Churchill, then Minister of Munitions, writing about the 1918 election campaign.

Different attitudes about what should happen to Germany at the Paris Peace Conference.

You will read in the next chapter about the Peace Conference of 1919. Lloyd George was one of the outstanding personalities of the Conference. He had a difficult task in balancing his own personal views about how to treat Germany with those of the British people he was representing.

He was under a lot of pressure to insist on a harsh peace, even though he knew this would be disastrous, in leaving Germany resentful, and more likely to cause trouble in future. In fact, by the time the conference assembled in January 1919, Lloyd George was not alone in realising that the more extreme demands of the British public could never be met.

SOURCE B

'Once a German, always a German' – a British poster of 1919.

SOURCE C

I think that everyone here takes the commonsense view that a dissatisfied Germany would be the worst of all evil legacies to Europe, but we are not the sole judges of the situation. Still I hope that our undoubted weight in international affairs may be sufficient to prevent an unprincipled peace.

A Liberal MP writing about the peace conference to a friend, April 1919.

QUESTIONS

1 How did Lloyd George want to treat Germany at the end of the war? Why did he have this attitude?

2 Study Source B. Explain why this poster was published in 1919.

Paper 2-type assessment: Britain and the First World War

The use of propaganda

Study the sources carefully. Then answer **all** the questions.

SOURCE A

Even for those who were not keen to join the army, there were enormous pressures to sign up. The government carried out a skilful propaganda campaign which portrayed the Germans as evil beasts. It was said that they had bayonetted babies and murdered nuns on their march through Belgium. Recruitment posters emphasised the need to help the country and to protect women and children from the horrors of war. Men who did not join up were made to feel like cowards.

An extract from a recent history book describing attitudes at the beginning of the war.

SOURCE B

RED CROSS OR IRON CROSS?
WOUNDED AND A PRISONER OUR SOLDIER CRIES FOR WATER.
THE GERMAN "SISTER" POURS IT ON THE GROUND BEFORE HIS EYES.
THERE IS NO WOMAN IN BRITAIN WHO WOULD DO IT.
THERE IS NO WOMAN IN BRITAIN WHO WILL FORGET IT.

A British poster issued early in the war.

SOURCE C

A Call from the Trenches.

(Extract from a letter from the Trenches.)

"I SAW a recruiting advertisement in a paper the other day. I wonder if the men are responding properly – they would if they could see what the Germans have done in Belgium. And, after all, it's not so bad out here – cold sometimes, and the waiting gets on our nerves a bit, but we are happy and as fit as fiddles. I wonder if __________ has joined, he certainly ought to."

Does '__________' refer to you?

If so

ENLIST TO-DAY.

God Save the King.

A recruiting advertisement in the *The Times*, 15 April 1915.

SOURCE D

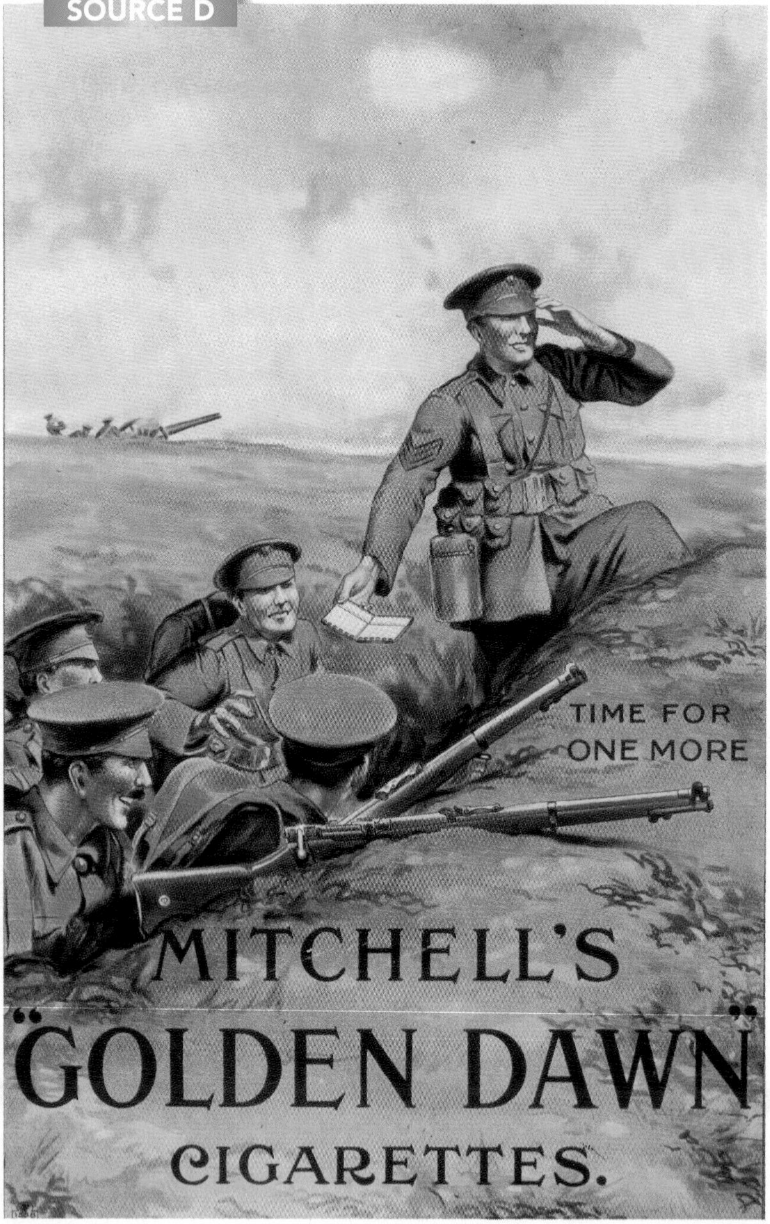

A British poster advertising cigarettes in 1915.

SOURCE E

Extract 1
When the fall of Antwerp was announced the bells were rung in Cologne and all over Germany.

Written in the German newspaper, *Kolnische Zeitung.*

Extract 2
According to the *Kolnische Zeitung* the clergy at Antwerp were compelled to ring the church bells when the town was captured.

Written in the French newspaper, *Le Matin.*

Extract 3
According to what the British newspaper, *The Times*, has heard from Cologne, via Paris, the unfortunate Belgian priests who refused to ring the church bells when Antwerp was taken were sentenced to hard labour.

Written in the Italian newspaper, *Corriere della Sera.*

Extract 4
According to information which has reached *Corriere della Sera*, from Cologne, via London, it is confirmed that the barbaric conquerors of Antwerp punished the unfortunate Belgian priests for their heroic refusal to ring the church bells by hanging them as living clappers to the bells, with their heads down.

Written in *Le Matin.*

SOURCE F

We had been brought up to believe that Britain was the best country in the world. We were taught at school that we were better than other people – didn't we always win the last war? Now we wanted to show the Germans what we could do.

Private George Morgan, 16th battalion West Yorks Regiment, explains why he signed up in 1914.

SOURCE G

The airship was on fire and it was floating down. I could only think of people inside it being roasted to death. I was disgusted to see kind, good-hearted people dancing in the street as the men in that airship were dying. When I said it was a terrible thing, my friends said, 'but they're Germans, they're the enemy, they've been bombing us.' That's what the war did. It turned decent, gentle people into monsters.

An eye-witness description of the shooting down of a Zeppelin during the First World War.

SOURCE H

When the news came through that the Accrington Pals had been wiped out. I don't think there was a street in Accrington and district that did not have its blinds drawn.

The son of one of the Accrington Pals remembering the day the town heard about the losses in the Battle of the Somme. 720 of the Pals took part in the attack on the first day of the Somme (1 July 1916). Of these 584 were killed, reported missing or wounded.

QUESTIONS

1 Study **Source A**.
How much could a historian studying the use of propaganda in the First World War learn from this source?
Use the source and your own knowledge to explain your answer. (6 marks)

2 Study **Sources** B and C.
Which of these two sources do you think would have had the greater impact on the British people?
Use the sources and your own knowledge to explain your answer. (8 marks)

3 Study **Source D**.
'This is an advertisement for cigarettes, not a piece of propaganda, so it is of no value to a historian studying the use of propaganda in the First World War'
Use the source and your own knowledge to explain whether you agree with this interpretation. (6 marks)

4 Study **Source E**.
Does this source prove that propaganda was just lies?
Use the source and your own knowledge to explain your answer. (6 marks)

5 Study **Sources F** and **G**.
Which of these two sources do you think would be most useful to a historian studying the effects of propaganda in the First World War?
Use the sources and your own knowledge to explain your answer. (8 marks)

6 Study **Source H**.
Do you think this source would have made the British people more or less likely to believe anti-German propaganda?
Use the source and your own knowledge to explain your answer. (6 marks)

7 Study **all** the sources.
'The use of propaganda in the First World War was subtle and extremely clever'.
How far do the sources in this exercise agree with this interpretation?
Use the sources and your knowledge to explain your answer. (10 marks)

Paper 2-type assessment: The Liberal Reforms

Old Age Pensions and National Insurance

Study the sources carefully. Then answer **all** the questions.

SOURCE A

A photograph showing living conditions for a London East End family in the early years of the twentieth century.

SOURCE B

David Lloyd George became Chancellor of the Exchequer in 1908. In his first budget speech he said that the government was going to introduce old age pensions. Old people would no longer be dependent on the Poor Law or the kindness of their friends and relatives. 'We are', he said 'lifting the shadow of the workhouse from the homes of the poor'.

An account of the work of Lloyd George, from a school textbook written in 1999.

SOURCE C

When the Old Age Pensions began, life was transformed for the aged. They were relieved of anxiety. They were suddenly rich. Independent for life! At first when they went to the Post Office to get their pension tears of gratitude would run down the cheeks of some – and there were flowers from gardens and apples from trees for the girl who merely handed them the money.

An extract from a novel by Flora Thompson. She had once been a Post Office worker handing out the benefits.

SOURCE D

Darby is 72, with a cataract in one eye and very little sight in the other. His wife Joan was 71 last October. They have lived on money given to them by their son and the meagre earnings from Joan's cleaning work. Interviewed by a reporter Darby chuckled and said 'It isn't wealth. No you couldn't call it wealth. But it's something for sure. The pension is not a charity. It's a right,' Darby said proudly.

An article in the *Daily Express* on 2 January 1909.

SOURCE E

Dear Sir,

The strength of this kingdom, in all its past struggles, has been its great wealth and the sturdy independent character of its people.

The measure will destroy both.

It will take the wealth from its possessors by unjust taxation and will sap the character of the people by teaching to rely, not on their own efforts, but on the State.

A letter written to *The Times* newspaper in 1908 complaining about the decision to introduce pensions.

SOURCE F

THE PHILANTHROPIC HIGHWAYMAN.

Mr. Lloyd-George. "I'LL MAKE 'EM PITY THE AGED POOR!"

A cartoon from *Punch* in 1909. It shows Lloyd George as a highwayman carrying out a robbery to pay for old age pensions.

SOURCE G

THE RIGHT TICKET FOR YOU!
YOU ARE TRAVELLING ON A SAFE LINE
GOVERNMENT LINE
1913
MALE WORKER PAYS 4D
EMPLOYER PAYS 3D
STATE PAYS 2D
YOUR RETURN
DURING ILLNESS
10/- Per Week FOR 26 WEEKS
5/- AFTERWARDS (TILL 70) WHILE INCAPABLE OF WORK
FREE DOCTOR & MEDICINE
30/- Maternity Grant
SANATORIUM BENEFIT
AND ARE ASSURED
A SAFE RETURN

A government poster advertising the National Insurance Act. It was introduced in 1911 to provide payments for sickness and unemployment. This poster refers to the health insurance scheme.

QUESTIONS

1 Study **Source A**.
How useful do you think this source is for showing us what it was like to be poor in the early years of the twentieth century?
Use the source and your own knowledge to explain your answer. (6 marks)

2 Study **Source B**.
Do you think it is true that the Liberal government introduced old age pensions just to keep people out of the workhouse?
Use the source and your own knowledge to explain whether you agree with this interpretation. (8 marks)

3 Study **Sources C** and **D**.
Which of these sources do you think gives the better impression of the impact of old age pensions?
Use the sources and your own knowledge to explain your answer. (6 marks)

4 Study **Sources E** and **F**.
How similar are these two sources?
Use the sources and your own knowledge to explain your answer. (8 marks)

5 Study **Sources G** and **H**.
'These two sources are particularly important to a historian studying the impact of the Liberal reforms because they were issued by the government.' How far do you agree with this statement?
Use the sources and your own knowledge to explain your answer. (10 marks)

6 Study **all** the sources.
Do you think it is possible to decide how great an impact the Liberal reforms had from the sources in this exercise?
Use the sources and your own knowledge to explain your answer. (12 marks)

SOURCE H

THE DAWN OF HOPE.

Mr. LLOYD GEORGE'S National Health Insurance Bill provides for the insurance of the Worker in case of Sickness.

Support the Liberal Government
in their policy of
SOCIAL REFORM.

A government poster advertising National Health Insurance. The doctor sitting by the bed is Lloyd George.

Paper 2-type assessment: The Suffragettes

How important were the Suffragettes in helping win the vote for women?

Study the sources carefully. Then answer **all** the questions.

SOURCE A

We believe that if we get the vote it will mean better conditions for our unfortunate sisters. We believe that only through new laws can any improvements be made and that new laws will not be passed until women have the same power as men to put pressure on governments.

We have tried every way. We have presented larger petitions than were ever presented before and succeeded in holding greater public meetings then men ever held. But we have been criticised and had contempt poured upon us.

Violence is the only way that we have to get the power which every citizen should have – the same kind of power that the worst of men have. The same kind of power that the wife-beater has, the same power that the drunkard has.

Emmeline Pankhurst speaking in her defence in court in 1912.

SOURCE C

'Hasn't Mrs Pankhurst the sense to see that the very worst kind of campaigning for the vote is to try to intimidate or blackmail a man into giving her what he would gladly give her otherwise'.

David Lloyd George, a member of the government, speaking in 1913 after his house had been bombed by Suffragettes.

SOURCE B

A poster issued in 1912 by a group of woman artists supporting votes for women.

SOURCE D

By 1913 the activities of the militant Suffragettes had reached the stage at which nothing was safe from their attacks. Churches were burnt, public buildings and private residences destroyed, bombs were exploded, the police and individuals were assaulted and meetings broken up. The feeling amongst MPs, caused by the extravagant and lawless action of the militants, hardened their opposition to the women's demands. So on 6 May the House of Commons voted against giving women the vote by a majority of 47.

Viscount Ullswater, a senior official in the House of Commons in 1913, writing in 1925 about the campaign for votes for women.

SOURCE F

THE CAT AND MOUSE ACT
PASSED BY THE LIBERAL GOVERNMENT
WSPU
THE LIBERAL CAT
ELECTORS VOTE AGAINST HIM!
KEEP THE LIBERAL OUT!
BUY AND READ 'THE SUFFRAGETTE' PRICE 1D

A Suffragette postcard from 1913. It is attacking the Liberal Government for passing the 'Cat and Mouse Act'.

SOURCE E

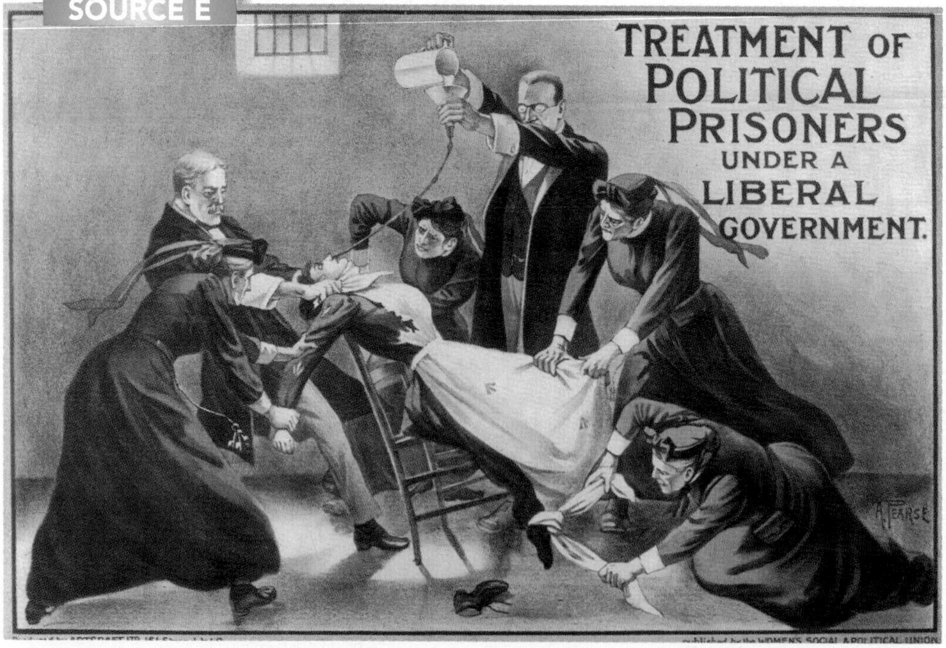

TREATMENT OF POLITICAL PRISONERS UNDER A LIBERAL GOVERNMENT.

A Suffragette poster, probably published for the 1910 election. It shows the force-feeding of a Suffragette on hunger strike.

SOURCE G

It must be remembered that the behaviour of the Suffragettes served a very important purpose. Without it the government could have (and did before 1913) stated that there was no real 'evidence' that women even wanted the vote. The militants destroyed this theory. By destroying property, staging demonstrations and creating riots, the militants kept 'the cause' constantly in the public eye.
The effects of World War are important because they raised women in the eyes of Parliament and all men who remained in Britain – and they also raised many women's estimation of themselves. But the militancy of the Suffragettes is the main reason why women gained the vote in 1918.

An extract from an article written by a male member of the British Suffrage Society in 1996.

SOURCE H

It was in the year 1918 that disaster took place. A member of the House of Commons stood up and said, 'If you are extending the vote to our brave soldiers, how about our brave munition workers?' That argument was difficult to resist. Then...How about our brave women munition workers?' And having agreed to the first argument it was impossible to resist the second.

An extract from the memoirs of Lord Birkenhead, a Conservative politician.

QUESTIONS

1 Study **Source A.**
What could a historian studying the Suffragettes learn from this source?
Use the source and your own knowledge to explain your answer. (6 marks)

2 Study **Source B.**
'This source is obviously biased, so it is of no value to a historian studying attempts by women to win the vote'. Do you agree?
Use the source and your own knowledge to explain your answer. (8 marks)

3 Study **Sources C** and **D.**
Do you agree that these two sources show that the Suffragettes did not have the support of the men in the country?
Use the sources and your own knowledge to explain your answer. (8 marks)

4 Study **Sources E** and **F.**
Why do you think these two pictures were produced?
Use the sources and your own knowledge to explain your answer. (8 marks)

5 Study **Sources G** and **H.**
How similar are these two sources?
Use the sources and your own knowledge to explain your answer. (8 marks)

6 Study **all** the sources.
'The Suffragettes were vital in helping women win the vote'. How far do the sources in this exercise support this interpretation?
Use the sources and your own knowledge to explain your answer. (12 marks)

Core Part I:

International relations 1919–c.1939

2 International relations 1919–c.1939

In early 1919 representatives of the victorious powers in the First World War met in Paris to draw up peace treaties to end the war. The failure of these treaties to create a stable and fair peace settlement made it certain that Europe would face further international problems and disputes. The Treaty of Versailles, imposed on an unwilling and embittered Germany, was particularly controversial, and left the Germans determined to reverse its terms at the first opportunity.

Yet the peacemakers of 1919 sincerely believed they had given the world the chance of a peaceful future. They set up the League of Nations to resolve international disputes and prevent countries from ever going to war again. Unfortunately the USA refused to join the League, which was therefore weak from the start. The League made a number of useful attempts in the 1920s to reach international agreements to prevent future conflict leading to war. However, the impact of the Great Depression after 1929 made nations less willing to work together, and the League's authority was fatally undermined by its failure to deal with Japanese aggression in China, and to prevent the Italian invasion of Abyssinia in 1935–6.

During the 1930s, the greatest threat to international peace was Hitler's desire to rebuild the military might of Germany and to reverse the territorial losses incurred in the Treaty of Versailles. Ignoring limits placed on Germany by the treaty, he built up the armed forces and followed an aggressive foreign policy which saw Austria, Czechoslovakia and finally Poland fall under Nazi control. Britain and France had followed a policy of appeasement during the 1930s, hoping that differences between them and Hitler could be resolved by negotiation. By September 1939 it was apparent that this policy had failed.

This topic is examined in Paper 1 of the examination. Paper 1-type exercises are included at the end of each section. Mark schemes, sample answers and comments can be found in the accompanying Teacher's Resource Pack.

Were the peace treaties of 1919–23 fair?

In January 1919 representatives from 32 countries met in Paris for a conference that would make the peace settlement at the end of the First World War. The tasks they faced were huge. The Europe of 1914 had been swept away by the impact of war. Nobody knows how many died in the war – at least 8 million fighting men and a further 8 million civilians is a reasonable guess. The Russian and Austro-Hungarian empires had collapsed, the former replaced by an unpredictable communist dictatorship pledged to destroy capitalism throughout the world. Large areas were left devastated by the fighting, and the European economy was shattered by the costs of war.

In these circumstances, to agree a peace settlement that everyone, victors and defeated, found fair and acceptable would have been an impossible task. What is remarkable is that the peacemakers achieved as much as they did. The peace treaties made with the defeated nations in 1919–20 redrew the map of Europe, set up the League of Nations – the first international organisation for maintaining world peace – and brought freedom to many ethnic groups previously under foreign rule.

QUESTIONS

1 Why was it so difficult to make a peace settlement which would please everyone?

2 How were the important decisions made during the peace conference?

3 What were the main differences in the aims of the 'Big Three'?

What were the motives and aims of the 'Big Three' at Versailles?

Of the nations that assembled in Paris to make peace, three possessed the power to make decisions which, more often than not, the others would have to accept. These were the great powers that had won the war: the USA, France and Britain. They were represented at the peace conference by President Wilson, and prime ministers Clemenceau and Lloyd George, known collectively as the 'Big Three'. Italy and Japan were the other members of the Council of Ten (there were two members from each of the five powers), which met daily at the conference to take all the important decisions.

The 'Big Three' had very different ideas about the peace settlement. The traditional interpretation of their relationship is that Wilson was the unworldly idealist, whose plans were undermined by the unscrupulous Europeans; that Clemenceau was cunning and cynical, determined that France should have its revenge on Germany; and that Lloyd George acted as a balance between the other two, doing his

SOURCE A

Woodrow Wilson (President of the USA, 1913–21).

best to make the treaty less harsh on Germany. Although this interpretation is in some ways valid, the truth is more complicated.

Once the conference met, all three came to realise that compromises would be necessary. They frequently and strongly disagreed. All got their way on some issues, and failed to do so on others. Although he championed the rights of different nationalities to rule themselves, in dealing with Italy's and Japan's territorial demands Wilson was prepared to give way and to ignore this principle of self-determination. Had he not done so, they would have refused to sign the treaties. Lloyd George fought hard to keep German territorial losses to a minimum, and argued for more German border areas to be given plebiscites (a vote on which country to join), but he was also capable of insisting on increases in reparations payments to suit British interests. When Clemenceau insisted on the German frontier being pushed back to the Rhine, Wilson threatened to quit the conference and return home. The French had to be satisfied with the demilitarisation of the Rhineland. But like all compromises, the final treaties satisfied nobody.

Wilson was a man of strong principles, who found it hard to accept other people's views. At first, he kept the USA out of the war, until by 1917 he had become convinced that 'to make the world safe for democracy' the USA would have to fight the Germans. However, once the war was won, Wilson wanted a fair settlement that would guarantee future world peace. In January 1918 he outlined his 'Fourteen Points', the principles that he believed should guide peacemaking when the war ended (see page 53). The most important was self-determination – people of different national groups had the right to rule themselves.

At Paris, Wilson tried to have every decision debated by all 32 nations. But this was too slow, and most nations were interested only in their own problems. Wider issues had to be decided by the great powers. Wilson was increasingly forced to compromise on his Fourteen Points, and had to place his hopes in the new League of Nations to put right any problems with the peace treaties. Wilson's authority was weakened by lack of support for his ideas in the USA. Many Americans were determined never to be dragged into Europe's troubles again. Electoral gains made by his opponents at home meant that whatever he agreed in Paris might be rejected. In March 1920 the US Senate finally failed to give the majority need[illegible] the peace treaties to be ratified.

SOURCE B

Georges Clemenceau (Prime Minister of France, 1917–20).

SOURCE C

David Lloyd George (Prime Minister of Britain, 1916–22).

s of the Versailles settlement.

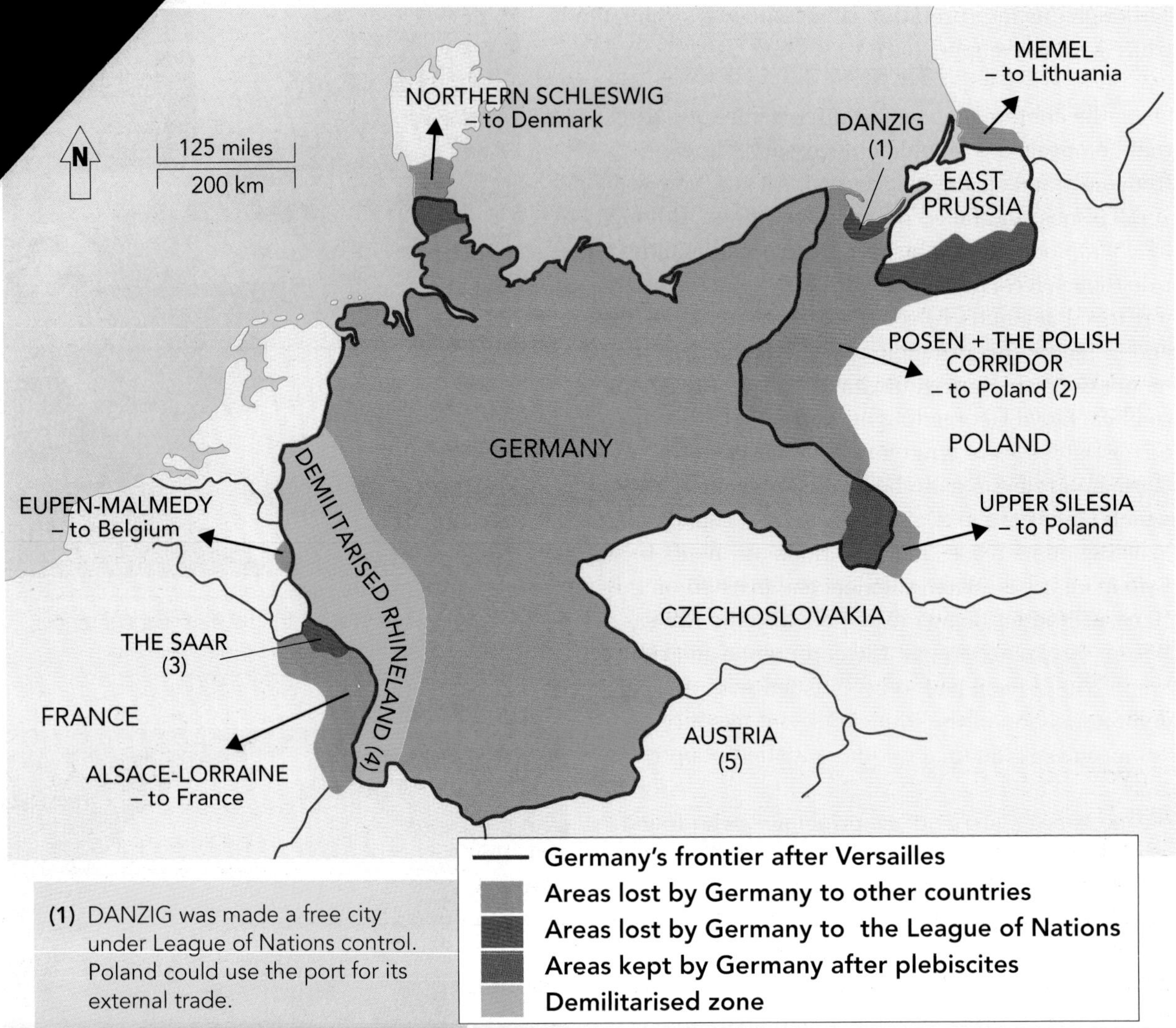

(1) DANZIG was made a free city under League of Nations control. Poland could use the port for its external trade.

(2) THE POLISH CORRIDOR gave Poland access to the sea. It also split East Prussia from the rest of Germany.

(3) THE SAAR was put under League of Nations control for fifteen years. France was given the production of the Saar coalfields as part of reparations payments.

(4) THE RHINELAND was to be permanently demilitarised by Germany. It would be occupied by the Allies for fifteen years.

(5) ANSCHLUSS (union) between Germany and Austria was forbidden.

Germany's colonial losses

Germany's colonies in Africa were given to the victorious powers as mandates. This means they were governed by one of the victorious powers until they were ready for independence.

Germany's colonies in the Pacific were also allocated as mandates.

- New Guinea – to Australia
- Samoa – to New Zealand
- Pacific islands north of the Equator – the Marshalls, Marianas and Carolines – to Japan

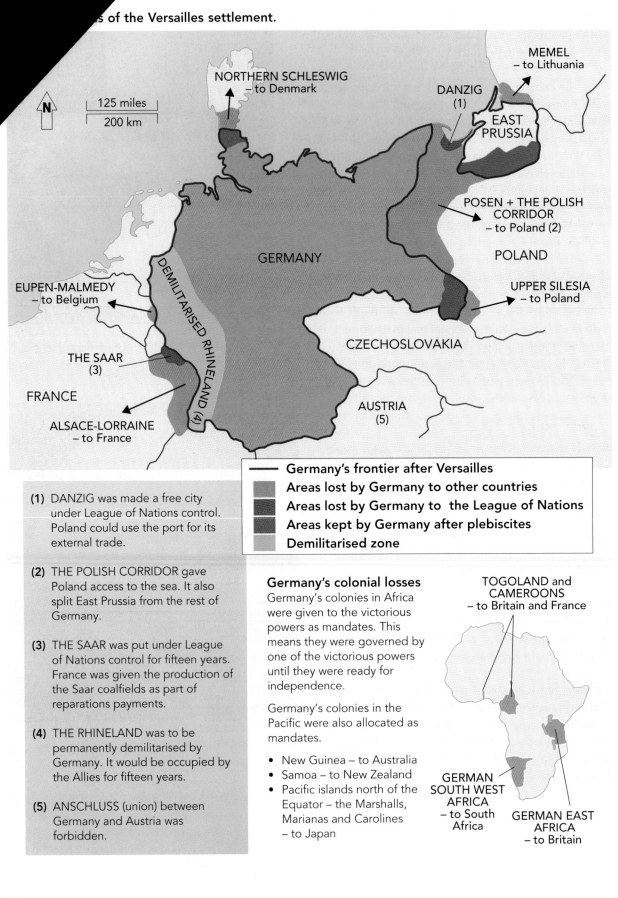

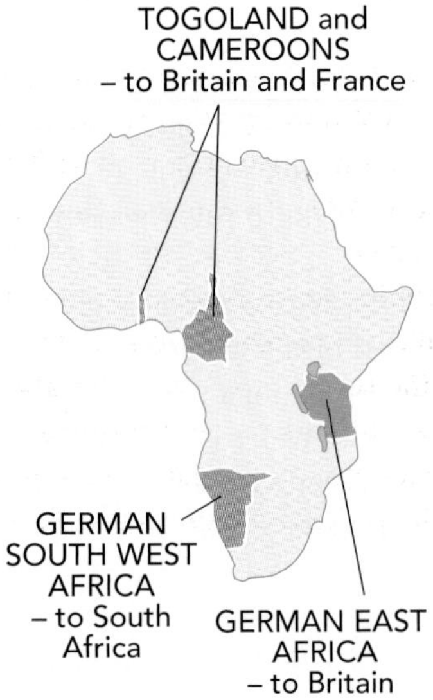

Clemenceau became French prime minister in 1917 when defeat in the war seemed a real possibility. He rallied the country, and led it to victory. As chairman of the peace conference, he was personally willing to compromise in order to find a settlement acceptable to all the victorious powers, but he knew what his countrymen expected. France had borne the brunt of the fighting on the Western Front. Much of north-east France was devastated. The Germans had systematically looted areas under their occupation, and deliberately destroyed mines, railways, factories and bridges during their retreat. The French expected Germany to pay for this destruction, and wanted to ensure that Germany could never invade France again.

Like the other conference participants, Clemenceau found it hard to achieve his aims. Neither Britain nor the USA shared France's enthusiasm for punishing Germany. Still less did they want to provide guarantees for French security in future. Clemenceau's demand for the German frontier to be pushed back to the Rhine was bluntly rejected. France was not given the Saar, although it did receive its coal production for fifteen years. The reparations issue was referred to a commission, which did not report until 1921. When the terms of the Treaty of Versailles became known, it was condemned throughout France. Within a few months, Clemenceau's government was overthrown and his political career ended.

Lloyd George and the treaty

Lloyd George became leader of Britain's coalition government in 1916. In December 1918 his government won a massive election victory by promising to 'squeeze the German lemon till the pips squeak'. The British blamed the Germans for the war and wanted to make them pay; some even suggested that the Kaiser should be hanged. Lloyd George probably knew early on that a harsh peace would store up trouble, but he was constrained by British public opinion and election promises.

Lloyd George was determined to preserve Britain's interests as the greatest naval power. He disliked Wilson's idea of 'freedom of the seas', which was referred to the League of Nations for discussion. He also wanted the German fleet sunk – a matter that the Germans resolved by sinking all their ships, held captive at Scapa Flow. By the completion of the treaty, however, British public opinion was shifting, and Lloyd George was prepared to make some amendments to the terms. As a trading nation, Britain knew that German recovery was essential to the European economy, and that large reparations payments would make this impossible. The British were not prepared to help France keep Germany weak.

The Fourteen Points

1. No secret treaties.
2. Freedom of the seas.
3. The removal of economic barriers.
4. The reduction of armaments.
5. Settlement of all colonial claims.
6. Germans to leave Russian territory and a settlement of all questions affecting Russia.
7. Germans to leave Belgium.
8. French territory freed and Alsace-Lorraine returned to France.
9. Italian frontiers adjusted to take into account the nationality of the population.
10. The peoples of the Austro-Hungarian Empire to be given self-determination.
11. Germans to leave Romania, Serbia and Montenegro and international guarantees of their independence to be given.
12. The people of the Ottoman Empire to be given self-determination, and the Dardanelles to be permanently opened to international shipping.
13. An independent Polish state to be created with access to the sea.
14. A general association of nations to be formed to give guarantees of political independence to great and small states alike.

The terms of the Treaty of Versailles, June 1919.

This was the treaty signed by the Allies with Germany.

War Guilt
Germany had to accept the blame for the war.

Article 231 of the treaty:
'Germany accepts responsibility for causing all the loss and damage to which the Allied governments have been subjected as a consequence of the war imposed upon them by the aggression of Germany.'

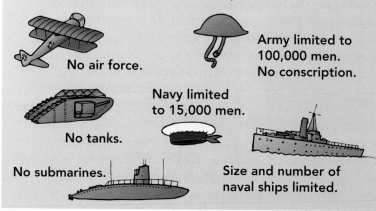

Military restrictions
Tight restrictions were placed on Germany's armed forces.

No air force.

Army limited to 100,000 men. No conscription.

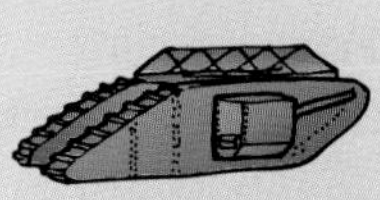

No tanks.

Navy limited to 15,000 men.

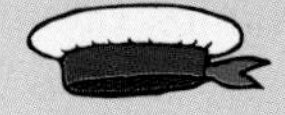

Size and number of naval ships limited.

No submarines.

The League of Nations
The first item in all the peace treaties with the defeated nations was the 'Covenant' (the rules) setting up the League of Nations.

Reparations
As Germany accepted the blame for the war, the Allies could demand payment for all the damage caused. Germany was required to pay compensation – reparations – to the Allies.

A Reparations Commission was set up to fix the amount. It reported in 1921. Germany was presented with a demand for £6600 million.

Why did all of the victors not get everything they wanted?

According to the British historian R. Henig, 'The Treaty represented an uneasy compromise between Wilson's idealism, French security requirements, and British pragmatism [common sense].' The British and French would not accept Wilson's vision of a new international order based on the Fourteen Points, and the British and the Americans would not back up France in making a peace that would keep Germany weak. To make matters worse, the British very quickly came to see the Treaty of Versailles as a mistake. Quite clearly, none of the victors got the peace they wanted, not least because they all wanted a different kind of peace. However, even when the nations first assembled in Paris, they were not free to shape the peace as they wished. Four important factors limited their freedom of action.

1 Wartime commitments and secret treaties

While the war was going on, a number of promises of territory were made to certain countries to encourage them to fight. Now that the war was over, these nations would expect the promises to be kept. Italy had joined the war on the Allies' side after the secret Treaty of London (1915) was signed, promising it a share in any partition of the Ottoman Empire or of German colonies, as well as significant areas of the Austro-Hungarian Empire. Japan's claims on China and parts of the German Pacific Empire had also been supported by the British in 1917. Wilson was horrified to hear of the extent of these commitments, most of which went against his principle of self-determination. Britain and France were much less enthusiastic about keeping their side of these bargains once the fighting stopped, but sometimes they could not avoid it.

Although the more extreme of the Italian demands for territory were resisted by the Allies at the peace conference, Italy still made substantial gains from Austria in South Tyrol, Trentino and Istria (but not the port of Fiume, which was given to Yugoslavia). However, Italian dissatisfaction at not receiving what had been promised led directly to the first crisis of the post-war period. Italian nationalists under the poet D'Annunzio seized Fiume in September 1919 and held it for a year. They were eventually driven out by Italian forces on the understanding that Fiume would become a free city under the League of Nations. This solution did not last long. In 1924 Fiume was retaken by the Italian dictator, Mussolini.

Despite Chinese protests and refusal to sign the Treaty of Versailles, British commitments to Japan made it impossible for Wilson to resist Japanese claims to Shantung and the harbour of Kiaochow, which had been leased by Germany from China since 1890.

2 The collapse of the Russian and Austro-Hungarian Empires

In early 1917 the Russian monarchy had collapsed under the pressures of fighting a losing war against Germany and Austria-Hungary. By the end of the year, Russia was defeated. In March 1918 Russia's new Bolshevik government signed the Treaty of Brest-Litovsk with the Germans. Under the harsh terms of this treaty, Russia gave up huge areas on its western borders: Finland, the Baltic States, its Polish provinces and the Ukraine. Although the treaty was annulled by Germany's defeat, most of the lost territory (the exception was the Ukraine) was not recovered by Russia, which was embroiled in civil war until 1920. The populations of these areas were quite distinct national groups. As neither Germany nor Russia would rule them, they would rule themselves. The peacemakers might discuss or adjust the frontiers of these states, but Germany's defeat and Russia's collapse brought them into existence.

Similarly, in Austria-Hungary the war brought the end of the monarchy. This sprawling central European empire contained dozens of different national groups. Some, such as the Czechs and Slovaks, declared their independence while the war still continued. As the empire fell apart, new countries emerged in its place. When the peace conference met, the new states of Austria, Hungary, Czechoslovakia and Yugoslavia already existed. True, their boundaries had not been finally decided, but the peacemakers did not make extensive changes to them.

3 The terms of the armistice

When nations make peace at the end of a war, they first agree the terms on which they will stop fighting (the armistice), before they meet to discuss and agree the terms of the peace treaty that formally ends the war. The First World War was exceptionally damaging and bitterly fought. As it came to an end, the defeated powers sought an armistice, but the victors were determined that its terms should be so severe that there would be no chance of hostilities breaking out again. The armistice terms came to have an important effect on the terms of the peace treaties themselves. For example, in the armistice agreed with Germany, the principle of reparations was accepted. Germany also agreed to leave Alsace-Lorraine, and that its armies would evacuate all areas on the left bank of the Rhine. Each of these found its way into the final peace treaty, as did other military restrictions

QUESTIONS

1 What were the Germans' main territorial losses in the Treaty of Versailles?

2 How else did the treaty limit Germany's power?

3 Why were the victors not free to make the peace they wanted?

placed on Germany by the armistice. Thus terms that were intended primarily to bring the fighting to an end actually became part of the treaty that punished Germany.

4 Public opinion

All the politicians at the Paris peace conference were under pressure to meet the expectations of public opinion. The problem was that people in different countries wanted different outcomes. The Italians were determined to gain the territory that they thought would make them a great power. The French wanted to make Germany pay, and so did the British, although they had a leader who increasingly doubted the wisdom of doing this. The Americans were not really enthusiastic about being involved in European affairs at all. Wilson, Clemenceau, Lloyd George and the Italian Prime Minister, Orlando, all found that they were not free to make the peace they wanted, as public opinion at home would not let them.

SOURCE D

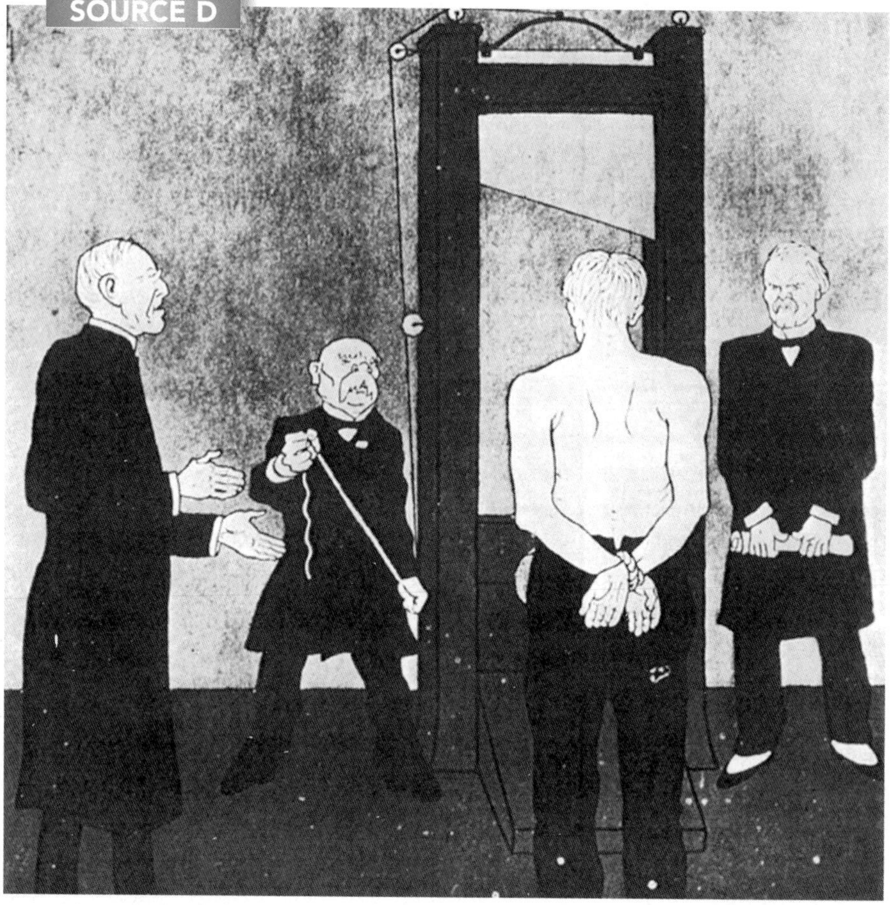

A cartoon about the Treaty of Versailles. It shows the figure of Germany about to be guillotined. The other three figures (left to right) are Wilson, Clemenceau and Lloyd George.

What was the immediate impact of the peace treaty on Germany up to 1923?

Although Germany lost the First World War, the reality of defeat took some time to hit the German people. Their country had not been invaded, and right up to the last few weeks of the war their leaders had continued to pretend that they were winning.

The Germans had good reason to believe that the Allies would treat them mercifully. They assumed that peace would be based on the principles of the Fourteen Points. The Kaiser, whom many blamed for the war, was now out of the way, overthrown in the German Revolution of November 1918 and replaced by a new democratic, republican government. However, German confidence was misplaced. The harsh terms of the armistice clearly indicated the kind of peace

QUESTION

Source D shows characters from the USA, France, Britain and Germany. Which of these countries do you think the cartoon comes from? Explain your answer, using your knowledge of the Treaty of Versailles, and referring to details of the cartoon.

that would eventually be made. More ominously, none of the defeated nations was allowed representatives at the Paris peace conference. The final terms of the Treaty of Versailles were presented to the Germans with no negotiation – a 'diktat' (dictated peace), as they called it.

The Germans were stunned by the severity of the treaty. They considered rejecting it outright, but the alternative was a resumption of the war. The government knew it had no choice but to sign, and was promptly blamed by the entire German nation when it did so. Extremist opponents of the government blamed the 'November Criminals' (those who had asked for peace in November 1918) and claimed that they had 'stabbed Germany in the back'. Many Germans were only too ready to believe the myth that their country had not really lost the war, but had been betrayed by disloyal Jews and socialists. From the very start, Germans did not accept the treaty as a just peace, and many were prepared to do everything they could to make sure the treaty did not work.

The weak Weimar Republic

In the confused and violent aftermath of the war, the Weimar Republic (Germany's new government) was much weakened by being blamed for agreeing to the treaty. Extremists from right and left struggled to overthrow the republic. Even the army was not totally loyal to its own government. It was angry about the military restrictions in the treaty. Many ex-soldiers refused to disarm after the war, and became members of Freikorps. These were semi-official bands of soldiers, who helped the government crush its left-wing enemies. The trouble was that they were very unreliable allies for the republic to have, and were notorious for their extreme nationalist views. In 1920, when the government, under pressure from Britain and France, tried to enforce the military restrictions in the Versailles Treaty, a force of Freikorps under Wolfgang Kapp occupied Berlin with the intention of overthrowing the republic. The army did nothing to intervene. This attempted revolution – known as the 'Kapp Putsch' – failed only when a general strike organised as a protest against the putsch brought communications to a standstill and demonstrated the support of the working people for the government.

The issue that Germans resented most about the Treaty of Versailles was being forced to accept responsibility for the war (the 'War Guilt' clause) and to pay reparations. It was not just Germans who thought reparations were an impossible burden for Germany to bear. In his book *The Economic Consequences of the Peace*, published in 1919, the famous British economist John Maynard Keynes argued that, by keeping Germany's economy weak, reparations would undermine trade between nations and therefore harm everyone. In fact, the sum of £6600 million fixed by the Reparations Commission in 1921 was a small fraction of the amounts that had been talked about in the immediate aftermath of the war. But the treaty was so unpopular in Germany that any politicians who argued that Germany should try to pay ran the risk of assassination; indeed, several were murdered for this reason.

SOURCE E

Paul von Hindenburg, President of Germany, 1925–34.

SOURCE F

French troops in the Ruhr.

By 1921 the German economy was in serious trouble. Burdened by huge amounts of debt from the war, the government was printing money to meet its expenditure and inflation was rising fast. This provided the Germans with a perfect excuse for delaying reparations payments. By the end of 1922, France was running out of patience. If Germany could ignore reparations, what other terms of the treaty might become worthless?

In January 1923 France and Belgium sent troops into the Ruhr, Germany's most important industrial region, to seize its produce as reparations. In response, the German government ordered a campaign of passive non-co-operation in the Ruhr. The workers went on strike and the government paid them not to work. This meant printing even more money, which produced the 'Great Inflation' of 1923 and left the German economy effectively bankrupt. Before long, even the French could see that there was little chance of receiving reparations, and that the invasion of the Ruhr was pointless. But the German government knew it could not ignore realities for ever. Sooner or later, the issue of reparations would have to be faced.

By the end of 1923 a new German government under Gustav Stresemann had accepted the principle of fulfilment – obeying the terms of the Treaty of Versailles. Promised huge loans from the USA to help rebuild the German economy, it introduced a new, sound currency and brought inflation under control. The Dawes Plan of 1924 determined the amount of reparations the Germans should pay each year, and approved the promised American loans. Over the years, Germany received far more in loans than it paid in reparations. In 1925 the French withdrew their soldiers from the Ruhr. It seemed that Germany was finally reconciled to the Treaty of Versailles, and could look forward to a future of peace and prosperity.

Peace treaties with other defeated nations, 1919–23

The Treaty of St Germain, September 1919.

This was the treaty signed by the Allies with **Austria**. Austria accepted the break-up of the Austro-Hungarian Empire. Austria and Hungary were left as small independent states.

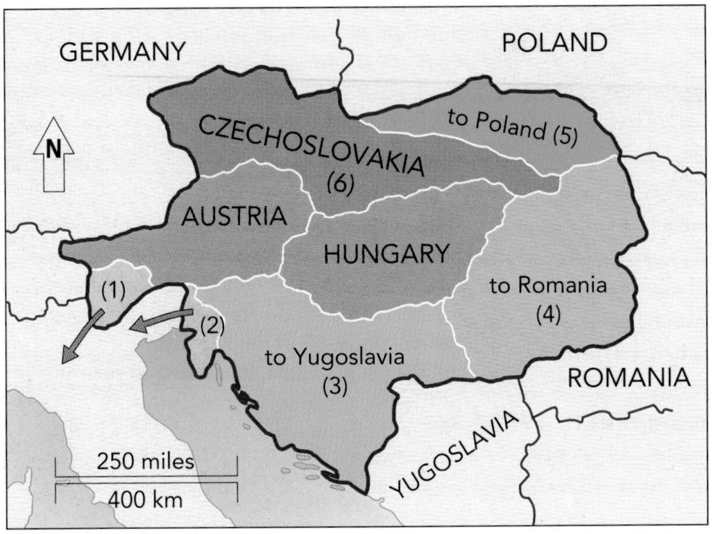

(1) South Tyrol and Trentino to Italy.

(2) Istria and Trieste to Italy.

(3) Croatia, Bosnia and Herzegovina to Serbia, creating Yugoslavia.

(4) Transylvania to Romania.

(5) Galicia to Poland. The new state of Poland also received territory from Germany and Russia.

(6) The new state of Czechoslovakia was created.

Reparations

Austria agreed to pay reparations, but the collapse of the Bank of Vienna in 1922 meant nothing was paid.

Military restrictions

Austria was permitted an army of no more than 30,000 men.

The impact of defeat

- It was impossible to give every national group self-determination. Most of the new states contained dissatisfied minorities who continued to create problems.
- Splitting up the empire created economic problems. Roads and railways had not been built to suit the new states, and the new nations had their own taxes on trade, where previously trade had been free.
- Several small, weak states now existed where there had previously been one large state.

The Treaty of Neuilly, November 1919.

This was the treaty signed by the Allies with **Bulgaria**.

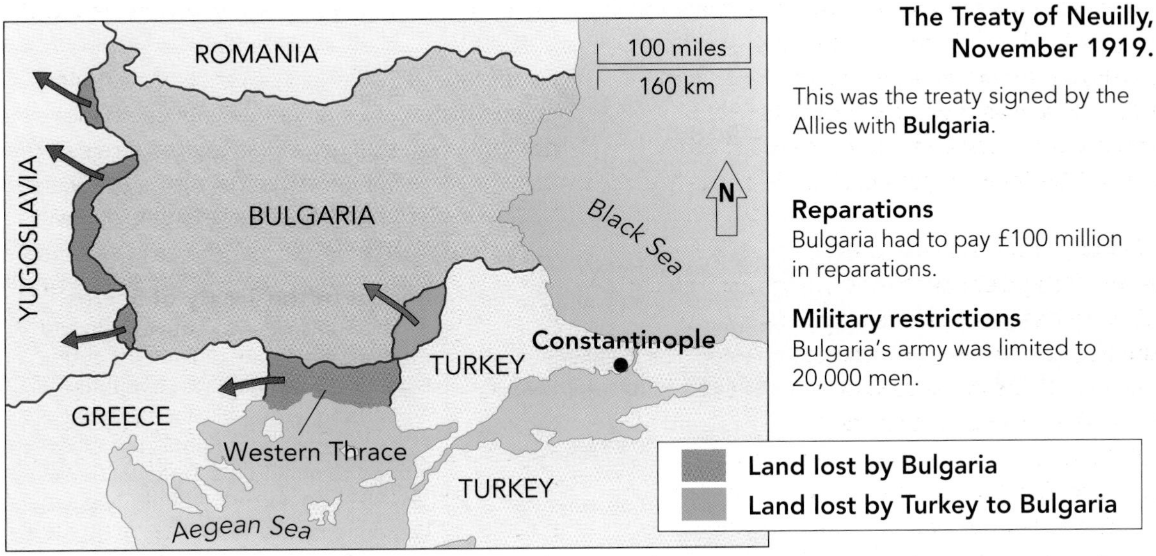

Reparations

Bulgaria had to pay £100 million in reparations.

Military restrictions

Bulgaria's army was limited to 20,000 men.

The Treaty of Trianon, June 1920.

This was the treaty signed by the Allies with **Hungary**. With the Treaty of St Germain, it marked the break-up of the Austro-Hungarian Empire.

Reparations

Hungary agreed to pay reparations, but the collapse of Hungary's economy in the early 1920s meant nothing was ever paid.

Military restrictions

Hungary was permitted an army of no more than 35,000 men.

The impact of the defeat

- A communist state under Bela Kun was established in 1919. He was overthrown later in the year and a military dictatorship set up under Admiral Horthy.
- The Hungarians continued to resent a settlement that left up to 3 million Magyars (Hungarians) under foreign rule.

The Treaty of Sèvres, August 1920, amended by the Treaty of Lausanne, July 1923

These treaties were signed by the Allies with **Turkey**.

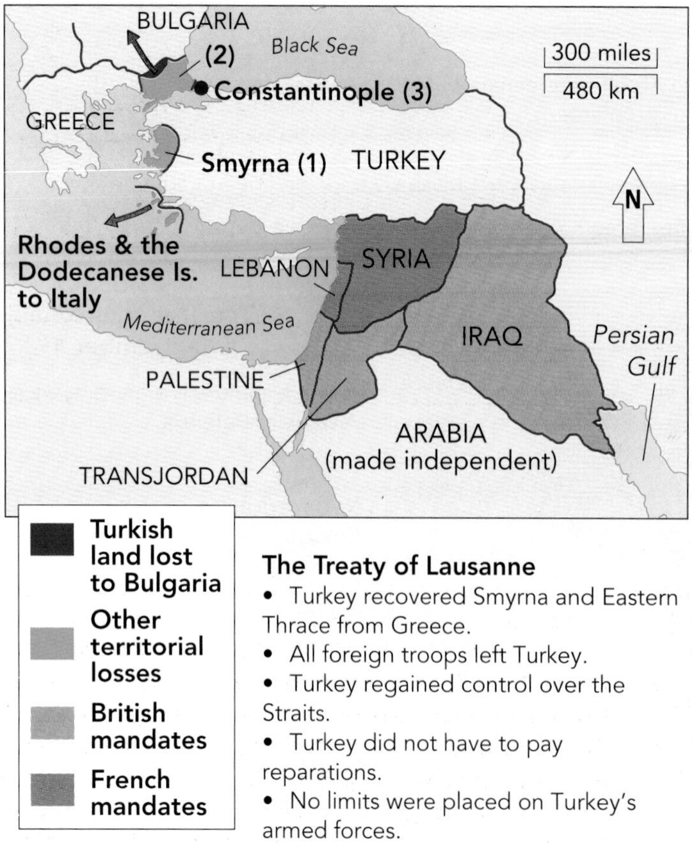

The Treaty of Lausanne

- Turkey recovered Smyrna and Eastern Thrace from Greece.
- All foreign troops left Turkey.
- Turkey regained control over the Straits.
- Turkey did not have to pay reparations.
- No limits were placed on Turkey's armed forces.

The Treaty of Sèvres

(1) Smyrna and **(2)** Eastern Thrace were lost to Greece. In Europe Turkey was left with only the small area around Constantinople.

(3) The Straits of the Dardanelles and the Bosphorus were opened to ships of all nations.

The Ottoman Empire was split up. Arabia was made independent. Turkey's other possessions in the Middle East were made League of Nations mandates and allocated to Britain and France.

(4) An independent Armenian State was to be created. The Allies could keep troops in Turkey to ensure the treaty was obeyed.

Impact of the Treaty of Sèvres

- The Turks were so outraged by the terms of the Treaty of Sèvres that the Sultan's government was overthrown in an uprising led by Mustapha Kemal.
- Rather than fight Kemal, the Allies agreed to amend the Treaty of Sèvres. This led to the signing of the Treaty of Lausanne in July 1923.

Could the treaties be justified at the time?

There is no doubt that the treaties which established the peace settlement at the end of the First World War imposed very strict terms upon the defeated countries.

- Germany lost all its colonies and, in total, 13 per cent of its land. Nearly six million German citizens now found themselves living outside Germany's borders. The Germans were also forced to agree to pay huge reparations and carry out massive reductions in their armed forces.
- Austria saw its empire disbanded and was also forced to pay reparations to the Allies. It too had its armed forces reduced. Similar penalties were also imposed on Bulgaria and Hungary.
- The Turks were so angered by their territorial losses that they rose up and overthrew their own government. The Allies then agreed to less severe terms in the Treaty of Lausanne in 1923.

The view held by most historians since 1919 is that the treaties were too harsh and were likely to lead to future war. It would only be a matter of time before the Germans, in particular, set about seeking revenge. On the day that the Treaty of Versailles was signed a leading German newspaper published a criticism of the terms of what it called 'a disgraceful treaty'. It made it clear that 'There will be vengeance for the shame of 1919'.

SOURCE G

Lloyd George told one of his officials that the treaty was '...all a great pity. We shall have to do the same thing all over again in twenty-five years at three times the cost'.

An extract from a book on the Treaty of Versailles, written in 1969.

SOURCE H

This is not peace. It is an armistice for fifteen years.

The judgement of Marshall Foch on the Treaty of Versailles. Foch was the French commander-in-chief of the Allied armies in the final year of the war.

SOURCE I

It was a peace of revenge. It sowed a thousand seeds from which new wars might spring. It was as though the Devil had sat beside Clemenceau and whispered madness into the ear of Wilson and grinned across the table at Lloyd George.

An extract from a book written by a British historian in 1929.

SOURCE J

PEACE AND FUTURE CANNON FODDER

The Tiger: "Curious! I seem to hear a child weeping!"

This cartoon by Will Dyson was published in a British newspaper in 1919. The 'Big Four' are seen leaving Versailles. Dyson shows Orlando, the Italian prime minister, as well as Lloyd George (at the back), and Wilson (far right), while Clemenceau, the prime minister of France (in front) stops as he hears a child weeping. The child represents 'the class of 1940'. Dyson thought that the terms of Versailles would lead to further war in 1940. He was wrong by only four months!

This view was shared not only by many people in Germany, but others elsewhere – even some of those involved in actually drawing up the terms of the treaty (see sources G–J).

Was the treaty a mistake?

Although the strict terms of the Treaty of Versailles aroused much criticism, this did not mean that the treaty-makers had simply acted foolishly or were not aware of what they doing.

- The 'Big Four' met after the most terrible war in history. They were determined to make sure that war would not happen again. Consequently they wanted to weaken Germany so that it would not be able to invade France again. Although the causes of the war were complex, by 1918 many people had come to believe that German military ambition was to blame. Consequently Germany had to be weakened to ensure future peace. This was done and a new organisation to maintain peace, the League of Nations, was established.
- After the loss of so many lives there was a strong desire for revenge amongst the people of the victorious nations. This was particularly true in France, where much of the fighting had taken place. In Britain there were many people who wanted to see the Kaiser brought to trial and hanged. If the Treaty of Versailles is considered in the light of such views, it can be seen that perhaps it could have been a lot worse for the German people.
- Some of the decisions the peacemakers had to make were extremely difficult. The Austro-Hungarian Empire was breaking up, large areas of Europe had been devastated, communism was spreading and Europe's economy was in tatters. There was a need to restore stability – and quickly. This the peacemakers did.
- The terms of the treaty were strict, but they were not entirely unexpected. When the Armistice was signed in November 1918 the Germans knew they would have to pay reparations, surrender territory and have their armed forces reduced. These were the usual consequences of defeat in war. At the end of the Franco-Prussian War in 1871 the Germans made the French pay five billion francs and stationed troops in France until it was paid. When the Russians asked for peace terms with the Germans in March 1918 the resulting Treaty of Brest-Litovsk took away more than a quarter of Russia's farmland and population. It is for that reason that some historians think that the Germans might have imposed even harsher terms on the Allies if they had won the war (see Source K).

Perhaps, therefore, those historians who have condemned the Treaty of Versailles have been over-critical. Nowadays most historians think that the peacemakers did a reasonable job considering the problems they faced.

SOURCE K

THE RECKONING.

PAN-GERMAN. "MONSTROUS, I CALL IT. WHY, IT'S FULLY A QUARTER OF WHAT *WE* SHOULD HAVE MADE *THEM* PAY, IF *WE'D* WON."

A cartoon from a British magazine published in 1919. The German in the caption is talking about the terms of the Treaty of Versailles: 'Monstrous I call it. These reparations are only a quarter of what we would have made them pay if we had won'.

Paper 1-type assessment: The Treaty of Versailles

SOURCE A

"PERHAPS IT WOULD GEE-UP BETTER IF WE LET IT TOUCH EARTH"

A cartoon from a British newspaper, 1921. Aristide Briand of France and David Lloyd George of Britain are looking at the effects of reparation payments on Germany.

QUESTIONS

Section A Questions

1a Study Source A. Explain the message of this cartoon. Support your answer by referring to details of the cartoon and your own knowledge. (6)

b Explain why the Treaty of Versailles imposed such strict terms on Germany. (9)

Section B Questions

2a How did the Treaty of Versailles try to make sure there would not be another war? (4)

b What did George Clemenceau of France hope to achieve in the Treaty? (6)

c 'The most important factor in deciding the terms of the Treaty of Versailles was Woodrow Wilson's desire for a fair and just peace'. Do you agree with this statement? Explain your answer. (10)

To what extent was the League of Nations a success?

The peacemakers at Versailles knew that they had not solved all the problems of the post-war world, but they looked to the League of Nations to complete their work. This international organisation, set up to preserve world peace, was dealt a serious blow by the USA's refusal to join, but still did much to encourage co-operation between nations. It had some successes, particularly in the 1920s, in persuading nations to resolve conflicts peacefully. However, the Great Depression, starting in 1929, created a more unstable international climate, in which aggressive nations, prepared to use war to achieve their aims, challenged the principles of international peace and co-operation on which the League was based. The League proved too weak to stand up to Japanese aggression in Manchuria, and could not prevent the Italian invasion of Abyssinia. By the mid-1930s it had lost its authority and had ceased to play an effective part in international affairs.

QUESTIONS

1. What was the work of the following in the League of Nations: the Assembly, the Secretariat, the Council?
2. In what ways was the League weak from the start?

How far did weaknesses in the League's organisation make failure inevitable?

The Covenant of the League of Nations (setting out its aims) was written into each of the peace treaties. Wilson hoped this would ensure that the League was accepted by all nations. However, from the start, the League shared many of the weaknesses of the treaties themselves. The defeated powers were not consulted about the League and were not invited to join. The victorious powers did not really agree among themselves about the League. Wilson's idealism and belief in co-operation between nations were not shared by the cynical and worldly wise Europeans. Lloyd George went along with the idea to keep Wilson happy, and the French agreed on the basis that anything which might give them additional security against Germany was worth trying.

SOURCE A

An American cartoon of 1919, showing America's reluctance to join the League.

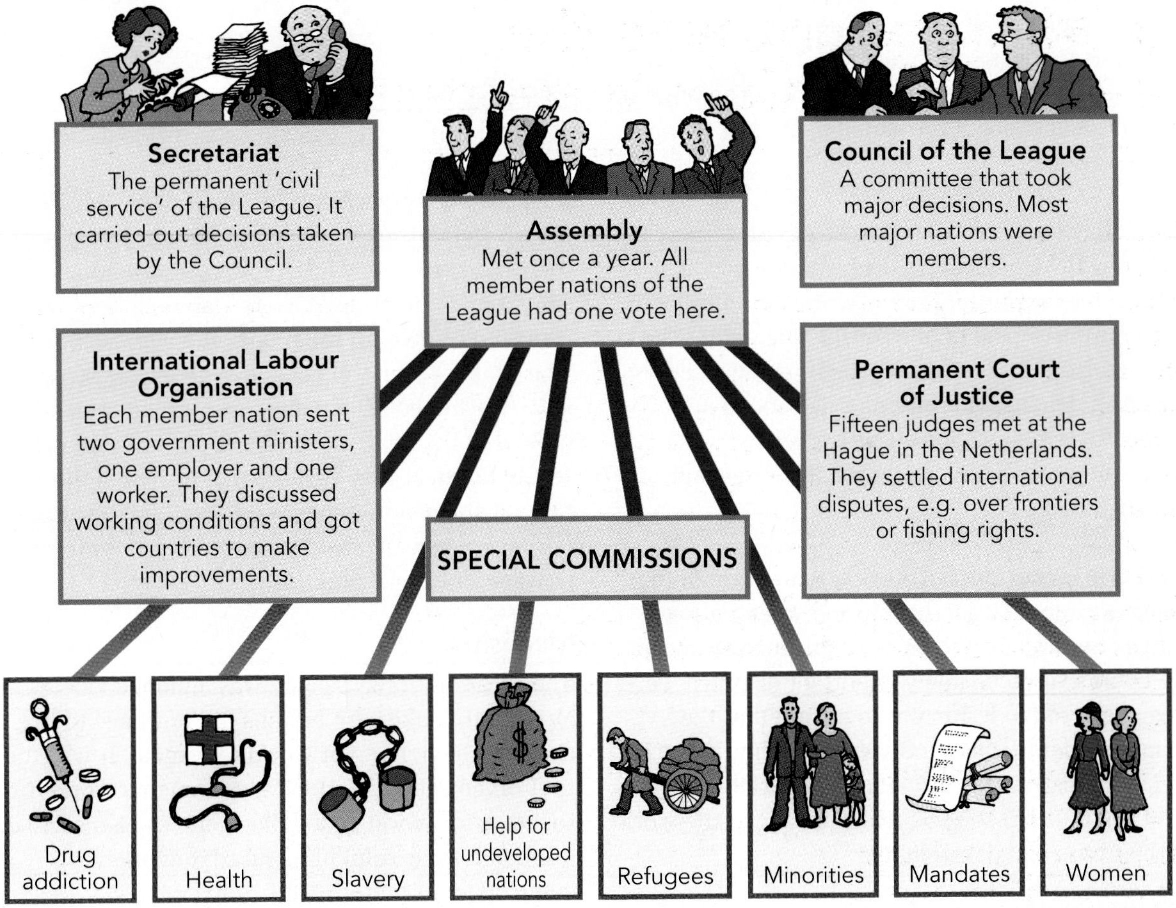

Secretariat
The permanent 'civil service' of the League. It carried out decisions taken by the Council.
Assembly
Met once a year. All member nations of the League had one vote here.
Council of the League
A committee that took major decisions. Most major nations were members.
International Labour Organisation
Each member nation sent two government ministers, one employer and one worker. They discussed working conditions and got countries to make improvements.
SPECIAL COMMISSIONS
Permanent Court of Justice
Fifteen judges met at the Hague in the Netherlands. They settled international disputes, e.g. over frontiers or fishing rights.
Drug addiction
Health
Slavery
Help for undeveloped nations
Refugees
Minorities
Mandates
Women

The structure of the League of Nations.

Most important of all, Wilson's failure to persuade the US Congress to accept the treaties meant that the USA never joined the League. The absence of the world's most powerful nation seriously undermined the League's authority to deal with international problems.

The structure and organisation of the League

To carry out its work, the League needed a structure that would enable nations to meet, discuss and resolve international problems. It was decided that the League would be based in Geneva, Switzerland. All member states could send representatives to the Assembly. This was the League's parliament. It met every year and had ultimate authority over the League's actions. In the Assembly, all nations were equal and had one vote. The Assembly was too large to react quickly to international crises, so a smaller group called the Council was set up, which met more frequently.

To promote international co-operation and to achieve international peace and security:

- by the acceptance of obligations not to resort to war;
- by the prescription of open, just and honourable relations between nations;
- by the firm establishment of international law as the rule of conduct between governments;
- by the maintenance of justice and a scrupulous respect for all treaty obligations in the dealings of organised peoples with one another.

Extracts from the Covenant of the League of Nations.

The great powers attempted to control the Council. Britain, France, Italy and Japan were permanent members and were originally matched by representatives from four other states. The number of additional states represented increased to nine over the years.

The Council supervised the work of commissions set up by the Covenant to deal with particular issues. The most important of these commissions were for disarmament and for the mandates. The League also established a range of committees and agencies, dealing with international social and economic issues, such as health, drugs, prostitution, working conditions, refugees and women's rights.

The Permanent Court of Justice was set up in the Hague to rule on legal disputes between nations, but as countries had to agree in advance to accept the court's verdicts, many important disputes were never referred to it. Finally, to ensure that the League's operations functioned smoothly, it had its own administrative staff – the Secretariat. This was the League's civil service, which arranged the work of the Council and Assembly.

Membership

The League had 42 members when it was set up, and this number increased over the years. However, it was not just the USA that was not a member. At first, all the defeated nations were excluded. They were later allowed in – Germany joined in 1926, although it left again when Hitler came to power in 1933. Russia was also excluded because other nations refused to recognise its communist government. It was finally admitted to the League only in 1934. Other founder members of the League, such as Japan and Italy, subsequently left it. So the League was never an organisation of all states, or even of all the most important states.

The League was dominated by Britain and France, which disagreed significantly over the role that it should play. Britain regarded the League as a harmless talking-shop, but did not want to give it real authority or power. France, on the other hand, wanted the League to enforce the terms of the peace treaties. This difference in attitude between the two powers most involved in the League's work inevitably weakened it.

Security issues

The real test for the League came when it had to deal with aggression. In theory, the Council could raise armed forces from member states, but in practice countries were very reluctant to agree to this. The Covenant said the League should use sanctions to deter aggressors – all members would refuse to trade with them until the aggression ceased. However, the League was only as strong and determined as its members, and nations often looked to the League to solve problems that they would not deal with themselves. Although the League could sometimes pressurise small nations into obedience, it was too weak to deal with great powers like Japan and Italy.

Idealism

The creation of the League was an idealistic attempt to make sure nations did not have to live through the horrors of world war again. It was the first organisation in which governments worked together for world peace. Its agencies also carried out much successful humanitarian work. Its campaigns for better health and working conditions, to help refugees return to their homes and to free slaves did much to improve people's lives across the world. The International Labour Organisation (ILO) encouraged governments to recognise trade unions, and to improve workers' pay and pensions. Even when governments did not accept everything proposed by the League's agencies, public awareness of a whole range of social issues was increased.

However, the idealism of the League was also a weakness. All member states, large and small, had equal voting rights, and all decisions (in both the Assembly and the Council) had to be unanimous. This was fine when members agreed with each other, but not when they disagreed.

The work of the commissions illustrates how the League was powerless to make progress against the wishes of individual states. The Covenant committed all members to reducing armaments, yet the Disarmament Commission found this impossible to achieve. The French regarded

SOURCE B

A British cartoon commenting on the ability of the League of Nations to deal with the threat of war.

disarmament as giving away their security, while the Germans, who had been disarmed in the Treaty of Versailles, thought they had a right to rearm, at least to the level of other powers. Not until 1932 was the commission finally able to set up a Disarmament Conference. By then, much of the spirit of co-operation and trust that the League originally enjoyed had disappeared. The Conference could agree nothing, and France's refusal to disarm was the perfect excuse for Hitler to walk out of the Conference (and the League) in 1933.

The Mandates Commission was only slightly more successful. The mandated powers were supposed to administer the mandates on behalf of the League and to prepare them for eventual independence. In practice, they treated them more or less as colonies. Iraq's independence in 1932 was the only example of a mandate being freed in the inter-war period.

Conclusion

The circumstances in which the League was set up, and in particular the refusal of the USA to join, left the League with serious weaknesses. The League was not well equipped to deal with cases of aggression, and had no armed forces of its own. The League worked well when members wished to co-operate, and through its agencies had many worthwhile achievements. However, the creators of the League were too optimistic and idealistic in expecting all nations to accept the League's authority.

QUESTIONS

1 Look at Source A.
What can you tell from this cartoon about American attitudes towards the League of Nations? Explain your answer using details from the cartoon.

2 Look at Source B.
Do you think the cartoonist believed that the League would be successful in preventing war? Use details of the cartoon to explain your answer.

How successful was the League in the 1920s?

Successes and failures in peacekeeping

The peace treaties of 1919–20 did not resolve all the territorial disputes caused by the war. As we have seen (refer back to page 60), the Turks were so outraged by the peace settlement that they refused to accept it. They went on fighting, mainly against the Greeks, until the Allies were ready to agree to the Treaty of Lausanne in 1923. The Italians were dissatisfied with their gains, and managed to hold on to Fiume after D'Annunzio's occupation of 1919–20. The Poles were especially active, grabbing much of the area of Teschen from Czechoslovakia in early 1919 (the League finally fixed this border between the two countries in 1920). More importantly, the Poles were at war with Russia until 1921, gaining much of the Ukraine and Belorussia.

In the face of continuing violence and uncertainty, the League only gradually established a role for itself in dealing with international crises. Even when it did become involved, its record in resolving crises was mixed.

Successes and failures for the League of Nations in the 1920s.

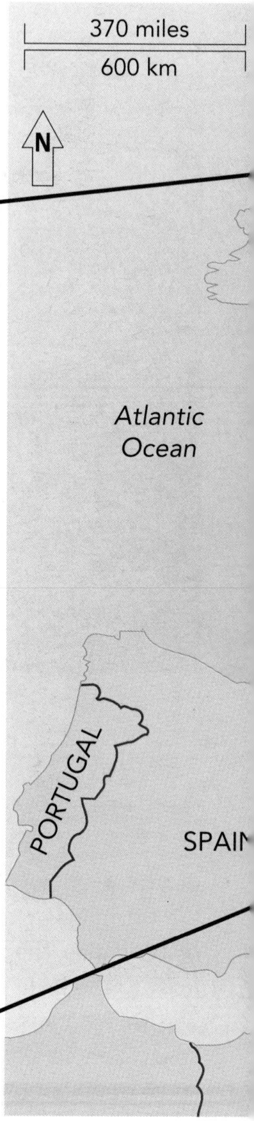

The Aaland Islands (1921). These islands are in the Baltic Sea about half way between Sweden and Finland. Both nations claimed the islands and seemed ready to fight over them, but they invited the League to reach a judgement on the dispute. It decided the islands should be awarded to Finland, and Sweden accepted this.
Verdict on the League: A satisfactory outcome, but only because the nations in the dispute were willing to accept the League's authority.

Economic collapse in Austria and Hungary (1922–3). In 1922–3 Austria and Hungary faced bankruptcy. Their economies had not recovered after the war, and now, burdened with reparations payments, it seemed that they would simply collapse. The League arranged international loans for the two countries, sending commissioners to supervise how the money was spent. In effect, the League temporarily took over the economic management of the two countries. With this help, both Austria and Hungary were able to begin economic recovery.
Verdict on the League: The League's action was prompt and effective.

Corfu (1923). In August 1923 five Italian surveyors, who were working for the League of Nations in mapping the Greek-Albanian frontier, were shot and killed on the Greek side of the border. Mussolini, the new Italian dictator, took advantage of the situation, demanding compensation from the Greek government. When this was not forthcoming, he bombarded and occupied Corfu, an island off the Greek coast. This action was in complete defiance of the principles of the League, of which Italy was a prominent member. The Council wanted to condemn Italy, but the great powers would not permit it. Instead they put pressure on the Greeks to accept Mussolini's demands. Only when the Greeks had apologised and paid up did Mussolini withdraw his forces from Corfu.
Verdict on the League: A disaster – confronted by a great power willing to use force, the League had backed down.

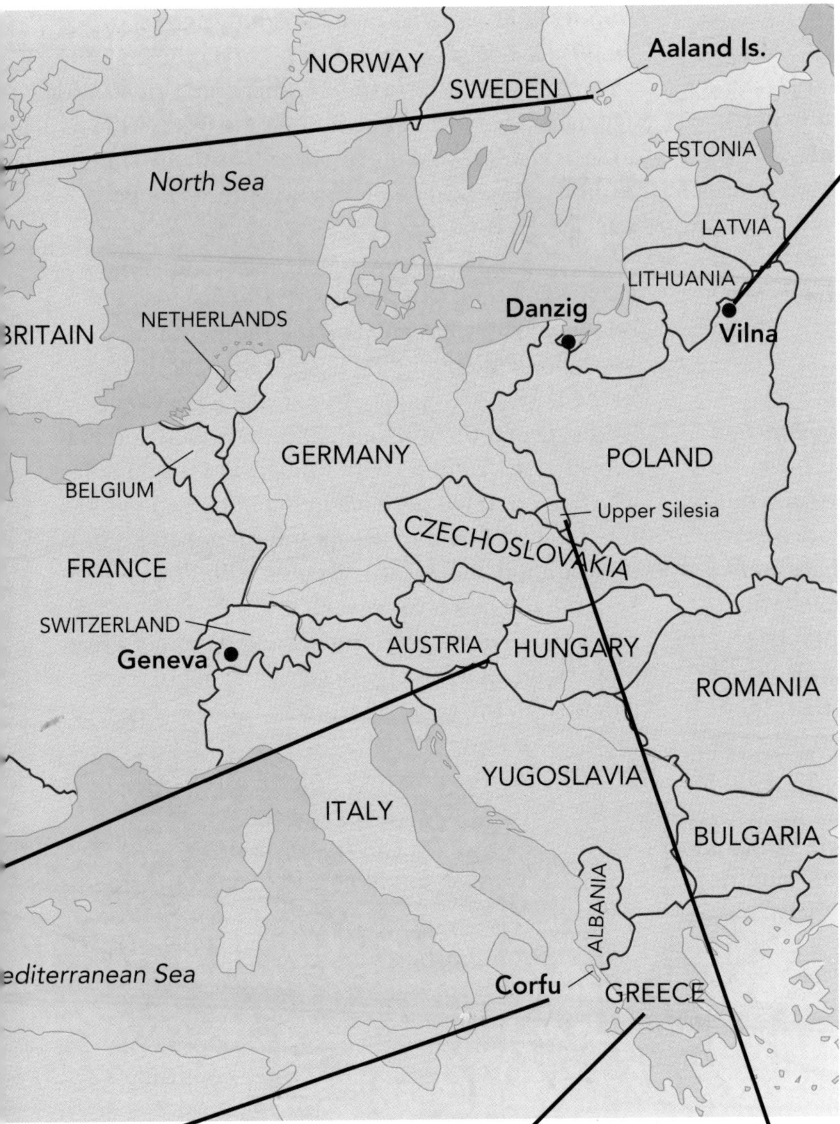

Vilna (1920). This area was claimed by both Lithuania and Poland. It was included in the new state of Lithuania set up at the end of the war, but it had a majority Polish population. In 1920, during the Russo-Polish War, Vilna was occupied by Polish forces, which later refused to leave. This seemed a clear case of one League member (Poland) showing aggression against another (Lithuania), but the League was very reluctant to become involved.

Taking action against Poland would have required armed forces, but League members were not willing to supply them. In addition, Britain and France saw Poland as a strong barrier against Germany and communist Russia, and did not wish to upset it. The League tried to negotiate a deal, but in 1923 it confirmed Poland's occupation of Vilna. Sporadic fighting between the two sides continued until 1927.

Verdict on the League: Weak and useless.

Upper Silesia (1921). Upper Silesia was one of several plebiscite areas defined in the Treaty of Versailles. The people who lived in these areas could vote on which country should have the territory. Upper Silesia contained large numbers of Poles and Germans, and since the area was particularly important for its industry, both Poland and Germany were determined to acquire the territory. In the plebiscite held by the League in March 1921, the people voted in favour of Germany by 700,000 votes to 480,000. The League decided to partition (share) the area. Germany received over half the land and population, while the Poles had most of the industry. This caused great bitterness in Germany, but both countries accepted the decision.

Verdict on the League: A messy compromise, but whatever the League decided would have displeased someone. In difficult circumstances, it did as well as it could.

The Greek-Bulgarian Dispute (1925). After the Treaty of Neuilly, the border between Greece and Bulgaria remained a source of tension between the two nations. After a number of violent incidents, the Greeks invaded Bulgaria in October 1925. On this occasion the League intervened effectively. It condemned the Greek action and pressurised them to withdraw, which they did.

Verdict on the League: Successful action brought a return to peace – exactly what the League was for. But cynics suggested that the League was only willing to take firm action when no great powers were involved.

Conclusion

The League had its successes and failures in dealing with international crises in the 1920s. It was at its best when dealing with small nations that were prepared to accept its authority. However, when the great powers had vital interests at stake, they ignored the League. Thus the League could do nothing about the French invasion of the Ruhr in 1923. Moreover, there were already signs that it would prove incapable of dealing effectively with determined aggressors.

A number of important international agreements were signed by the great powers in the 1920s without reference to the League. It was as if the great powers felt that some matters were too important for the League to handle. There were many such agreements, but two examples will illustrate the point. The League was notably unsuccessful in achieving disarmament. However, by the Washington Naval Agreement of 1922 the USA, Britain, Japan, France and Italy agreed to limit their fleets. No major ships would be built for ten years, and the size of the American, British and Japanese fleets would be in the ratio 5:5:3, with France and Italy having about half as many ships as Japan. The League played no part in reaching this agreement.

Even when the great powers met to discuss relations with Germany and the future of the Versailles settlement, the League was not invited. In the Locarno Treaties of 1925, signed between Germany and the wartime Allies, Germany formally accepted its frontiers with France and Belgium. It also agreed to the permanent demilitarisation of the Rhineland, and to accept international arbitration in any future disputes with France. Locarno did much to create a more friendly relationship between Germany and the other great powers, and led directly to Germany being admitted to the League in 1926.

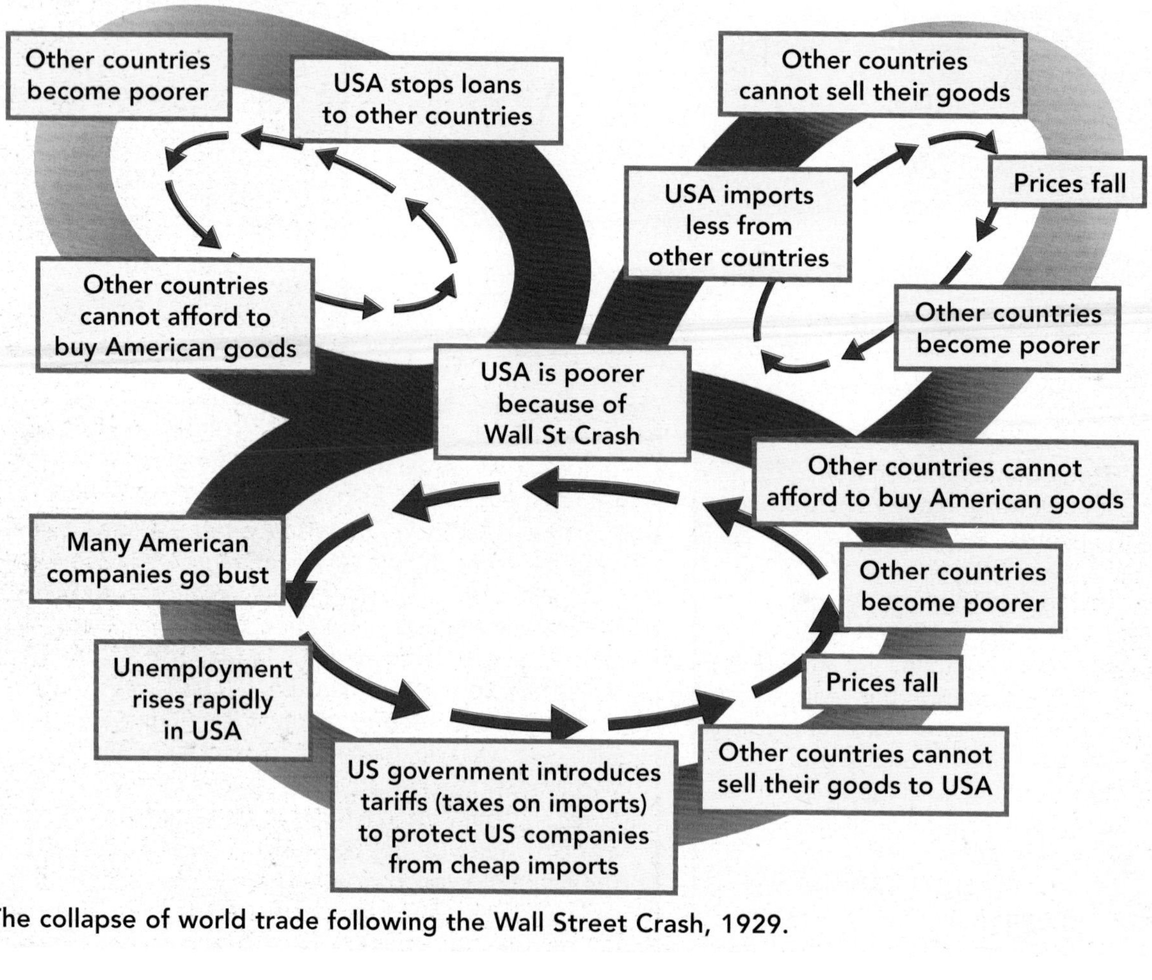

The collapse of world trade following the Wall Street Crash, 1929.

How far did the Depression make the work of the League more difficult?

The Great Depression was sparked off by the Wall Street Crash – the collapse of the US stock market – in October 1929. The slump in US share prices was a disaster not just for America, but for the world economy. The wave of bankruptcies that followed the crash sent the US economy into a downward spiral that had a deep impact on world trade. Hardly a country in the world remained unaffected. The only exception was the Soviet Union, whose economy was not dependent on trade with other nations. The slump in world trade made all other nations poorer, and unemployment soared as industries ground to a halt.

Although this was an economic crisis, it soon had harmful political effects, which impacted on the work of the League of Nations. The Great Depression did much to destroy the goodwill on which the League had depended in the 1920s. The 1930s brought increasing tension and conflict, as nations struggled to cope with the effects of the crash. Their failure to find peaceful ways of doing this culminated in the Second World War.

Unemployed shipbuilding workers in England on a protest march from Jarrow to London in 1936.

SOURCE C

SOURCE D

Members of the Italian Fascist Youth organisation receiving their rifles in the presence of Mussolini.

Unemployment

Millions of workers lost their jobs because of the crash. Across the industrialised states, unemployment was five times higher in 1932 than it had been in 1929. In the USA, 30 per cent of the working population was unemployed. Not surprisingly, the unemployed demanded action from the politicians. However, the politicians had little idea how to cope with the situation. Their first reaction was to assume that the slump was temporary and would soon correct itself. Meanwhile, the unemployed became ever more desperate. The effects of unemployment were different from country to country, but everywhere governments became uncertain, unstable and preoccupied more with solving their own problems than with tackling international difficulties.

Extremism

In some countries, notably Germany, the Depression helped extremist political parties come to power. Voters were tempted to follow any politician who offered a solution to unemployment. They felt they had nothing to lose, as democracy had failed them. These extremist parties were often nationalist – they had a hatred of other nations, and were concerned only with their own national interests. Where such parties came to power, they often showed an unwillingness to accept international agreements and a willingness to use force to achieve their aims. The League of Nations found it almost impossible to deal with the more violent international climate of the 1930s, as nations simply ignored its authority.

Militarism

Extremist leaders looked to foreign policy success to distract the attention of their people from troubles at home. Dictatorships re-armed their countries and prepared their populations for war. Political parties like the Fascist Party in Italy and the Nazis in Germany were like armies – they even had their own uniforms. In these countries, ordinary life was militarised. People who did not accept party discipline were punished. Workers lost their rights. Opposition was not tolerated. Women and children, as well as men, were expected to join party organisations. Militarism in a powerful country, like Germany, posed a great threat to other countries. Sooner or later the dictatorships would use their power. The consequences of increasing militarism in Germany are described later. Two other powers whose militarism did much to destroy international peace in the 1930s were Japan and Italy.

Increasing militarism in Japan

Japan was already established on the Asian mainland: its victory over Russia in the war of 1905 had given Japan control over much of Manchuria, and in 1910 it had annexed Korea. Moreover, Japan emerged from the First World War as the most important power in Asia, acquiring colonies in the Pacific and control over German territories leased from China. Yet Japan was not satisfied by these gains for several reasons:

- Rapid population growth and industrial development meant that Japan had to import food and raw materials.
- The Allies' refusal to refer to racial equality in the peace treaties of 1919–20 was deeply offensive to the Japanese.
- The Japanese government had accepted an inferior position in the Washington Naval Agreements (1922), which permitted Japan only three ships to every five built by Britain and the USA. The Japanese military took this as a sign that they could not trust their politicians to protect Japan's interests.

Tension between the military, who wanted a policy of aggressive expansion in Asia, and the politicians, who were much more cautious, grew worse during the 1920s. The army began to act without government approval. In 1928 it had the local warlord in Manchuria, Chang Tso Lin, assassinated because it thought the government's policy of friendship towards Chang was wrong. The army simply wanted to take Manchuria over.

There were also increasing economic difficulties towards the end of the 1920s. The price of rice began to collapse because of over-production, and Japan's farmers saw their incomes fall sharply. Moreover, the export of silk, mostly to the USA, was seriously affected by the Depression. By 1932 the price was only one-fifth of what it had been a decade earlier. Japanese industry was also in a bad state – production and employment fell by 30 per cent between 1929 and 1931. While the government seemed unable to cope with these developments, the army's policy of territorial conquest and expansion seemed to offer the people some hope.

In September 1931 (see pages 75–6), the army staged the Mukden incident, which led to the seizure of Manchuria and the establishment of the Japanese puppet state of Manchukuo. The government in Tokyo had advance warning of these plans, but did not intervene. Politicians needed great courage to stand up to the army, since assassinations were common. In May 1932 a group of soldiers murdered the prime minister, Inukai Tsuyoshi, in his own house. In February 1936 a full-scale military revolt in Tokyo was crushed only after many politicians and government officials had been murdered. Such events undermined normal political life. After 1932 Japan's governments were dominated by military men, and followed ever more aggressive policies, culminating in the invasion of China in 1937.

QUESTIONS

1. Explain how the Great Depression made the work of the League more difficult.
2. Why did militarism develop in
   a Japan
   b Italy
   during the 1920s and 1930s?
3. Look at Source E. What was the cartoonist's opinion of Japanese actions in China?

Increasing militarism in Italy

Italy, like Japan, emerged from the First World War dissatisfied with the gains it had made. The years immediately after the war were marked by great instability as the country tried to cope with its economic problems. Unemployment rose rapidly, and extremists on left and right struggled to take control.

By 1922, Mussolini's Fascist Party, or Blackshirts, had emerged as the dominant group. After staging his 'March on Rome' in October that year, Mussolini was invited by the king to become prime minister. It took some time for him to take complete control of the country, but by 1926 he was firmly established as dictator – he preferred the title 'Il Duce'.

SOURCE E

Mussolini making a speech.

Once in power, Mussolini put into practice the extreme right-wing policies of his Fascist Party. Opposition was crushed and other political parties were banned. He took command of the economy, controlling working conditions, pay and prices by law. His achievements seemed impressive. New roads were built, marshes were drained, dams were constructed for hydroelectric power, and railways were electrified. In foreign affairs, Mussolini quickly made a name for himself. He built up Italy's armed forces, and was not afraid to use the threat of violence. The Corfu incident of 1923 showed that Mussolini would follow an aggressive, nationalistic foreign policy.

Like other nations, Italy was hit badly by the Great Depression. When unemployment rose, Mussolini turned to foreign adventures to distract the Italian people from the troubles at home. The first victim was the African state of Abyssinia. Mussolini's invasion of 1935–6 went unchecked by other nations, and did much to destroy the credibility of the League of Nations. From 1936 Italy sent troops to support to the Nationalist side in the Spanish Civil War. At first, Mussolini was suspicious and jealous of the German dictator Adolf Hitler. But the signing of the Rome–Berlin Axis in 1936 marked the first move towards the alliance of Italy and Germany in the Second World War.

QUESTION

Look at Source E.
What impression does this photograph give you of Mussolini as a politician?

Why did the League fail in Manchuria and Abyssinia?

Failure in Manchuria, 1931–3

Manchuria is a part of northern China – fertile and rich in natural resources such as coal and iron ore. In the 1920s China was weak, and in many areas local leaders called warlords were more important than the national government. Japan took advantage of this weakness to expand its interests in Manchuria.

The Japanese already had an army (known as the Kwantung army) stationed in southern Manchuria to protect the territory gained from Russia in 1905. They also owned the South Manchurian Railway. The Chinese regarded the area as theirs, and claimed that they had been forced, first by Russia and later by Japan, to accept foreign domination of Manchuria. By the late 1920s many Chinese were moving into Manchuria to settle, attracted by the availability of land and work. At the same time, the Chinese government was beginning to stand up to the warlords, and the Japanese feared that the Chinese might soon be strong enough to challenge them in Manchuria.

SOURCE F

The Sleeping Giant Begins to Feel It

An American cartoon of 1937, commenting on the Japanese invasion of China.

Exasperated by what they believed was their own government's weakness in dealing with China, in September 1931 officers of the Kwantung army staged the Mukden incident. The exact sequence of events remains unclear. However, on the night of 18 September, there was an explosion on the South Manchurian Railway just outside the city of Mukden. The Japanese claimed that this was sabotage by the Chinese, who subsequently opened fire on Japanese railway guards. The Chinese denied this, claiming that all their soldiers in the area were in barracks at the time. Whatever the truth of the matter, the incident was very convenient for the Kwantung army and gave it an excuse to begin the takeover of Manchuria.

There is no doubt that the Japanese government was appalled by these events, but as the invasion progressed successfully, an outburst of nationalism swept Japan, leaving the government no choice but to accept what had occurred. In 1932 Manchuria was renamed Manchukuo, and the last Chinese emperor, Pu Yi, swept from power in his own country in 1911, was installed by the Japanese as a puppet ruler.

How would the League of Nations react? At first, the occupation of Manchuria looked like an obvious case of aggression by Japan. However, the Japanese had long-standing economic rights there, agreed by treaty with the Chinese. Most nations were inclined to regard Manchuria as a Japanese sphere of interest, and were not keen to get involved. In addition, the Japanese had successfully sown confusion about the true circumstances of the Mukden incident, and insisted that they were just defending themselves from Chinese attacks. Nevertheless, when China appealed for the League's help, it could not ignore what was going on. The League instructed Japanese forces to withdraw, but it was ignored, and the further advance of the Japanese into Manchuria left little doubt of their intentions.

In truth, there was little that the League could do if Japan remained determined to ignore its authority. For most League members, events in East Asia seemed very distant. China's internal turmoil was well known, and many League members secretly sympathised with Japan's attempts to impose 'order' on the region. The League decided to set up a Commission of Inquiry under Lord Lytton, which was sent to the area to gather information and report on what had happened. When the report was published in late 1932, it condemned Japan's actions. The members of the League accepted Lytton's conclusions. The Japanese response was simple: they ignored the report and left the League.

The occupation of Manchuria did not end Japanese aggression in China. Early in 1932 Japanese and Chinese troops clashed in Shanghai, and during four weeks of fighting Japan bombed parts of the city. In February 1933 the Japanese occupied Jehol province, which bordered on to Manchuria. These actions were just a prelude to the full-scale invasion of the Chinese mainland that commenced in July 1937. In the months that followed, fighting spread through much of China, and by 1938 many of China's most important cities were under Japanese occupation. Many historians regard July 1937 as the true starting date of the Second World War.

SOURCE G

Japanese troops after a victory over Chinese forces in December 1931.

The League had been exposed as powerless to deal with Japanese aggression in Manchuria. However, because these events took place in East Asia and not in Europe, they were not too damaging to the League's authority. It was easy for the League's supporters to continue to believe that, if a similar crisis occurred in Europe, where vital interests of the great powers were at stake, the League would be able to cope with it.

SOURCE H

On arrival at the site of the explosion, the patrol was fired upon from the fields on the east side of the line. Lieutenant Kawamoto immediately ordered his men to deploy and to return the fire. The attacking body, estimated at five or six, then stopped firing and retreated northwards. The Japanese patrol at once started in pursuit and, having gone about 200 metres, were again fired upon by a larger body, estimated at between three and four hundred.

The Japanese account of events given to the Lytton Inquiry.

SOURCE I

Instructions had been received that special care was to be taken to avoid any clash with Japanese troops in the tense state of feeling which existed at the time. On the night of 18 September, all the soldiers of the 7th Brigade, numbering about 10,000, were in the North Barracks. The west gate in the mud wall surrounding the camp, which gave access to the railway, had been closed. At 10 p.m. the sound of a large explosion could be heard, immediately followed by rifle fire.

The Chinese version of events given to the Lytton Inquiry.

SOURCE J

An explosion undoubtedly occurred on or near the railroad between 10 and 10.30 p.m. but the damage was not sufficient to justify military action. The military operations of the Japanese during this night cannot be regarded as legitimate self-defence.

An extract from Lord Lytton's report, published in October 1932.

QUESTION

Read Sources H, I and J.

Did Lord Lytton believe either the Japanese or the Chinese? How can you tell?

Failure in Abyssinia, 1935–6

In October 1935, Italy, one of the founder members of the League of Nations, attacked Abyssinia, a poor, undeveloped state in north-east Africa. Most historians believe that the resulting crisis was a death-blow to the League, which found it impossible to take effective action to stop the Italian aggression.

Abyssinia was almost the only part of Africa not under European control and, being located next to the Italian colonies of Eritrea and Somaliland, it was an obvious target for Mussolini's colonial ambitions. Italy had attempted to conquer Abyssinia before, and one of Mussolini's aims was to avenge the humiliation suffered by the Italians at the Battle of Adowa (1896). Despite the Treaty of Friendship that Italy had signed with Abyssinia in 1928, it was clear by 1934 that Mussolini was planning war. In December 1934 a clash between Italian and Abyssinian troops at the oasis of Wal Wal gave Mussolini the excuse he needed. Although the League attempted to intervene in the dispute, tension increased and by September 1935 war seemed near.

The League was in an impossible situation. Both Italy and Abyssinia were member states, bound in theory to accept the League's authority in settling their dispute. But it was obvious that Mussolini wanted war. If he invaded Abyssinia, the League would have to take action. But what action? Everything would depend on the attitude of Britain and France, the two great powers in the League. If they were determined enough, Mussolini might be forced to back down. However, they needed Mussolini's friendship because they saw him as a potential ally against Germany.

In January 1935, the French foreign minister, Laval, met Mussolini in Rome. A number of secret agreements were made, some of which concerned Abyssinia. Laval thought he was making economic concessions in North Africa so as to win Mussolini's friendship. But Mussolini interpreted France's approach as an indication that he could do as he liked in Abyssinia. In any case, Mussolini assumed that Britain and France, both major colonial powers themselves, would not object to Italy acquiring another African colony of its own. There was some surprise, then, when Britain tried to warn Mussolini off from invading Abyssinia. In September, Sir Samuel Hoare, the British foreign secretary, made a vigorous speech to the Assembly of the League, calling for collective resistance to any Italian aggression.

In spite of the warnings, Italy's invasion of Abyssinia commenced on 3 October 1935. The Abyssinian forces stood little chance against the modern Italian army, but the country was huge and the roads poor, so the Italian troops were not able to advance quickly. At first, it seemed the League would take the strong action that Hoare had demanded. Within a week the League had condemned Italy as an aggressor, and soon afterwards it imposed sanctions, by which League members were forbidden to trade with Italy. Crucially, however, the sanctions were not extended to basic war materials such as coal, iron and oil. Even Mussolini later admitted that this would have stopped the invasion within a week. But Britain and France were unwilling to risk provoking Mussolini more than necessary. As a result, they kept the Suez Canal open to the Italians, allowing Mussolini to supply his armies in Abyssinia.

Behind the scenes, Britain and France undermined the apparently tough actions of the League. Desperate for a settlement with Italy, Hoare and Laval met in December and agreed a plan that was designed to bring the invasion to an end. Abyssinia would be split up, with Italy gaining much of the fertile lands in the north and the south of the country. Another huge area in the south would be reserved for Italian economic expansion and settlement. Abyssinia would be reduced to half its original size, and limited to the barren, mountainous region. The only compensation for Abyssinia would be a narrow strip of land providing access to the Red Sea – the so-called 'corridor for camels'. The Hoare–Laval Plan was never put to Abyssinia or Italy. Almost immediately, details of it were leaked to the press, causing a public outcry. Hoare and Laval were forced to resign. However, the damage had been done. Everyone now knew that the British and French had been talking tough, but were not prepared to back up their threats with action. Just the opposite – they seemed willing to reward Mussolini for his aggression.

SOURCE K

A British cartoon of 1936 commenting on Mussolini's invasion of Abyssinia.

The League was, of course, completely powerless when its most important members would take no effective action. Abyssinia was left helpless against the Italians, who now pressed home the invasion with greater determination. Only the difficulty of the terrain could slow the advance of the Italian troops, who were using modern weapons such as bombers, tanks and poison gas, against Abyssinian troops often armed only with spears. On 5 May 1936 Italian troops entered the Abyssinian capital, Addis Ababa, in triumph.

Three days earlier the Abyssinian emperor, Haile Selassie, had fled the country. He travelled to Geneva, where on 30 June he addressed the Assembly of the League of Nations. He spoke for three-quarters of an hour, summarising the events of the war and protesting against the failure of the League to deal with the invasion. His speech marked the end of the League's existence as an important international organisation. Nobody took it seriously in future, and it played no significant part in the events which, from 1936, rushed its members towards another world war.

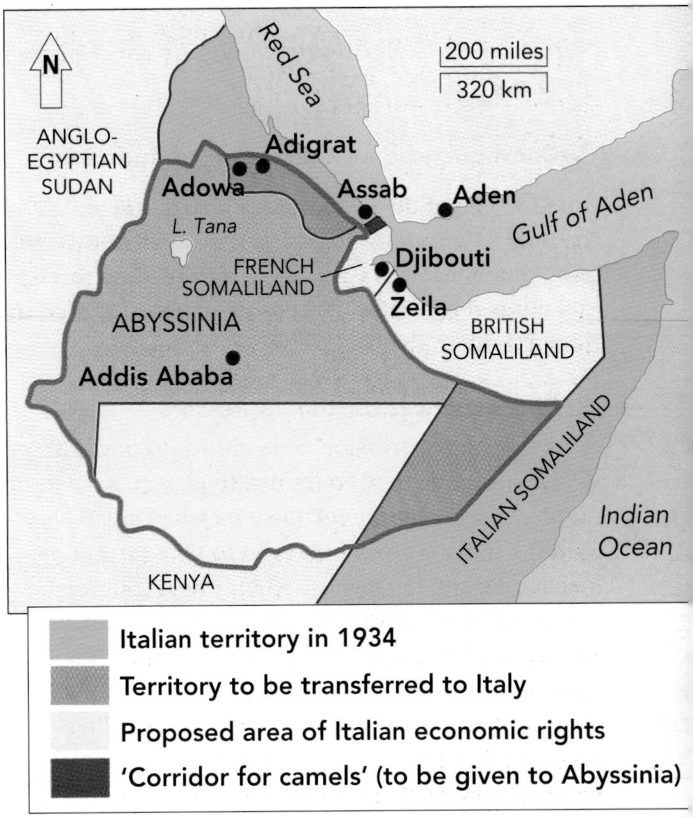

The Hoare–Laval Plan.

SOURCE L

I, Haile Selassie, Emperor of Abyssinia, am here today to claim that justice which is due to my people, and the assistance promised to it eight months ago, when fifty nations asserted that aggression had been committed in violation of international treaties.

Haile Selassie addressing the Assembly of the League of Nations, 30 June 1936.

SOURCE N

The real death of the League was in December 1935, not 1939 or 1945. One day it was a powerful body imposing sanctions, seemingly more effective than ever before; the next day it was an empty sham, everyone scuttling from it as quickly as possible. What killed the League was the publication of the Hoare–Laval Plan.

The judgement of the British historian, A.J.P. Taylor, on the impact of the Abyssinian crisis on the League.

SOURCE M

The bombing was magnificent sport. One group of Abyssinian horsemen gave me the impression of a budding rose unfolding as the bomb fell in their midst and blew them up.

Description by Mussolini's 19-year-old pilot son of one attack in Abyssinia by the Italian air force.

QUESTIONS

1 Look at Source K.
What was the cartoonist's opinion about the invasion? Use details of the cartoon to explain your answer.

2 Why was the League so ineffective in dealing with the Abyssinian crisis?

3 Why was the Abyssinian crisis a death blow to the League, when the Manchurian crisis was not?

What were the consequences of the failures of the League in the 1930s?

1 Consequences for the victims of aggression

The failures of the League over Manchuria and Abyssinia left weak nations defenceless against aggression by powerful neighbours. Manchuria and Abyssinia were occupied by foreign powers and abandoned by the League. Other nations realised that they could no longer look to the League for security.

2 Consequences for the aggressors

Violence and aggression were shown to pay. Although Italy and Japan left the League, they continued to play an active part in international affairs. They kept the territory they had gained and suffered no penalty. They were encouraged to take further aggressive actions. Japan persisted in its attacks on China (Source O). Italy intervened in the Spanish Civil War, and later occupied Albania (April 1939).

3 Consequences for Britain and France

The weakness of Britain and France in dealing with the Abyssinian crisis mirrored the weakness of the League itself. Up to 1936 they could pretend that collective security was the way to deal with international aggression. From 1936 onwards they had to find different ways of dealing with the dictators. Above all, they had to accept that nobody would do this for them. Although they continued to appease Hitler (see page 83), re-armament began in earnest as the democracies faced up to the fact that, in the end, they might have to fight another war.

4 Consequences for the League of Nations

The Manchurian and Abyssinian crises destroyed the idea of collective security by demonstrating that League members would not act together firmly in the face of determined aggression. This also destroyed the credibility of the League as a peacekeeping organisation.

SOURCE O

Japanese soldiers celebrating the capture of Hankow, China, in 1938. The League had failed to stop this attack.

Paper 1-type assessment: The League of Nations

SOURCE A

A German cartoon of 1936 commenting on the Abyssinian crisis. The soldier is saying to the League: 'I am sorry to disturb your sleep, but I wanted to tell you that you don't need to bother yourself about this Abyssinian business any more. It's been settled elsewhere.'

QUESTIONS

Section A Questions

1a Study Source A. Explain the message of this cartoon. Support your answer by referring to details of the cartoon and your own knowledge. (6)

b Explain why the Italian invasion of Abyssinia was important in the history of the League of Nations. (9)

Section B Questions

2a What were the aims of the League of Nations? (4)

b Explain why not all the major powers joined the League of Nations when it was set up. (6)

c 'The most important factor in the failure of the League of Nations was the fact that the USA was not a member.' Do you agree with this statement? Explain your answer. (10)

Why had international peace collapsed by 1939?

The Second World War started barely twenty years after the first had finished. Hopes of establishing permanent peace were destroyed by the Great Depression and the rise to power of aggressive, militaristic regimes in Germany, Italy and Japan. Hitler's takeover in Germany in 1933 was a major turning point. His foreign policy challenged the Treaty of Versailles directly and put Europe on the path to war. Whether or not Hitler planned war from the start remains uncertain, but his constant demands for territory and his willingness to threaten violence to achieve his aims finally forced Britain and France to resist him.

What were the long-term consequences of the peace treaties of 1919–23?

The peace settlement after the First World War left many nations, both victors and losers, dissatisfied. Some of the problems caused by this were resolved, more or less peacefully, during the 1920s. But in Germany resentment against the Treaty of Versailles persisted. As early as 1920, Hitler stated in the Nazi Party Programme that he would get rid of the Treaty of Versailles, gain *Lebensraum* (living space) for the Germans by conquering land to the east, and unite all Germans in a new German Empire (Reich). Since other nations could be expected to resist these aims, Hitler's policies would mean that Germany would have to become a great military power again – something forbidden in the Treaty of Versailles.

However, it was not just extremists like Hitler who wanted to overturn the terms of the peace settlement. The aims of Stresemann, German foreign minister between 1923 and 1929, were in some respects similar to those of Hitler (see Source A). Of course, there was a great difference between moderates like Stresemann and extremists like Hitler. Stresemann was willing to work co-operatively with other nations to achieve his aims peacefully, whereas Hitler was prepared to use force. Nonetheless, it was clear that Germany did not accept the settlement of 1919–23, and this left Germany's future unresolved.

Once the international system of collective security began to crumble under the impact of the Great Depression, the way was open for Hitler to make Germany a great power again. He was helped by the weakness of the system set up to enforce the peace settlement. The League of Nations had no armed forces. The idea of collective security was fine as long as nations wanted peace, but it gave no security against determined aggressors.

SOURCE A

Three great tasks confront German foreign policy in the near future. In the first place the solution of the reparations problem in a way tolerable to Germany. Secondly the protection of Germans abroad – those 10 to 12 million who now live under a foreign yoke ... The third great task is the readjustment of our eastern frontiers: the recovery of Danzig and the Polish corridor and a correction of the frontier in Upper Silesia.

From a letter written in 1925 by Stresemann, the German foreign minister.

SOURCE B

If only we could sit down at a table with the Germans and run through all their complaints and claims with a pencil, this would greatly relieve all tension.

Neville Chamberlain speaking in 1938.

SOURCE C

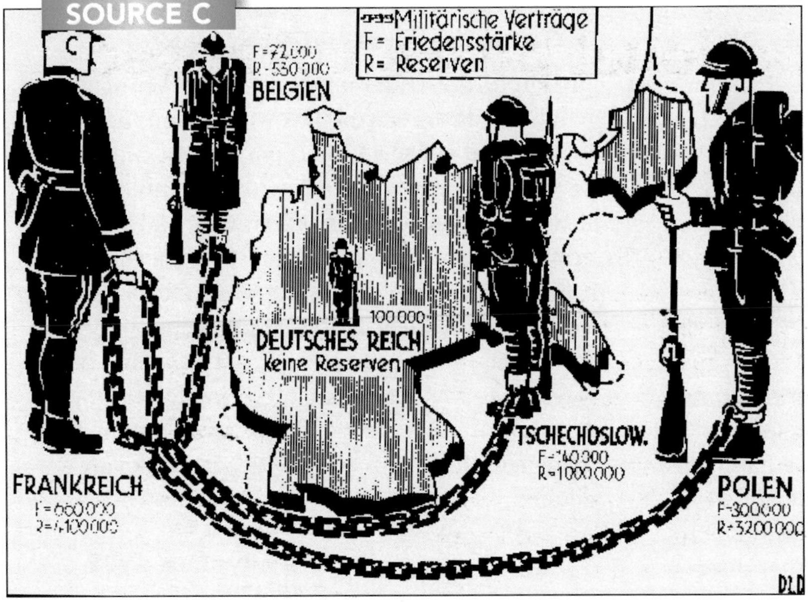

A Nazi propaganda cartoon against the Treaty of Versailles. It shows Germany, its army limited by the Treaty of Versailles, surrounded by hostile neighbours.

SOURCE D

Neville Chamberlain.

Moreover, Britain and France found it hard to agree about how to treat Germany. The British felt that Germany had been harshly treated at Versailles, and saw nothing wrong in making concessions. The French were fearful of Germany becoming strong again. Desperate to avoid another war, Britain and France responded to Hitler's demands with a policy of appeasement – making concessions to him in the hope that he would be satisfied.

Appeasement

Appeasement is most closely associated with Neville Chamberlain (British prime minister, 1937–40), but the policy was followed by Britain almost from the time Hitler came to power. By the 1930s most British politicians did not believe that all the terms of the Versailles settlement could be maintained; it was vital to reach an agreement with Germany that would settle its grievances once and for all.

Appeasement assumed that Hitler would keep his side of a bargain, but Hitler was an unscrupulous dictator who was prepared to use violence to get what he wanted. Chamberlain himself doubted whether appeasement would finally work, but like most politicians in Britain and France, he would try almost anything to avoid war.

QUESTIONS

1 How did the policies of Hitler and Stresemann differ?

2 Why were Hitler's aims a threat to world peace?

3 Study Source C.
How can you tell that the cartoonist was opposed to the Treaty of Versailles? Explain your answer, referring to details of the cartoon.

How did Hitler destroy the Treaty of Versailles?

Between 1933 and 1936 Hitler destroyed the Treaty of Versailles, finding this surprisingly easy to do. One reason was his determination and willingness to take risks. Another was the weakness of other nations and their unwillingness to stop him.

1 Germany leaves the League of Nations and the Disarmament Conference, October 1933

The League of Nations Disarmament Conference started in 1932 and dragged on unsuccessfully into 1933. The Germans said they would be happy to accept disarmament if every nation disarmed. If not, they wanted to increase their armaments to French levels. The French would neither disarm nor allow German re-armament. This gave Hitler an excuse to quit the conference while pretending that Germany wanted peace. In fact, almost from the moment Hitler came to power, Germany had been re-arming. On the same day he withdrew Germany from the League of Nations. Many in Britain blamed France for the failure of the Disarmament Conference.

2 The population of the Saar votes to rejoin Germany, January 1935

The Treaty of Versailles had placed the Saar, an important coal-mining area on the Franco-German border, under League of Nations administration for fifteen years. In January 1935 the people of the Saar voted by 477,000 to 48,000 to return to Germany. This overwhelming vote was a tremendous propaganda success for Hitler, who increased its international impact by promising to make no further claims on French territory, so giving up German claims to Alsace and Lorraine, which had also been lost in the Treaty of Versailles.

3 German air force and army, March 1935

In March 1935 Hitler announced that Germany had a military air force (the Luftwaffe), and that he was introducing conscription (compulsory military service) to expand the army to half a million men. It was an open secret that Germany had been re-arming for some time, but this announcement was a clear rejection of the military restrictions in the Treaty of Versailles. Britain, France and Italy formed the so-called Stresa Front, condemning German re-armament, and agreeing to work together to preserve existing treaties. But as Hitler expected, they were not prepared to take any action.

4 Anglo-German Naval Treaty, June 1935

This treaty allowed the Germans to build a navy 35 per cent of the size of Britain's. It seemed to guarantee Britain permanent naval superiority over Germany, and was consistent with Britain's policy of trying to control and satisfy legitimate German demands. In fact, it merely permitted Germany to ignore the naval restrictions in the Treaty of Versailles, including those on the possession of submarines and battleships, and to build up a navy as quickly as possible. By signing this treaty, Britain officially recognised that the military terms of the Treaty of Versailles were dead. Britain had consulted neither France nor Italy before signing – the Stresa Front had collapsed.

5 German re-occupation of the Rhineland, March 1936

While the Rhineland remained demilitarised, Germany was vulnerable to attack from the west. Pursuing a more aggressive policy in the east meant that the Rhineland would first have to be made secure. On 7 March 1936, Hitler took a big

SOURCE E

I think it would be a mistake to seem to be on the side of France about the secret re-arming of Germany. To do that means that we appear to re-endorse that wicked Versailles Treaty and to justify the evil policies of France towards reconciliation over the past ten years. God knows, the danger from Germany is bad enough, but the dangers from France in the last few years have been equally grave.

From a letter written in 1934 by a British Labour Party politician. The letter helps to explain why Hitler could get away with his re-armament plans.

gamble by marching his troops into the demilitarised zone. His armies were not prepared for war, and he could not know how Britain and France would react. But the French would not act on their own, and the British saw no reason to risk war in order to stop Hitler 'marching into his own backyard'. Hitler had used force, and nobody had tried to stop him. In future, the threat of war would lie behind all of Hitler's demands.

6 The Rome–Berlin Axis and the Anti-Comintern Pacts

Hitler's successes made it easier for him to develop closer relationships with possible allies such as Italy and Japan. The Rome–Berlin Axis (1936) was not a formal alliance, but an informal agreement between Hitler and Mussolini to work more closely together. Thus both Italy and Germany gave support to the nationalists in the Spanish Civil War. This war, which broke out in 1936, gave Hitler an opportunity to test much of his new military equipment. The Anti-Comintern Pact (1936) committed Germany and Japan to hostility towards the Soviet Union, and Italy joined the pact in 1937. A full military alliance between Germany and Italy (the Pact of Steel) was signed in 1939, and expanded in 1940 to include Japan.

SOURCE F

PAX GERMANICA
THE GOOSE-STEP.
"GOOSEY GOOSEY GANDER,
WHITHER DOST THOU WANDER?"
"ONLY THROUGH THE RHINELAND—
PRAY EXCUSE MY BLUNDER!"

A British cartoon of 1936 about the remilitarisation of the Rhineland. The 'goose-step' was the style of marching used by the German army.

How far was Hitler's foreign policy to blame for the outbreak of war in 1939?

Anschluss, March 1938: why did Hitler bother to invade Austria?

Austria is a German country both by language and by culture. Hitler had been born and raised in Austria, and his desire to unite all Germans was well known. Although the Treaty of Versailles forbade the union of Germany and Austria (Anschluss), it seemed obvious that he would try to bring it about. A strong Nazi Party already existed in Austria. In 1934 Nazis murdered the Austrian chancellor, Dollfuss, during an attempted takeover which failed only when Mussolini, the Italian dictator, threatened to intervene. At this time, Mussolini was suspicious of Hitler, and regarded Austria as being in Italy's sphere of interest.

In 1936, Dollfuss' replacement, Schuschnigg, agreed to appoint Nazis to the government. In return, Germany promised to respect Austria's independence. But in January 1938 Austrian police raided Nazi headquarters in Vienna and found plans to take over the government. On 12 February, Schuschnigg met Hitler at Berchtesgaden and agreed to appoint Seyss-Inquart, a Nazi supporter, as Minister of the Interior,

QUESTIONS

1 Study Source F. What does it tell you about British attitudes to the remilitarisation of the Rhineland? Explain your answer, referring to the cartoon.

2 Why do you think Britain followed a policy of appeasement towards Hitler?

3 How did Hitler make Germany a great power again?

and to lift all restrictions on Nazi Party activities.

By making concessions to Hitler, Schuschnigg hoped to preserve Austria's independence. However, Schuschnigg also announced that a plebiscite would be held for the Austrians to decide whether or not Austria would remain an independent nation. If the vote went in Schuschnigg's favour, Hitler's plans for the gradual takeover of Austria would be undermined.

On 11 March, Hitler demanded that the plebiscite be postponed. When the Austrians agreed, he demanded the replacement of Schuschnigg by Seyss-Inquart. The plan was for Seyss-Inquart to become chancellor and then request German help to restore order in Austria. At 8 p.m. Seyss-Inquart was appointed chancellor, and the Germans invaded Austria the following day.

It was one of the worst planned invasions in history. German tanks had to refuel at petrol stations along the road to Vienna, and German commanders had to use tourist guides to plan their routes. But there was no resistance from the Austrians and the invasion was completed without bloodshed. Austria was absorbed into Germany. The Anschluss had occurred.

This time, Mussolini did not object. Since the creation of the Rome–Berlin Axis in 1936, Hitler and Mussolini had worked together more closely. Without Italy's protection Austria was doomed. Britain and France would not intervene. Although many people in those countries were worried by Hitler's methods, most were reassured by a plebiscite held on 10 April, in which over 99% of Austrians approved the Anschluss.

The Czechoslovakian crisis, 1938

After the Anschluss, it was clear that Czechoslovakia would be the next country to attract Hitler's attention. A free and hostile Czechoslovakia would make it impossible for Germany to fight a war in the west. Czechoslovakia's geographical position, with its land thrusting deep into German territory, would be a direct threat to Germany. Although not a large nation, Czechoslovakia was well defended and had a modern and well-equipped army.

SOURCE G

GOOD HUNTING

Mussolini. "All right, Adolf—I never heard a shot"

A British cartoon of February 1938. Mussolini (on the left) is saying to Hitler, 'All right, Adolf, I never heard a shot.' In 1934 Mussolini had defended Austrian independence, but by 1938 the relationship between Italy and Germany had become much closer.

QUESTION

Study Source G.
What does this cartoon tell you about Hitler's policy towards Austria? Explain your answer, referring to details of the cartoon.

However, it had one crucial weakness, which Hitler planned to exploit. Its population included several ethnic minorities, among them 3.5 million ethnic Germans living in the Sudetenland, a part of Czechoslovakia along the German-Czech border. The Sudeten Germans could be used to stir up trouble against the Czech government.

A Czech–German war?

The Czechs knew that to surrender the Sudetenland would make them defenceless against Germany, since all Czechoslovakia's frontier defences against Germany were in the Sudetenland. Handing these over would mean that Hitler could easily take over the rest of Czechoslovakia whenever he wanted. It began to look as though war between Germany and Czechoslovakia might break out. If so, then France and probably Britain would go to Czechoslovakia's aid. However, neither Britain nor France wanted to fight against Germany.

Chamberlain was sure that a peaceful solution could be found to the Czech crisis. On 15 September 1938 he met Hitler at Berchtesgaden in Germany to discuss the crisis. Hitler made it clear that the crisis could be solved only by the transfer of the Sudetenland to Germany. Chamberlain indicated that he had no objection to this as long as the transfer was done peacefully.

A week later on 22 September, having in the meantime forced the Czechs to agree to the loss of the Sudetenland, Chamberlain returned to Germany to meet Hitler at Bad Godesberg. But Hitler now demanded that the Sudetenland be handed over by 1 October, and that claims on Czech territory by Hungary and Poland be met. If his demands were not met by 1 October 1938, Germany would invade Czechoslovakia. Europe was on the brink of war.

The Munich Conference

Chamberlain was desperate for any solution that would avoid war. When Mussolini, the Italian dictator, proposed a four-power conference, both Chamberlain and Hitler, who now saw the prospect of achieving his aims without having to fight, agreed to attend. On 29 September 1938, Chamberlain, Hitler, Daladier (the French prime minister) and Mussolini met in Munich and signed an agreement that gave Hitler the terms he had demanded at Bad Godesberg. It was also agreed that Czechoslovakia's new frontiers would be guaranteed by the four powers. This enabled the British and French to claim that Czechoslovakia had been saved.

In fact, the guarantee was meaningless. Hitler had no intention of keeping to it and soon both Poland and Hungary grabbed the territory that they wanted, while the traditional rivalry and dislike between the Slovaks and the more prosperous Czechs within what was left of the country further threatened the Czechoslovakian government.

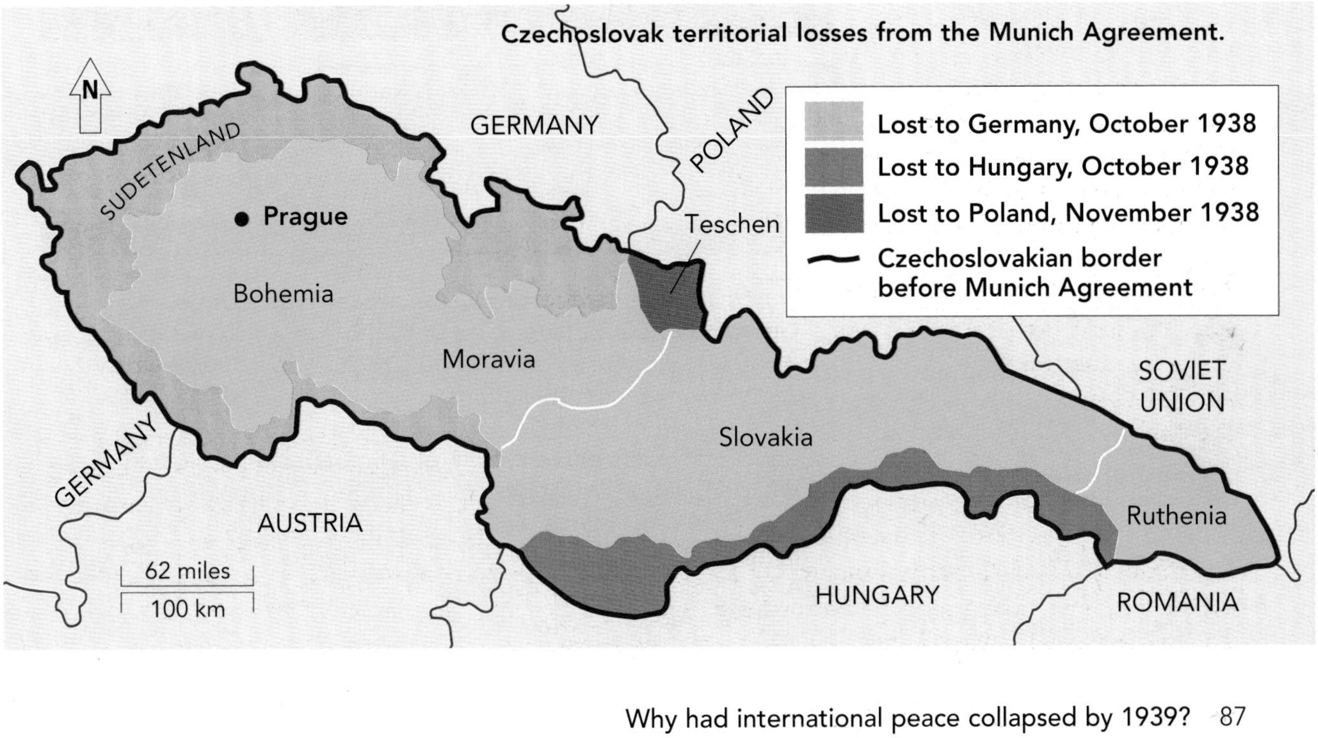

Czechoslovak territorial losses from the Munich Agreement.

'Peace for our time'

The Soviets were not invited to the Munich Conference. Everyone knew they would never agree to Hitler's terms. The Czechs were not even consulted, and had no choice but to agree. The day after the conference, Chamberlain met Hitler alone and they agreed an Anglo-German Declaration. The two countries promised never to go to war with each other again, and that they would settle all disputes between the two countries by consultation. It was a copy of this agreement that Chamberlain waved to the cheering crowds on his return to Britain. He announced to the British public, 'I believe it is peace for our time.'

By 10 October 1938 German troops had completed the occupation of the Sudetenland. Czechoslovakia was now defenceless against its enemies.

SOURCE H

Chamberlain's return from Munich. He is waving a copy of the agreement to the crowd.

An American historian, William Shirer, writing in 1959, summarised the damage that the Munich Agreement did to Czechoslovakia.

SOURCE I

The final settlement forced Czechoslovakia to cede to Germany 11,000 square miles of territory in which dwelt 2,800,000 Germans and 800,000 Czechs. Within this area lay all the vast Czech fortifications.

Czechoslovakia's entire system of rail, road, telephone and telegraph communications was disrupted. [It] lost 66% of its coal, 80% of its lignite, 86% of its chemicals, 80% of its cement, 80% of its textiles, 70% of its electrical power and 40% of its timber. A prosperous industrial nation was split up and bankrupted overnight.

Hitler destroys Czechoslovakia, March 1939

At Munich, Hitler had given Chamberlain meaningless promises about the future of Czechoslovakia. Chamberlain thought that the Munich Agreement had secured 'peace for our time'. He was wrong. Within six months Hitler's armies were on the march again. Czechoslovakia could not survive in its weakened state. Internally torn apart by the hostility between the Czechs and the Slovaks, and with much of its territory already seized by Germany, Poland and Hungary, it was incapable of defending itself. In March 1939, Hitler ordered his armies to occupy Bohemia and Moravia, two parts of Czechoslovakia that had been protected by the Munich Agreement. Slovakia then became nothing more than a puppet-state under German domination. Hungary took the opportunity to grab yet more territory – this time Ruthenia.

Czechoslovakia had ceased to exist. On 23 March 1939 Hitler also seized the territory of Memel from Lithuania. It was finally clear to everyone, including the British and French governments, that the policy of appeasement was dead. In an effort to deter any further German aggression, Chamberlain promised Poland that Britain would guarantee its independence.

SOURCE J

Be glad in your hearts. Give thanks to your God. People of Britain, your children are safe. Your husbands and sons will not march to battle. If we must have a victor, let us choose Chamberlain. For the Prime Minister's conquests are mighty and enduring – millions of happy homes and hearts relieved of their burden.

Comments on the Munich Agreement in the *Daily Express*, 30 September 1938.

SOURCE K

The events of the last few days are one of the greatest diplomatic defeats this country and France have ever suffered. There can be no doubt that it is a tremendous victory for Herr Hitler. Without firing a shot, he has achieved a dominating position in Europe.

Clement Attlee, the leader of the British Labour Party, speaking in Parliament on the Munich Agreement, October 1938.

SOURCE L

At the airport Daladier turned up his coat collar to protect his face from the rotten eggs he expected from the crowd. To his astonishment there were no eggs or shouts of 'We are betrayed'. Instead they were actually cheering him – shouting 'Vive Daladier', 'Vive la Paix' 'Vive la France!' Daladier turned to a colleague and whispered, 'The fools!'

From Daladier's own account of his return to France from the Munich Conference.

QUESTIONS

1 Why did Hitler find it so easy to bring about Anschluss?

2 Why were Britain and France prepared to sign the Munich Agreement (September 1938)?

3 Study Sources J, K and L. Why did judgements about the Munich Agreement differ so much?

SOURCE M

In the early hours of the morning of 15 March 1939, a meeting took place at the Reich Chancellery, Berlin, between Hitler and a delegation from the Czech government, led by the President, Emil Hacha. Hitler was about to bring the independence of Czechoslovakia to an end.

Hitler told the Czechs that at 6 a.m. his armies would cross their borders near points where the Luftwaffe had already seized their airfields. Any attempts at resistance would be broken by brute force. He paused. Of course, he said, they had a choice. If the defenders laid down their arms, the Führer would treat them with generosity, and even grant them a certain measure of freedom. He suggested the Czechs step into the next room and talk it over.

Awaiting them there were Goering [head of the Luftwaffe] and Ribbentrop [the German foreign minister], who literally chased them around a table covered with documents, thrusting papers at them, pushing papers at them, pushing pens into their hands, shouting that if they refused to sign, within two hours half of Prague [the Czech capital] would be bombed to ruins and their families slain.

Suddenly Goering shouted out, 'Hacha has fainted!' A single thought crossed the minds of the Germans: the world would say that Czechoslovakia's president had been murdered in the Reich Chancellery. Then Dr Theodor Morell – Hitler's personal doctor – gave Hacha an injection to try and revive him. A special telephone line to Prague had been rigged up; over it the revived president gave orders to his Cabinet to give in to the Germans. Morell gave him another shot, and he signed the papers. It was 3.55 a.m. Two hours later German troops swarmed over the Czech frontier. Hacha was appointed governor of the German protectorate of Bohemia and Moravia. But the world already knew who really ruled the country now. Hitler had told them. Before going to bed that night he issued a triumphant statement: 'Czechoslovakia has ceased to exist.'

Adapted from an account by an American historian, written in 1988.

Was the policy of appeasement justified?

There are strong differences of opinion between historians about appeasement. After the Second World War, many British historians shared the feeling of shame that Britain had not stood up to Hitler earlier, particularly as Chamberlain's claim to have brought back 'peace with honour' from Munich rested on the betrayal of Czechoslovakia. These historians portrayed Chamberlain as a weak man who was taken in by Hitler. More recently, though, some historians have begun to restore Chamberlain's reputation by explaining why he acted as he did, and how restricted his options were. Consider the arguments given for and against appeasement on the next few pages, and decide whether you think appeasement was justified.

The arguments for appeasement

1 Sympathy for Germany

At first, many people felt that there was some justice in Hitler's claims. The British accepted that the Treaty of Versailles was too harsh, and that Germany had a right to be treated more fairly and to be accepted as a great power. So in 1935 they were happy to make the Anglo-German Naval Agreement, which ignored the terms of the Treaty of Versailles. When Hitler remilitarised the Rhineland in 1936, there was a feeling that he was just 'marching into his own backyard', and when Anschluss occurred in 1938, the Austrians (who according to this view were really Germans anyway) were simply achieving the self-determination denied them at Versailles. Each single step that Hitler took could be justified, and it was always possible to believe that, with just one more concession, he would be satisfied and demand no more.

2 The desire for peace

It was perfectly understandable that Britain and France would want to find peaceful solutions to Germany's problems, and so avoid another war. Memories of the horrors of the First World War were still strong. Most Europeans placed their trust in the League of Nations and the idea of collective security. Decent, democratic politicians in Britain and France at first simply found it hard to accept that the rise of brutal, militaristic regimes in Germany, Italy and Japan would make it necessary again to prepare for war. To make matters worse, they were still coping with the impact of the Great Depression, and were concerned that their economies were just not strong enough to bear the costs of re-armament.

3 The threat of communism

In dealing with the aggressive nature of German policies in central and eastern Europe, Britain and France faced a serious problem. They could not actually protect countries like Czechoslovakia and Poland from attack, as they were too far away. The only great power that could protect these countries was the Soviet Union. But with good reason, Britain and France, and more so, Czechoslovakia and Poland, hated and feared Stalin's communist tyranny just as much as they hated Nazi Germany. Most western politicians could not make up their minds which of Germany and the Soviet Union was the greater threat.

4 Time to re-arm

The strongest argument for appeasement was that Britain was just not ready to fight. A re-armament programme to prepare Britain for war began only in 1936, and was not planned for completion until 1940. When the crises of 1938 occurred, Britain desperately needed more time to build up its strength. By giving into Hitler's demands at Munich, war was postponed for a year, and when it did eventually come, Britain had made just enough preparations to survive.

The arguments against appeasement

1 The appeasers misjudged Hitler

The appeasers made the crucial mistake of treating Hitler as they would treat each other – as a rational politician who was open to reasoned argument. They did not realise until too late that they were dealing with a determined, unscrupulous tyrant, who would interpret any concession as a sign of weakness. The more they gave him, the more he demanded.

2 Appeasement was morally wrong

Britain and France were so afraid of another war that they allowed Germany to break international agreements without punishment, and finally abandoned Czechoslovakia to its fate in return for meaningless promises. Appeasement was simply another word for weakness and cowardice.

SOURCE N

A cartoon from a British newspaper, 1936.

QUESTIONS

1 At what point do you think it became clear that appeasement had failed?

2 Do you think Chamberlain was right or wrong to follow a policy of appeasement? Explain your answer.

3 The appeasers missed excellent chances to stop Hitler

The appeasers were so busy looking for chances to give Hitler what he wanted that they missed good opportunities to resist him. After the remilitarisation of the Rhineland in 1936, Hitler admitted that any sign of military action by the French would have led him to withdraw his troops immediately. At Munich in 1938, Britain and France abandoned Czechoslovakia, a well-defended and well-armed country, which could have put up a significant resistance to German attack.

How important was the Nazi–Soviet Pact?

Hitler turns to Poland

After the destruction of Czechoslovakia, it was clear that Poland would be Hitler's next target. Germany had obvious claims on some Polish territory. The 'Polish corridor', which split East Prussia from the rest of Germany, had been taken from Germany by the Treaty of Versailles, as had the city of Danzig, which was now a 'free city' under League of Nations control. Hitler wanted these areas back. He also wanted Polish territory as *Lebensraum* (living space).

SOURCE O

A Soviet cartoon of 1936 showing western nations as Hitler's protectors.

Despite this, the Poles enjoyed a friendly relationship with Hitler's Germany until 1939. The Polish government sympathised with the Nazis' authoritarian and anti-Semitic (anti-Jewish) policies. They had even taken part in the destruction of Czechoslovakia after the Munich Conference by grabbing Teschen. At first, the Poles found it hard to take seriously Hitler's demands and increasing threats against them. They even thought their best hope of survival was to try and avoid making commitments to either of their two powerful neighbours, Germany and the Soviet Union.

Britain's promise

Britain's guarantee to preserve the independence of Poland made the Poles feel safer than they really were. There was little that Britain and France could do to stop a German invasion of Poland – it was too far away from them. So the attitude of Poland's other powerful neighbour, the Soviet Union, would be crucial. Would it help Poland against a German attack?

Discussions between Britain, France and the Soviet Union took place through early August 1939, but collapsed because of distrust between the two sides, and also because the Poles refused to let Soviet troops enter their territory in advance of an attack by Germany. The Soviets thought that Britain and France would be happy to see the Soviet Union doing all the fighting if war broke out with Germany.

The Nazi–Soviet Pact

On 23 August 1939 the sensational news broke of an agreement signed in Moscow by the foreign ministers of the Soviet Union and Germany, Molotov and Ribbentrop. They had agreed to a non-aggression pact – a promise not to fight each other. Secretly, they had also decided to split up Poland between them. Fascist Germany and the communist Soviet Union gave every appearance of being bitter political enemies. Nobody really believed that the pact made any difference to their mutual hatred. So why did they make an agreement not to fight each other?

Why was the Nazi–Soviet Pact important?

The pact left Britain and France to fight Germany alone. Hitler did not really believe they would go to war over Poland, but almost had second thoughts when Britain's reaction to the pact was the signing of a formal alliance with Poland on 25 August 1939. This time Britain and France would not be able to back down in the face of Nazi aggression. If they did, it would signal to the world that they could no longer be regarded as great powers, and unlike in 1938, re-armament meant that they were now more ready for war. But the Anglo-Polish alliance did not really change anything. It took only a few days for Hitler to recover his nerve and order that Poland be invaded on 1 September. When Hitler ignored Britain and France's ultimatum to call off the attack, they declared war on 3 September. Nevertheless, within three weeks Poland had been defeated, its armies completely

SOURCE P

It is not Danzig that is at stake. For us it is a matter of expanding our living space to the east. There is therefore no question of sparing Poland and we are left with the decision: to attack Poland at the earliest opportunity. We cannot expect a repeat of Czechoslovakia. There will be war.

Hitler speaking at a conference of his generals, 23 May 1939.

QUESTION

How far does Source O help you understand why the Soviet Union was prepared to make a pact with Germany in August 1939?

powerless against the *Blitzkrieg* (lightning war) launched by Germany. Two weeks into the fighting, Soviet armies invaded Poland from the east, at the same time occupying the Baltic states (Estonia, Latvia and Lithuania).

The pact makes war inevitable

The pact was the single most important short-term cause of the Second World War. This means that it explains how and why the war broke out at the time it did. Hitler had planned to invade Poland, and now he knew that he could do so without direct interference from any other great power. Once he attacked, Britain would be forced to honour its guarantee to Poland. Of course, this could not save Poland because there was nothing that Britain and France could do to stop the German invasion, but it would mean war.

Why did Britain and France declare war on Germany in September 1939?

Neither Britain nor France wanted to go to war with Germany in 1939. They would have preferred a peaceful solution to the Polish crisis and did their best to persuade the Poles to negotiate with Hitler over the disputed areas, Danzig and the Polish corridor. The problem was that the Poles did not want to negotiate – they knew from the example of Czechoslovakia that negotiating with Hitler could be fatal. Anyway, once the Nazi–Soviet Pact was signed, negotiations would have been meaningless as Germany and the Soviet Union had secretly resolved to split Poland between them.

QUESTIONS

1 Why do you think Germany and the Soviet Union signed the Nazi–Soviet Pact?
2 Do you agree that the Nazi–Soviet Pact was the most important cause of the war? Explain your answer.

Advantages for Germany of the Nazi–Soviet Pact

1 Hitler knew he could now invade Poland without having to fight the Soviet Union.
2 Hitler would be able to get back land lost to Poland at Versailles, and begin to acquire *Lebensraum*.
3 There would be no alliance between the Soviet Union, Britain and France to prevent Hitler carrying out his plans.

Advantages for the Soviet Union of the Nazi–Soviet Pact

1 The Soviet Union would not be drawn into a war with Germany over Poland.
2 The Soviets did not trust Britain and France enough to ally with them to save Poland, and now would not have to.
3 Poland was hostile to the Soviet Union and the two countries had fought a war in the 1920s. Much of Poland's territory had been taken from Russia when Poland was created. Now the Soviet Union could get this land back. This area would be a useful 'buffer zone' against any future German attack.
4 Stalin still believed that war with Germany would come eventually, but the pact gave him time to build up the strength of Soviet armed forces.

A 'state of war'

When Germany invaded Poland on 1 September 1939, Britain and France did not declare war immediately. They delayed, still hoping that there might be a chance to make Hitler change his plans. They knew they could not save Poland. However, they were both allied to Poland and had to take some action. On 3 September the British government sent Hitler an ultimatum (Source R). The French sent a similar ultimatum. When no reply was received by 11 a.m., Britain declared war on Germany.

Britain and France went to war because they were forced to. Hitler had finally pushed them to the point at which they had to resist. The alternative was national humiliation and acceptance of German domination of Europe.

Chamberlain speaking in the House of Commons, 3 September 1939.

SOURCE R

Unless not later than 11 a.m., British summer time, today September 3rd, satisfactory assurances have been given by the German government and have reached His Majesty's Government in London, a state of war will exist between the two countries from that hour.

The ultimatum from the British to the German government, 3 September 1939.

SOURCE S

This is a sad day for all of us, and to none is it sadder than to me. Everything that I have worked for, everything that I have believed in during my public life, has crashed into ruins.

SOURCE Q

A group of British people reading about the invasion of Poland, 3 September 1939.

Paper 1-type assessment: The collapse of peace

SOURCE A

"EUROPE CAN LOOK FORWARD TO A CHRISTMAS OF PEACE", SAYS HITLER

A British cartoon from October 1938.

QUESTIONS

Section A Questions

1a Study Source A. Explain the message of this cartoon. Support your answer by referring to details of the cartoon and your own knowledge. (6)

b Explain why Hitler followed an aggressive foreign policy in the period 1938-9. (9)

Section B Questions

2a What was agreed at the Munich Conference in September 1938? (4)

b Explain why Germany invaded Poland in 1939. (6)

c 'The most important cause of the Second World War was the weakness of Britain and France'. Do you agree with this statement? Explain your answer. (10)

3 Germany 1918–45

The Germany that emerged from the First World War was much weaker than the country that had entered it in 1914. The army was defeated, the economy was in ruins, and law and order was under serious threat as a number of extremist groups tried to seize power.

The Weimar Republic, set up immediately after the war to provide a new system of government for Germany, soon ran into difficulties. It was highly unpopular because of its association with the hated Treaty of Versailles and soon faced uprisings against its rule in Berlin and Munich. In 1923 the failure to keep up reparations payments led to the French occupation of the Ruhr and prices spiralling into hyperinflation.

The work of Gustav Stresemann helped restore the German economy and improve relationships with foreign countries. Germany entered a period of prosperity reflected in notable achievements in art and culture. However, the prosperity was based on loans from the USA and once these were withdrawn, the German economy collapsed. The consequences of the Wall Street Crash brought economic ruin to Germany and increased support for extremist parties, such as the Nazis.

In 1933 the Nazi leader, Adolf Hitler, became chancellor and set about restoring Germany's greatness. Under Nazi rule the economy improved and stability was restored. Later Hitler regained many of the territories Germany had lost at the Treaty of Versailles. But these successes came at a high price. Hitler's totalitarian regime limited personal freedom and dealt harshly with any opposition, potential or real. It also enforced Nazi beliefs on the supremacy of the Aryan race with horrific consequences for Slavs, gypsies and, especially, the Jews.

This topic is examined in Paper 1 of the examination. Paper 1-type exercises are included at the end of the chapter. Mark schemes, sample answers and comments can be found in the accompanying Teacher's Resource Pack.

Germany 1918–45

In 1914 the Germans had gone to war confident that victory would soon be theirs. But there was no quick victory, and when the war finally ended in 1918 it was the Allies who had won the victory, not Germany. A new system of government, the Weimar Republic, was established and soon faced political and economic crises. Although it rode out those crises and from 1924 to 1929 seemed to have brought stability and prosperity to Germany, it could not survive the Great Depression that followed the Wall Street Crash in 1929. From 1933 Hitler and the Nazis ruled Germany. Hitler's policies restored the economy and brought a German Empire that controlled most of Europe. But the success was short-lived and the cost enormous.

SOURCE A

We sat in our bunkers and heard about the mess behind the lines, about the dry rot setting in back home. We felt that the Frenchmen and Tommies were no longer our enemies, that there was worse to come. Real poison was being brewed in the witches' cauldron at home.

A German lieutenant describing his thoughts on hearing of the unrest in Germany in November 1918.

Was the Weimar Republic doomed from the start?

How did Germany emerge from defeat in the First World War?

In September 1918, Allied troops broke through the German Hindenburg line on the Western Front. Defeat in the war now looked inevitable. The British blockade of German ports had produced serious food shortages in Germany, and there were many calls for the country to make peace. In October, sailors at the naval base at Wilhelmshaven mutinied and there was a further mutiny at Kiel when the order was given for one last attack on the British navy. On 7 November, Kurt Eisner declared Bavaria to be a socialist republic, and all over Germany workers and soldiers formed councils similar to the soviets in Russia.

This 'German Revolution' so frightened Germany's leaders that they persuaded Kaiser Wilhelm to abdicate. President Wilson had already made it clear that there could be no peace if the Kaiser remained in office – and Germany desperately needed peace.

SOURCE B

Kaiser Wilhelm II. Two days before the end of the war, Wilhelm abdicated and went to live in exile in the Netherlands.

So on 9 November, Kaiser Wilhelm stood down and Friedrich Ebert, one of the leaders of the Social Democratic Party (SPD), announced that Germany was now a republic. Ebert himself was to be president and his colleague, Philipp Scheidemann, became chancellor (the senior government official, similar to our prime minister).

Problems for the new government

To restore order in Germany, the new government quickly signed the armistice with the Allies on 11 November 1918. Many Germans were shocked by the German surrender, even though there was really little choice. The decision to sign the armistice soon gave rise to the 'stab in the back' theory – the idea that Germany was betrayed by its politicians and should have fought on. Nationalists called Ebert's government 'The November Criminals'. The new republic had got off to a very unpopular start.

A major problem for Ebert was establishing how Germany should be governed. Some Germans wanted a system of government based on communism, as had recently been established in Russia. In January 1919 the Spartacus League, Germany's Communist Party, staged a revolt in Berlin in an attempt to seize power and make Germany a communist country. Ebert's government had few troops, as the army had been disbanded after the war. So the government formed units of volunteer soldiers. These 'Freikorps' (Free Corps) soldiers were bitter opponents of communism and crushed the revolt. On 15 January the leaders of the revolt, Karl Liebknecht and Rosa Luxemburg, were executed by the Freikorps. (Later, in 1920, when a Soviet republic was proclaimed in Munich, the Freikorps crushed that too.) The actions of the Freikorps led to bitter hostility between the SPD and the German Communist Party (KPD), which lasted throughout the time of the Weimar Republic.

QUESTIONS

1 What was the 'German Revolution' of 1918?

2 Why did some Germans call Ebert's government 'The November Criminals' ?

3 Why did the Freikorps play such a major role in Germany in the immediate post-war years?

SOURCE C

The Freikorps on parade.

Democracy established

Just four days after the execution of Liebknecht and Luxemburg, elections were held for a National Assembly, which would draw up a new constitution for Germany. The SPD won the most seats, but it did not have a majority. However, after joining in coalition with the Centre Party (Z) and Democratic Party (DDP), it had the support of more than three-quarters of the 423 deputies.

As there was unrest in Berlin, the National Assembly held its first meeting in the town of Weimar. So the constitution that it drew up was called the Weimar Republic.

The Weimar Republic

- Germany was to be a democracy. The Reichstag (Parliament) was to make laws and control the government.
- Men and women aged 21 and over could vote in elections for deputies to the Reichstag. Voting was by proportional representation (PR), so a party receiving 10 per cent of the votes had 10 per cent of the deputies.
- The head of the government was the chancellor.
- The head of state was the president, who was to be elected every seven years. The president could dissolve the Reichstag, order fresh elections and, in times of emergency, suspend the Reichstag and rule by himself (Article 48).

SOURCE D

A cartoon from a German magazine in July 1919. It was called 'Clemenceau the Vampire' and shows the French premier sucking the blood from Germany.

This new constitution had several in-built weaknesses. Between 1919 and 1933, no party won more than half the votes cast in elections for the Reichstag. As a result, the system of proportional representation meant that no party won more than half the seats. Consequently, whichever party formed the government could do so only by working with one or more other parties in a coalition. When faced with serious political problems, the various members of the coalitions often fell out. In addition, many people, such as the aristocratic families (Junkers), industrialists and members of the army, did not like the new democracy. They wanted Germany to have one strong leader, as it had before the war.

But whatever problems there were in the constitution of the Weimar Republic, they were nothing compared to the series of crises that the government had to face in the period 1919–24. The first of these, and in some ways the cause of all of them, was the peace settlement at the end of the First World War.

SOURCE E

We trusted the suggestion that the peace would be based on President Wilson's Fourteen Points. What is now given us is a contradiction of that promise. Such a dictated peace will provoke fresh hatred between the nations and, in the course of time, fresh killing.

President Ebert, condemning the proposed Treaty of Versailles in May 1919.

What was the impact of the Treaty of Versailles on the Republic?

The Treaty of Versailles was a vindictive treaty which punished Germany for its part in the war. Germany was split in two. It lost 13 per cent of its territory and 10 per cent of its population, and restrictions were placed on the size of its armed forces and the weapons those forces could have. Article 231 of the treaty (the 'War Guilt' clause) stated that Germany had to take full responsibility for starting the war and causing any damage that had occurred. This clause was the basis for the reparations payments that it was decided Germany should pay. No figure was set until 1921, when it was decided that Germany should pay £6600 million.

The Germans were furious at the terms of the treaty. They claimed that they had agreed to the armistice because they believed that the peace treaty would be based on Wilson's Fourteen Points. These had been published in January 1918 and were much less severe than the final treaty. The Germans also complained that they had been given no say in negotiating the treaty. They said it was a 'Diktat' (a dictated peace). Later opponents of the treaty were to argue that, if the German people had no say in drawing up the treaty, then they had no obligation to abide by its terms.

The new chancellor, Philipp Scheidemann, at first suggested that Germany should not sign the treaty. However, there was little choice as the Allies would probably have invaded if the Germans had refused to sign. So the treaty was signed – and the Weimar Republic became even more unpopular.

The Kapp putsch

The Spartacist uprising of January 1919 was only one example of political problems faced by the Weimar Republic. The Spartacists had been defeated with the help of the Freikorps, but this group itself caused the government great difficulties. Among its members were a group of extreme nationalists who opposed democracy and believed that the only way to prevent the spread of communism was through strong leadership and a strong army.

QUESTIONS

1 The Weimar Republic had a system of proportional representation. What does this mean?

2 Why did so many Germans object to the terms of the Treaty of Versailles?

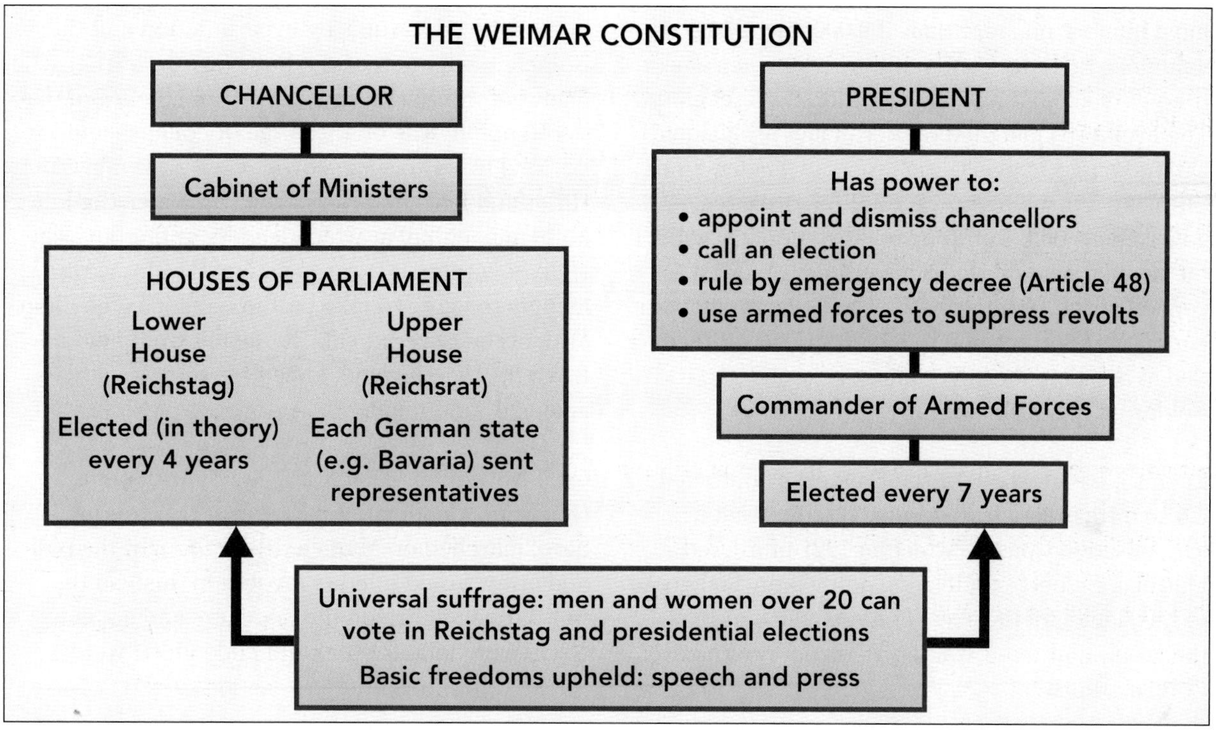
THE WEIMAR CONSTITUTION
CHANCELLOR
Cabinet of Ministers
HOUSES OF PARLIAMENT
Lower House (Reichstag)
Elected (in theory) every 4 years
Upper House (Reichsrat)
Each German state (e.g. Bavaria) sent representatives
PRESIDENT
Has power to:
• appoint and dismiss chancellors
• call an election
• rule by emergency decree (Article 48)
• use armed forces to suppress revolts
Commander of Armed Forces
Elected every 7 years
Universal suffrage: men and women over 20 can vote in Reichstag and presidential elections
Basic freedoms upheld: speech and press

SOURCE F

The Munich putsch. The scene in Munich on the morning of 9 November 1923.

The Treaty of Versailles said that Germany's army must number no more than 100,000, including the volunteer Freikorps units. But in 1920 when Ebert tried to disband the Freikorps, there was rebellion. The Freikorps marched on Berlin and proclaimed Dr Wolfgang Kapp as Germany's new leader. Since the army refused to fire on the Freikorps, the government fled. But Kapp was not popular with the people, who obeyed a government request for a general strike. Soon gas, water and electricity were cut off and Berlin came to halt. Kapp was forced to flee to Sweden, the government returned and the Freikorps was disbanded.

Even so, ex-members of the Freikorps continued to cause difficulties. They formed a group called 'Organisation Consul', which in 1921 murdered Matthias Erzberger, a leading politician who agreed to the signing of the Treaty of Versailles. In 1922 the group murdered Walther Rathenau, Germany's Foreign Minister.

The Munich putsch

In 1923 the Weimar Republic faced another attempt to overthrow it. By 1923 the German economy had been reduced to ruins by hyperinflation and the French occupation of the Ruhr (see page 103). The leader of the Nazi Party, Adolf Hitler, believed that the Republic was on the verge of collapse and decided to try to seize power. On 8 November 1923, Hitler and his supporters broke up a meeting in a Munich beer-hall at which leaders of the Bavarian state government were speaking. He forced the leaders to agree to take part in a putsch (rebellion) against the government. But he allowed them to leave the meeting and, once free, they quickly changed their minds.

On 9 November, 3000 Nazis, led by Hitler and General Ludendorff, the First World War army hero, marched on Munich. Hitler thought the police and army would join his revolution. Instead the police opened fire on the marchers and sixteen Nazis were killed. Hitler and Ludendorff were arrested for conspiracy.

Hitler used his trial to make long speeches criticising the government and setting out his plans for the future of Germany. The publicity he received turned him into a national figure. At the end of the trial, Hitler was sentenced to just five years in prison and he was released after nine months. Ludendorff was found not guilty. There were two other important outcomes of the trial. First, Hitler now realised that power could best be achieved in Germany through the ballot box rather than an armed uprising. Secondly, during Hitler's time in prison he began work on his book *Mein Kampf* (My Struggle). This book set out Hitler's main beliefs, although few people at the time can have thought that he would ever get the chance to put them into practice.

The economic crisis of 1923

During the First World War, the German government paid its bills by printing more banknotes. This sounds like a good solution, but in reality having more money in circulation means that prices rise. As prices rise, so workers demand more wages. This makes goods dearer to produce and so more expensive to buy. Workers therefore demand more wages and so it goes on. This is known as inflation.

When a country suffers high inflation, its currency is worth less to foreign countries, which expect more of it in exchange for their goods. This happened to Germany from 1914 onwards, but particularly during 1923.

In 1921 the Allies fixed the reparations that Germany had to pay at £6600 million. The Germans, like all the major powers in Europe, had spent huge sums on the war. After the war, valuable raw materials in Germany, such as coal and iron, were taken away as the Allies tried to make sure that Germany remained weak. Towards the end of 1922, Germany failed to make a reparations payment. The French and Belgians responded by occupying the industrial heartland of Germany, the Ruhr. They intended to take the value of the missing payments in goods. But the German government ordered a policy of passive resistance and German workers went on strike. Production fell and the French and Belgians could not take the goods they wanted.

SOURCE G

As soon as I received my salary, I rushed out to buy the daily necessities. My daily salary was just enough to buy a loaf of bread and one small piece of cheese or oatmeal. A friend of mine, a clergyman, came to Berlin with his monthly salary to buy a pair of shoes for his baby. He could only afford a cup of coffee.

A German journalist describes the effects of hyperinflation in Germany.

Although it seemed that the Germans had won this particular battle, they still had to pay their workers and meet their other bills. So they printed more and more banknotes. This led to a particularly severe type of inflation known as hyperinflation. In December 1921 a loaf of bread cost just under 4 marks. In September 1923 it cost one and half million marks. Obviously people's wages went up too, but not by that amount! Banknotes were collected in and re-stamped with different values. But it made little difference. Paper money became practically worthless and bartering became common as people settled their bills by paying in eggs or bread. Foreign goods were also so expensive that few Germans could afford them.

Hardest hit were people with savings who had saved carefully for their old age, and expected to have enough money to live in comfort in their retirement. Suddenly their savings would not buy a week's groceries. At first, many people in work found that their wages went up too, but as wages fell below the dramatic price rises, so people's living standards fell. Many people could not afford to eat properly and hunger was common.

QUESTIONS

1 What could a historian learn about Germany in the 1920s from the events of the Munich putsch?

2 a Why was there hyperinflation in Germany in 1923?

b Why was hyperinflation such a problem to the German people?

Of course, there were those who gained from the hyperinflation. People who had borrowed large sums of money suddenly found that they could pay it back out of a week's wages – and foreigners visiting Germany discovered that small amounts of their own currency could be traded for millions of marks.

Yet despite the few who gained, the situation was extremely serious. Thousands of Germans had become destitute and there was a real danger that law and order might break down. It was no coincidence that Hitler chose just this time to try to carry out the Munich putsch.

QUESTIONS

1 Read the text on page 105. How did Stresemann restore Germany's economy?

2 Why were Stresemann's measures in foreign policy so important?

3 What do you think Stresemann meant in Source J?

SOURCE H

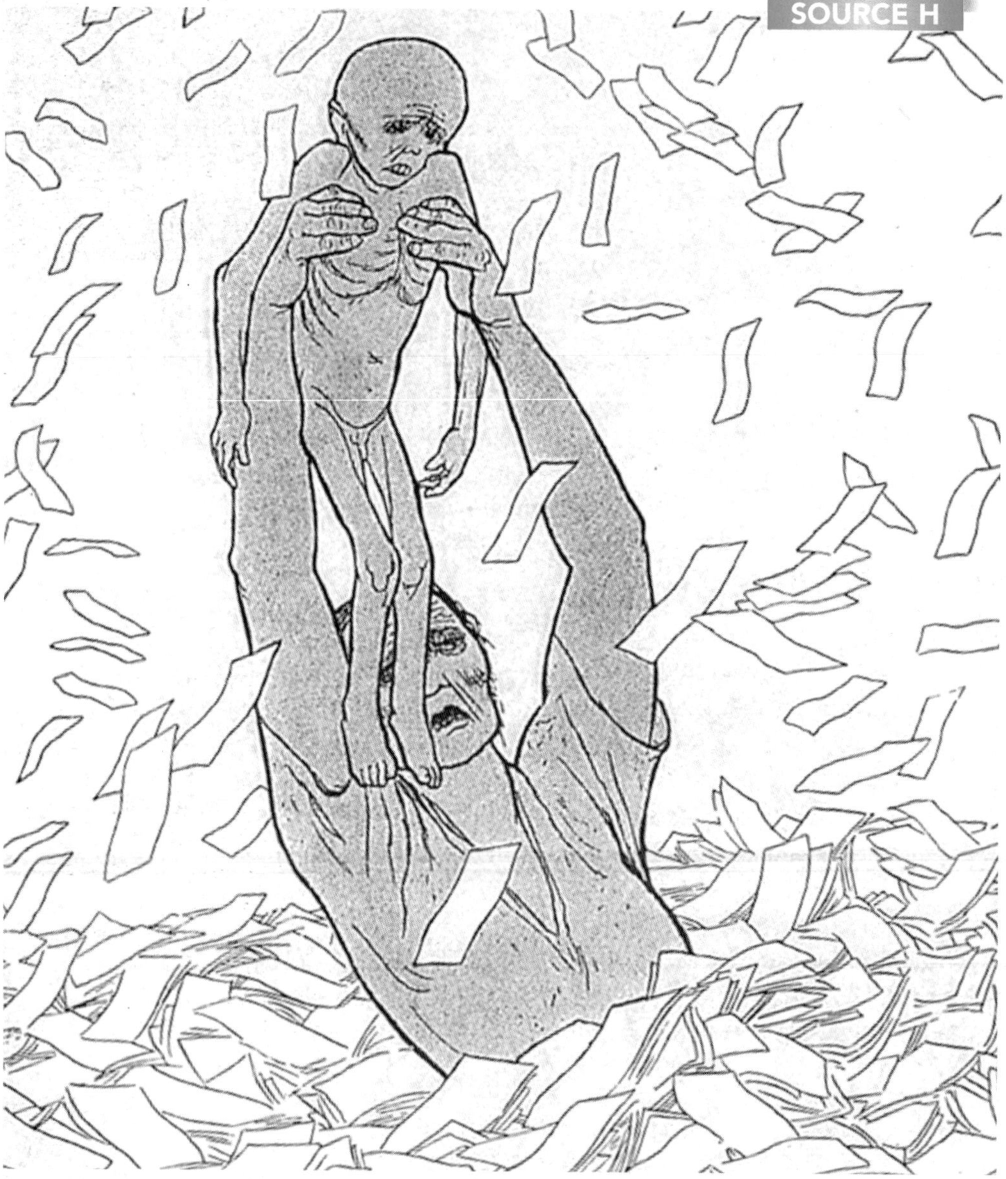

A cartoon from a German magazine in 1923. The mother is calling for bread while she and her child drown in paper money.

The Stresemann era 1923–9

By mid-1923 the German economy was in ruins and the Weimar Republic close to collapse. Yet within several years it had returned to prosperity and stability. How did this happen?

Much of the credit for the transformation must go to Gustav Stresemann, who became chancellor in August 1923. He was a committed nationalist, but believed that Germany's problems could be solved only by moderation and working with other countries.

One of his first acts was to introduce a new currency, the Rentenmark. At the same time, government spending was reduced (700,000 government employees lost their jobs). These measures helped end the hyperinflation and brought confidence back.

Stresemann also put down left-wing uprisings in Thuringia and Saxony, and dealt with the attempted putsch by the Nazis in Munich. For the rest of the 1920s, there was political stability in Germany and extreme parties, such as the Communists and Nazis, found it difficult to win large numbers of seats in the Reichstag.

Stresemann was chancellor for just four months, but he was foreign minister for five years. It was in this office that he had his greatest success. In 1924 he negotiated the Dawes Plan with the Allies. By this treaty, the USA agreed to loan Germany 800 million gold marks. It was also decided that the annual reparations payments should be reduced and Germany given longer to pay. In 1929 the Young Plan further extended the time that Germany had to pay reparations until 1988 (though payments actually ceased in 1930).

SOURCE I

Gustav Stresemann.

To what extent did the Republic recover after 1923?

These economic measures, together with further loans from the USA, helped the German economy to recover. Between 1924 and 1929 Germany received over 25 billion marks in loans, which enabled German industry to be rebuilt. Stresemann also had great success in improving relations with other countries. In 1925 he signed the Locarno Pact with France and Belgium, in which the countries agreed to respect the borders between them. Then in 1926 Germany joined the League of Nations. This acceptance of Germany back into the international community was reinforced in 1928 when it was one of 60 countries signing the Kellogg–Briand Pact against the use of war in foreign policy.

Stresemann was strongly criticised for being too willing to co-operate with Germany's former enemies. But he firmly believed that revision of the Treaty of Versailles could not happen overnight and had to be done by co-operation with foreign countries. Others, particularly Adolf Hitler, disagreed.

SOURCE J

A nation must not adopt the attitude of a child who writes a list of his wants on Christmas Eve, which contains everything that the child will need for the next fifteen years. The parents would not be in a position to give all this. In foreign policy, I often have the feeling that I am confronted with such a list.

Gustav Stresemann explaining why he signed the Locarno Pact when it appeared to accept the Treaty of Versailles.

This painting, called *The Party*, was painted by George Grosz. It shows the decadent night club life of the Weimar Republic.

SOURCE K

Art and culture under the Weimar Republic

The economic recovery experienced in Germany after 1924 was reflected in a cultural revival that could be seen in a variety of fields from architecture to opera. Under the Kaiser, there had been censorship in Germany. Now there was a new spirit of freedom, in which criticism of the government and even songs and books mentioning sex were allowed! Berlin became a thriving centre of the arts with over 120 newspapers and 40 theatres. German literature flourished, with Erich Remarque's *All Quiet on the Western Front* selling over half a million copies. German playwrights such as Bertolt Brecht won international fame, too. Painters such as George Grosz and Hannah Hoech became well known for their original style, and Walter Gropius founded the Bauhaus group, which brought in new ideas in architecture and sculpture.

Some Germans hated the new ideas in art and considered them decadent and unpatriotic. They wanted art to celebrate the traditional values of German society. They argued that the new artistic styles, popular music, jazz and clubs showed how Germany was going into moral decline.

What were the achievements of the Weimar period?

As you have read, the Weimar Republic inherited serious political and economic problems in 1919 and then faced even more difficult ones in the years up to 1923. Under these circumstances, it was a major success to maintain political stability in Germany and prevent a revolution from leading to more extreme government. By the mid-1920s, the German people seemed to have accepted the Weimar Republic and there was less demand for a return to the 'good old days' of the Kaiser.

After 1924 the successes of the Republic are much easier to see. Stresemann's work brought economic recovery and the reintroduction of Germany into the international community of nations. There was also significant achievement in the arts with Gropius, Brecht and Grosz winning international fame.

However, this 'golden age' of Germany was to some extent an illusion. Economic prosperity was based largely on foreign loans. At the same time, exports were falling and the government was spending huge sums on welfare and health care. Could it last? Already by 1928 there were serious disputes between unions and employers. Meanwhile, the farmers had never shared in the apparent prosperity. Prices for farm produce fell during the 1920s and many farmers were in debt.

The political stability was also wafer thin. In 1925 Hindenburg was elected president – and he was a strong supporter of the Kaiser. Many Germans resented the fact that the Treaty of Versailles had not been reversed and blamed the government for it.

While things were going well, the Weimar Republic's achievements looked impressive. Once things went wrong, they looked much less so.

SOURCE A

> Goodness! He's got a big gob. We could use him.

A comment made by Anton Drexler on first hearing Hitler speak in public.

Why was Hitler able to dominate Germany by 1934?

What did the Nazi Party stand for in the 1920s?

In January 1919, three Germans formed a small party called the German Workers' Party (DAP). Adolf Hitler joined the party in September 1919. He quickly showed a talent for public speaking, was invited to join the party's executive committee and was put in charge of propaganda. In 1920 he played a major part in writing the party's Twenty-Five Point Programme, setting out its beliefs. This programme showed the early anti-Semitism (anti-Jewishness) of the party, but also contained many socialist ideas. The socialist ideas were not thought to have been Hitler's suggestions.

SOURCE B

Deutsche Arbeiter-Partei (D. A. P.)
Ortsgruppe München
Abteilung:
Mitgliedskarte
für Herrn Adolf Hitler
München, den 1. Jan. 1920
Nr. 555
Schriftwart
Für den Arbeitsausschuß:
Drexler
Diese Karte gilt als Ausweis bei geschlossenen Versammlungen

Hitler's membership card for the German Workers' Party. He claimed he was the seventh member of the party, but his card shows he was 555th. Some historians say that the party started numbering at 500 to make it look better.

In April the DAP was renamed the National Socialist German Workers' Party ('Nazi Party' for short) and later in the year it bought a Munich newspaper, *Volkischer Beobachter*. This paper was well known for its anti-Semitic views – it had once had a headline saying 'Clean out the Jews once and for all'. The newspaper was used to spread Nazi views, and support for the party began to grow.

QUESTIONS

1 Why was German prosperity after 1924 'to some extent an illusion'?

2 What can we learn about Adolf Hitler from Source A?

SOURCE C

A Nazi propaganda poster showing the popularity of the Stormtrooper movement.

In 1921 Hitler became party leader and in the same year founded the Sturm Abteilung ('Stormtroopers' or 'Brownshirts'). The SA was a paramilitary organisation that paraded in full military uniform, wearing the Nazi 'swastika'. Its main task was to protect Nazi meetings and 'disrupt' those of its opponents. The military style of the organisation attracted many unemployed soldiers, and the Stormtroopers soon developed a reputation for brutality against Nazi opponents.

The Munich putsch and its consequences

By 1923 the Nazi Party had grown to 35,000 members, although support was based largely in Bavaria. Hitler was convinced that the Weimar Republic's problems gave him the opportunity to seize power, but his Munich putsch was unsuccessful and Hitler was imprisoned. The failed putsch had an important impact on the Nazi Party. Its leader was jailed, its newspaper in Munich was banned – and so was the party itself!

Why did the Nazis have little success before 1930?

While Hitler was in prison, some of his supporters formed the National Socialist Freedom Party, but in December 1924 (when Hitler came out of prison) the party won only fourteen seats in the Reichstag. Hitler was determined to try to win power by legal means, but the success of Stresemann's policies meant that there was very little support for extremists such as Hitler.

In 1925, however, Hitler persuaded the authorities to lift the ban on the Nazi Party and set about reorganising it. He made a bad start in February when he made a speech that was so critical of the government that he was banned from public speaking for two years. Hitler divided Germany into 34 districts and put a leading Nazi in charge of increasing support in each area. He also started the Hitler Youth and a personal bodyguard, the Schutzstaffel (SS). In 1926 he called a party conference and persuaded the members of his party to re-adopt the original Twenty-Five Point Programme.

By the end of 1926 the Nazi Party had 50,000 members, and in 1927 it held its first Nuremberg rally. It had become a nationally known party with a strong leader and effective propaganda. But despite all the hard work, the party was not making gains in terms of the number of deputies elected to the Reichstag. In the 1928 election, the Nazis won just twelve seats and were only the eighth largest party. Things were soon to change.

Why was Hitler able to become chancellor by 1933?

1 The economic crisis

In October 1929, two significant events had a dramatic effect on Germany. On 3 October, Gustav Stresemann died. Germany had lost one of its most able politicians. Then on 29 October, the Wall Street Crash began in the United States. As a result of the dramatic fall in share prices, many American businesses went bankrupt. American banks called in the loans they had made to Germany. Without these loans, German industry could not operate, especially as the American markets for their goods had now collapsed. Factories closed and millions of workers lost their jobs. Those in work had to take wage cuts and go on to short-time working. Germany had once more sunk into economic depression. Under these circumstances, the old hostility to the Weimar Republic resurfaced and people blamed the government for the crisis. People began to lose faith in parliamentary democracy and turn to those parties that offered a radical solution to Germany's problems – the Nazis and the Communists.

SOURCE D

Germany has lost her ablest politician. Gustav Stresemann lived and worked without stint for the internal reconstruction of his shattered country. As for peace and co-operation abroad, he laboured with immense energy. The task he took up when he became Chancellor would have frightened a smaller man. The domestic recovery of Germany and her new standing in Europe give measure to his achievement.

The obituary of Gustav Stresemann from the English newspaper, *The Times*, on 4 October 1929.

SOURCE E

We demand the union of all Germans in a Greater Germany.
We demand land and colonies to feed our people and settle our surplus population.
No Jew may be a member of the German nation.
All citizens shall have equal rights and duties.
We demand profit sharing in large industrial companies.
We demand the abolition of incomes unearned by work.

Extracts from the Twenty-Five Point Programme, 1920.

QUESTIONS

1 What was the purpose of the Sturm Abteilung?

2 How strong was the Nazi Party in 1927?

3 Look at Source E. How far does it explain why the Nazi Party grew in popularity in the 1920s?

2 The political crisis

In 1929 the government was a coalition led by Hermann Müller of the Social Democratic Party. His coalition could not agree on how to deal with the effects of the Depression and in March 1930 he resigned as chancellor. Müller was succeeded by Heinrich Brüning of the Centre Party. He did not have a majority in the Reichstag and had to rely on President Hindenburg, using Article 48 of the constitution to get his measures adopted. Between 1930 and 1932 the Reichstag met less and less frequently, and Hindenburg issued over a hundred presidential decrees.

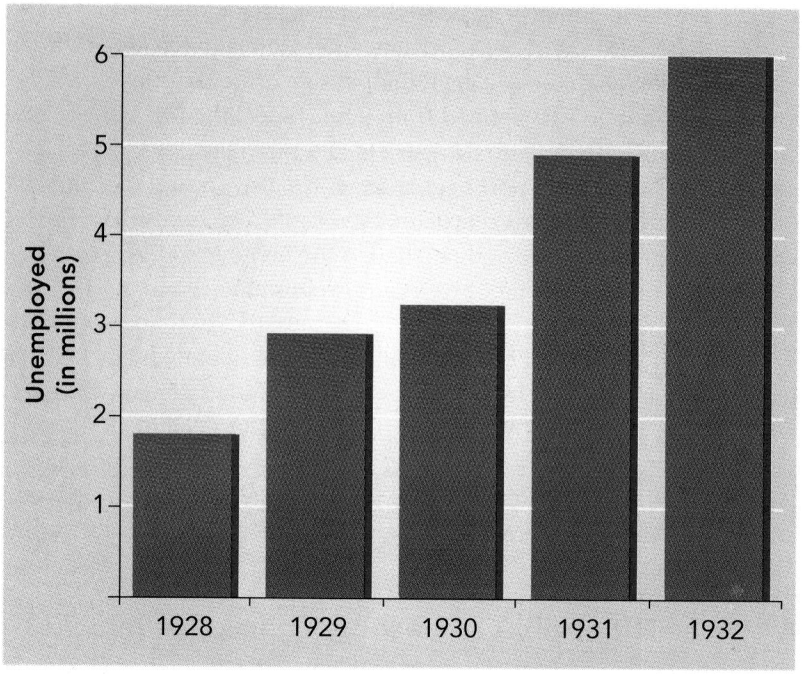

Unemployment in Germany, 1928–32.

During this time, Hitler exploited the government's problems by holding huge rallies and touring Germany, promising to restore Germany's economy. The socialist elements of the party's programme were forgotten as Hitler tried to win support from the German middle classes and industrialists. In the elections of September 1930, the Nazis won 107 seats. In the next election, in July 1932, they won 230 seats (although they dropped back to 196 in November 1932).

In 1932 Brüning was replaced as chancellor by von Papen, who was then overthrown by von Schleicher. Von Papen plotted revenge and in January 1933 persuaded Hindenburg to replace von Schleicher with Adolf Hitler. Von Papen was to be vice-chancellor. He thought that

Party	1928	1930	July 1932	Nov. 1932
Social Democrats	153	143	133	121
National	73	41	37	52
Centre	62	68	75	70
Communists	54	77	89	100
People's	45	30	7	11
Democrats	25	20	4	2
Nazis	12	107	230	196

Results of elections to the German Reichstag, 1928–32 (main parties only).

QUESTIONS

1. How do the table and the graph on this page help explain how the Nazis came to power?
2. Explain the steps by which Hitler came to power between 1929 and 1933.

SOURCE F

German women!
Our young people defiled.

It has been confirmed that in a German Grammar School for girls, 63% of the girls have had sexual intercourse and 43% have had some form of sexual disease. This is the result of the many years during which our people, and in particular our youth, have been exposed to a flood of muck and filth, in word and print, in the theatre and in the cinema.

An extract from a Nazi election leaflet in 1932.

support for the Nazi Party was now in decline and that Hitler could be manipulated to do what von Papen wanted. On 30 January 1933, Hitler became chancellor. But he was not a man to be manipulated.

How did Hitler consolidate his power in 1933–4?

The dramatic increase in the number of seats that the Nazis won in the Reichstag elections was an obvious reflection of the growth in their support. Who gave them this support and why?

The election of March 1933

Hitler had become chancellor, but he did not have genuine power. He headed a coalition government in which only three of the twelve Cabinet ministers were Nazis. The answer lay in holding a new election in which the Nazis would win sufficient seats to govern on their own.

An election was called for March 1933 and the Nazis set about persuading the German people to support them. Their main tactic was to emphasise the threat to Germany from the communists. Hitler fully exploited the advantages he had as chancellor by banning communist election meetings and shutting down communist newspapers. Thousands of Stormtroopers were enrolled as special constables. These men often 'overlooked' Stormtrooper brutality towards opponents of the Nazis which they saw in the streets.

Reasons for Nazi support

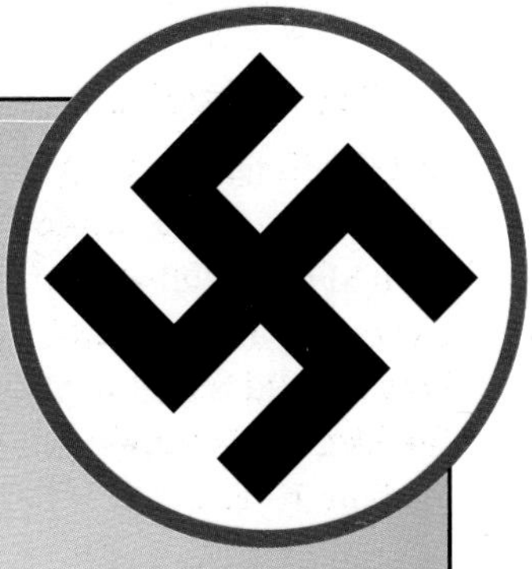

- The Nazi Party was anti-communist. This appealed to all those who feared what communism might bring, but particularly industrialists, who feared that a communist government would take over their businesses. Hitler conveniently dropped the socialist elements of the Nazi programme and in return won the support of the industrialists. One leading industrialist gave the party one million marks.
- The promise to reverse the Treaty of Versailles and restore Germany's military strength appealed to nationalists and to those who believed the 'stab in the back' theory about the end of the war. Most importantly, it won the support of Germany's armed forces.
- The promise to tackle unemployment obviously appealed to the millions who were out of work or feared losing their jobs as a result of the Depression. The promise of strong government also attracted the support of many middle-class Germans who remembered the difficulties of 1923.
- Many women were attracted to the party by its emphasis on family life and self-discipline. This message was reinforced by heavy propaganda campaigns (Source F).
- Hitler's anti-Jewish campaign may seem strange to us today, but it was highly effective. He knew that many people were having a hard time and wanted someone to blame. He told them that their difficulties were being caused by the Weimar Republic, the communists and especially the Jews (though no credible reason for blaming the Jews ever emerged). So Hitler provided a scapegoat and this helped increase his support.
- Hitler was a skilled public speaker and his colleague, Joseph Goebbels, made effective use of propaganda. Those who would have spoken up against the Nazis were often persuaded not to do so by a visit from the Stormtroopers.

The Reichstag fire

The most dramatic event occurred on 27 February 1933 when the Reichstag building in Berlin was burned to the ground. A Dutch communist, Marinus van der Lubbe, was caught in the building with matches and firelighters. He confessed to starting the fire, was put on trial and was later executed.

Hitler was delighted by what had happened. Here was the evidence of what he had been saying for years. The communists were trying to seize power by violent revolution. They had to be stopped. He had 4000 leading communists arrested and persuaded President Hindenburg to sign 'A Decree for the Protection of the People and the State'. Hitler used this decree to prevent the Nazis' political opponents from holding public meetings and to arrest more communists.

The Reichstag Fire was extremely convenient for the Nazis, and some historians have suggested that they had the fire started themselves. There is no objective evidence to suggest that they did, but it remains extremely doubtful that van der Lubbe was part of a communist conspiracy and he always denied this. The fire was probably the individual action of one mentally unstable communist, but it gave Hitler the opportunity to take action against his opponents.

The steps taken by the Nazis helped them to increase the number of deputies in the Reichstag to 288 out of 647. This was not the 50 per cent that Hitler wanted, but two things gave him a majority in the Reichstag. First, he banned the 81 communist deputies from taking their seats; and secondly, he won the support of the Centre Party by saying that he would not take any measures that would harm the Catholic Church. Germany now had a fully Nazi government.

SOURCE G

A cartoon published in the *Daily Express*, 5 March 1933. It shows how Hitler forced Germans to vote for him in the March election.

SOURCE H

The Reichstag building on fire.

SOURCE I

I decided to go to Germany to see for myself. Since the workers would do nothing, I had to do something by myself. I considered arson a suitable method. I did not wish to harm private people, but something that belonged to the state. I acted alone, no one helped me, nor did I meet a single person in the Reichstag.

A statement made by van der Lubbe to the police in March 1933.

SOURCE J

I was told that a young Dutchman had turned up in Berlin of whom we could make use. This Dutch communist, van der Lubbe, would climb into the Reichstag and blunder about conspicuously. Meanwhile, I and my men would set fire to the building...

We prepared a number of fires by smearing chairs and tables and by soaking carpets and curtains in paraffin. At exactly 9.05 we finished and left.

I am writing this confession because the SA has been betrayed by the evil plans of Goering and Goebbels. I shall destroy it the moment these traitors have been removed.

This account is part of the evidence published against the Nazis by communists in 1934. It is said to be a confession written by Karl Ernst, a senior member of the SA, in June 1934. He ordered that the document should be published only if he met a violent death. He died in the 'Night of the Long Knives' (see pages 114–5).

QUESTIONS

1 Why was Hitler so pleased by the Reichstag Fire?

2 How do you explain the differences between Sources I and J?

3 How far does Source G suggest that the German people might not have fully supported the Nazi Party in the March 1933 election?

How effectively did the Nazis control Germany 1933–45?

The Enabling Law

Hitler was not a supporter of parliamentary democracy and wanted to make changes to the German constitution to give himself greater power. He needed a two-thirds majority in the Reichstag to make such changes. His banning of the Communist Party and support from the Centre Party gave him this majority.

On 23 March 1933 the Reichstag met to discuss the passing of the Enabling Law. This would give Hitler the power to make laws without the Reichstag for a period of four years. In effect, it would make him a dictator in Germany. Hitler had the majority he needed, but to make sure he got his way he surrounded the building with Stormtroopers to intimidate those who wanted to vote against the measure. The Reichstag passed the law by 441 votes to 84 and effectively voted itself out existence. The Reichstag met only twelve times between 1933 and 1939, and passed just four laws – all without a vote. The only speeches made were by Hitler.

SOURCE A

The Reichstag has passed the following law:

In addition to the procedure outlined for the passing of laws in the constitution, the government is also able to pass laws. The laws passed by the government shall be issued by the Chancellor.

An extract from the Enabling Law giving the Nazi government the power to make laws.

The establishment of the Nazi dictatorship

After March 1933, Hitler used his new powers to turn Germany into a totalitarian state – that is, one where the state had control of all aspects of its citizens' lives. In July, the Law Against the Establishment of Parties stated that the Nazi Party was the only political party in Germany. Democracy in Germany was dead.

The 'Night of the Long Knives'

The Stormtroopers had been loyal servants of the Nazi Party since their formation in 1921. But once Hitler was in power, they became a problem. The Stormtroopers expected to be given well-paid jobs in the government as a reward for their loyalty. Their leaders also wanted Hitler to merge the SA with the German army and put the combined force under the command of Ernst Röhm, the SA leader. Such a move would have horrified the army commanders, who saw the Stormtroopers as little more than a rabble. Hitler was keen to have the support of the army, but he had another reason for moving against the SA. The SA leaders, particularly Ernst Röhm, had left-wing views which would offend the big businesses that had helped fund Hitler in the period up to 1933. Röhm might even emerge as a rival to Hitler's leadership of the party.

The solution to the problem was to bring the SA into line. On the night of 30 June 1934, Hitler ordered his elite bodyguard (the SS) to arrest and execute the leaders of the SA. Röhm and hundreds of other Stormtroopers were executed. Hitler also took the opportunity to settle a few old scores – he had von Schleicher, his predecessor as chancellor, put to death. People inside Germany and around the

QUESTIONS

1 a What was the Enabling Law?
  b Why was it so important?
2 What do you think the cartoonist was trying to say in Source B?
3 How believable do you find Source C?
4 Why did the Nazis carry out the 'Night of the Long Knives'?

world were shocked by what had happened, but Hitler's propaganda convinced many of them that Röhm and the other leaders were a genuine threat to the country. President Hindenburg even went as far as thanking Hitler for saving Germany from possible revolution.

A few weeks after this event, the ageing Hindenburg died. Hitler decided that the country no longer needed a president. Instead the office would be combined with that of chancellor, and Hitler himself would be known as 'Führer' (leader) of Germany. From 1934 the army swore an oath of allegiance to Hitler, not to the country of Germany as it had previously. It seemed that, as far as the Nazis were concerned, Hitler *was* Germany.

SOURCE C

We enter the house and surprise a sleeping band of conspirators, taking them prisoner at once. With unparalleled courage Hitler personally makes the arrests. I do not wish to dwell on the revolting scenes of debauchery that we witnessed, but let me quote the words of a simple Hitler guard who declared 'I only wish the walls would collapse so that the whole nation could witness these happenings and understand how good it is that our leader acts in this way.'

An extract from a radio broadcast made by Goebbels on 1 July 1934. It describes how Hitler's guards arrested Stormtroopers, who were seen as enemies of the state.

SOURCE B

A cartoon published in an English newspaper on 3 July 1934.

How did the Nazis use culture and the mass media to control the people?

An essential part of the Nazi control of Germany was the use of propaganda. The German people were bombarded with the party message to ensure that Hitler's regime had popular support.

In 1933 the Ministry for People's Enlightenment and Propaganda was set up under Joseph Goebbels. He saw his duty as twofold. He had to get the Nazi message across and at the same time ensure that any views hostile to Nazism were suppressed. So Goebbels' ministry controlled the radio, the press and all areas of culture, such as films, literature, art and the theatre. Journalists were given detailed instructions about what to write in their newspapers (Source E) and what could be broadcast on radio. The Nazis made sure that the radio was easily available to all Germans. Radios were so cheap that the German people had more of them per head of the population than even the wealthy Americans.

In addition, all films, plays and literature had to conform to Nazi beliefs or they could not be performed or published. In this way, 'undesirable' influences, such as jazz or Black American music, could be kept from the German people.

SOURCE E

In the next issue there must be a lead article, featured as prominently as possible, in which a decision of the Führer, no matter what it may be, will be discussed as the only correct one for Germany.

Instructions issued to the press by the Ministry of Propaganda and Enlightenment in 1939.

SOURCE D

Crowds at the 1936 Nazi Party rally in Nuremberg.

In May 1933 there was a public book burning in Berlin when Goebbels watched Berlin students set fire to a collection of books that had been looted from libraries in the city. Altogether the writings of over 2500 writers were banned. Many of these writers were famous authors from the Weimar Republic. Similar restrictions were placed on musicians, poets and playwrights. In contrast, those putting forward acceptable views of Germany, like Wagner, were positively encouraged.

There were also great public displays of Nazism to promote support. Posters and photographs of Hitler, together with swastika flags, were to be found all over Germany. Hitler was always portrayed as a strong and confident leader. Perhaps the most famous of these public displays were the Nuremberg rallies. Each year an enormous rally of soldiers and party officials took place in a stadium especially designed for the occasion. Other processions and rallies were held throughout the year to celebrate special events, such as the Führer's birthday in April.

The greatest propaganda coup for Hitler came in 1936 when the Olympic Games were held in Berlin. The games were used to promote German technical efficiency and the supremacy of the Aryan race. A brand new stadium was built holding 100,000 spectators, and television cameras were used for the first time. Foreign visitors were highly impressed with the excellence of the facilities and the efficiency of the organisation. Of course, Hitler ensured that the negative sides of Nazism, such as the restrictions on personal freedom and the mistreatment of the Jews, were kept in the background.

To Hitler's great joy the German team won 33 gold medals, 26 silver and 30 bronze – far more than any other team. However, he was less pleased about the performance of the American athlete, Jesse Owens. Owens was black, and according to Nazi racial theories inferior. Yet he was the star of the games, winning four gold medals and breaking eleven world records. Not surprisingly, Hitler refused to shake hands with the man who single-handedly showed Nazi racial theory to be nonsense.

SOURCE F

Jesse Owens in action at the 1936 Berlin Olympic Games.

QUESTIONS

1 Why was propaganda so important to the Nazis?

2 The Nazis could hardly burn all the books of which they disapproved, so what was the point of public book-burning ceremonies?

3 Why do you think Hitler refused to shake Jesse Owens' hand at the 1936 Olympics?

How much opposition was there to the Nazi regime?

It is very difficult to judge the amount of opposition to the Nazis because officially no opposition was recognised. The Nazi propaganda machine gave the impression that everyone loved the Führer and that the German people were all grateful to him for restoring Germany's greatness. In reality, many people objected to the personal restrictions placed upon them and to the treatment of the Jews in Germany. But there was a big difference between objecting to some of Hitler's policies and active opposition. And, of course, the Nazis made sure that opposition to their rule was extremely dangerous. Consequently, there was little effective opposition to the Nazi regime and it was only during the strains of the Second World War that opposition to the Nazis became apparent to the outside world.

In 1933 Hitler had used the Enabling Law to ban all political parties other than the Nazis. His two main opponents, the Social Democratic Party (SPD) and the Communist Party (KPD), went underground and published anti-Nazi propaganda, but little of it reached the German people.

Opposition from artists and authors was more common, but here the opposition was more concerned with the restrictions on artistic freedom. Some spoke out against the restrictions, but most chose either to suffer in silence or to emigrate. One of the most famous emigrants was the physicist Albert Einstein, who later helped to develop the atomic bomb.

The Nazis were aware of the importance of maintaining good relationships with the Church in Germany. Many Germans were committed Christians and opposition from the Church would prove very difficult to counter.

At first the Christian churches seemed to be keen to work with the Nazis. The government's encouragement of family values and campaign against immorality in Germany was very much in keeping with Christian beliefs. In 1933 the Catholic Church and the Nazis signed an agreement called the Concordat. The Church agreed not to make comments on political matters if the Nazis did not interfere in religion. Hitler failed to keep his promise, however. He interfered more and more in church matters: for example, closing down Catholic Youth movements because they rivalled his own Hitler Youth. In 1937 Pope Pius XI denounced Nazism as anti-Christian and in 1941 a letter from the Pope criticising the Nazis for their abuse of human rights was read out in Catholic churches. Hitler responded by sending nuns and priests to labour camps.

SOURCE G

Two 'swing types'. Their pictures were issued to shock the German public.

Relations with Protestant churches also deteriorated sharply under the Nazis, when Hitler set up the Reich Church to keep control. Some 800 Protestant churchmen, such as Pastor Niemoller, were sent to labour camps for speaking out against the Nazis. Co-operation with the churches had turned to confrontation.

Some army generals were highly suspicious of the Nazis. One of the most prominent was General Ludwig Beck, who disagreed with Hitler's expansionist foreign policy. Hitler's reaction was to sack large numbers of generals in 1938, including General Beck.

Although the Hitler Youth movement was very popular with many German youngsters, some objected to the restrictions it placed on them. They did not want regimentation and training for the army or motherhood. Instead they were more

SOURCE H

Members of the Navajos Gang in Cologne in 1940.

interested in dancing to American and English songs and listening to jazz music. The Nazis condemned these members of the 'Swing' movement as degenerate and issued pictures to help identify them.

Other problems came from gangs such as the Navajos Gang or Edelweiss Pirates. These groups were usually made up of 14–17-year-olds (between the age of leaving school and signing up for the army). Many liked to beat up members of the Hitler Youth and in some cities, such as Cologne, they became a genuine problem for the authorities. If their activities had been restricted to bullying the Hitler Youth and leading a 'degenerate' lifestyle, things might not have been too bad. But during the Second World War, their activities became more serious as they helped spread Allied propaganda and sometimes helped Allied airmen to escape. In 1944 a group of Edelweiss Pirates took part in an attack on the Gestapo in which a senior officer was killed. As a result, twelve pirates were publicly hanged.

When the Second World War began to go badly for the Germans, some of the opposition to the Nazis actually turned to open resistance as they tried to overthrow the regime.

A group of university students in Munich led by Hans and Sophie Scholl formed the White Rose movement. They handed out pamphlets appealing for people to oppose the policies of the Nazi regime. In 1943 the government arrested and executed the Scholls and other leading members of the organisation.

SOURCE I

They are everywhere. There are more of them than there are Hitler Youth. They don't agree with anything. They don't go to work either; they are always down by the canal.

A German complaining about the number of Edelweiss Pirates in Oberhausen in 1941.

QUESTIONS

1 How well did Hitler get on with the Church in Germany?

2 Why were the Nazis so concerned about organisations such as the Edelweiss Pirates?

3 How difficult was it to oppose the Nazi regime?

There was increasing opposition to the Nazis from within the German upper classes. Although they had originally supported the way that the Nazis brought stability back to Germany, by 1940 they were tired of Nazi brutality and feared that Hitler's aggressive foreign policy might lead to Germany's ruin.

Two main upper-class organisations opposed the Nazis. The Kreisau Circle was led by Helmuth von Moltke, from one of Germany's most famous aristocratic families. They wanted to see the Nazis overthrown, but were not men of violence. In 1944 their group was discovered and the leaders were executed.

A second group was the Beck–Goerdeler Group, named after Ludwig Beck and Karl Goerdeler. The two leaders of this group realised that the only way to rid Germany of Hitler was to assassinate him. In July 1944 one of their supporters, Count Claus von Stauffenberg, placed a briefcase with a bomb in it under a table at a meeting attended by Hitler. The bomb went off, but Hitler was not seriously injured. Those responsible for the 'July Plot', including Beck and Goerdeler, were executed. Field Marshal Rommel, one of Germany's greatest generals, committed suicide to avoid the disgrace of a trial.

How effectively did the Nazis deal with their political opponents?

Although the Nazis' main weapons for enforcing compliance with their rule were persuasion and propaganda, behind the flags, displays and radio broadcasts was a ruthless system for dealing with their opponents.

The main organisation was the Schutzstaffel (SS). It was formed in 1925 as an elite bodyguard and from 1929 came under the leadership of Heinrich Himmler. After the purge of the SA in 1934, it was the Nazis' main security force. Gradually the SS split into three main sections. One was responsible for national security. Another, the Waffen SS, was a group of highly skilled and dependable soldiers who fought alongside the regular army. A third group, the Death's Head Units, ran the concentration camps and later the death camps.

SOURCE J

A German cartoon published in 1934 entitled 'Life in the Third Reich.'

The Geheime Staatspolizei (Gestapo) was a state police force set up by Hermann Goering in 1933. It was led by Reinhard Heydrich and was ruthless in dealing with opposition to the Nazis. Its task was to 'discover the enemies of the state, watch them and render them harmless'. The Gestapo had the power to arrest and detain suspects without trial. An extensive web of informers ensured that the authorities quickly learned of anyone plotting against them.

From 1933 the German courts were 'Nazified'. Hitler set up the People's Court to try people who opposed the Nazi regime. Judges had to be loyal Nazis and could be guaranteed to give the 'right' verdict. Under such a system, the number of political prisoners increased dramatically. Between 1930 and 1932 just 8 people were found guilty and executed. Between 1934 and 1939, 534 people were executed. By 1939 there were 162,734 people under 'protective arrest'.

The Nazis also made use of concentration camps – labour camps where 'enemies of the state' could be sent. Discipline was very hard and food very poor. Few people survived a stay in the camps. At first, most prisoners were communists or trade union leaders. Later other 'undesirable' groups were also sent to the camps (e.g. eastern Europeans, Jews, homosexuals and religious fundamentalists). In 1942, when the Nazis came up with their 'Final Solution' to the 'Jewish problem', many of these concentration camps became death camps (see pages 130–1).

What was it like to live in Nazi Germany?

How did young people react to the Nazi regime?

The Nazis were particularly anxious to win the hearts and minds of the young in Germany. They knew that, no matter how much propaganda they used, there would always be some adults who rejected their ideas. But if the young could be indoctrinated into the Nazi way of thinking, then those views were likely to stay with them for the rest of their lives.

SOURCE A

A recruiting poster for the Hitler Youth.

This was the major purpose of the Hitler Youth, which had been founded in 1926. By the time the Nazis took power in 1933, it had 100,000 members.

Boys aged between 6 and 10 joined the Little Fellows; then from 10 to 14 they went on to the Young Folk; finally, from 14 to 18 they became members of the Hitler Youth. Girls joined the Young Girls between 10 and 14, and from 14 to 17 they joined the League of German Maidens.

These youth organisations provided ideal opportunities for the leaders to put across Nazi beliefs, and members were encouraged to report their parents or teachers if they criticised the Nazi regime. But they had another purpose too. The Hitler Youth was really a training ground for the army, and great emphasis was placed on physical activity and military training. Girls did not join the army, but they were still encouraged to keep fit in preparation for motherhood – the opportunity to give birth to future soldiers.

Year	Membership	Population of Germany aged 10–18
1933	2,292,041	7,529,000
1934	3,577,565	7,682,000
1935	3,394,303	8,172,000
1936	5,437,601	8,656,000
1937	5,879,955	9,060,000
1938	7,031,266	9,109,000
1939	7,287,470	8,870,000

Membership of the Hitler Youth, 1933–9.

At first, membership of the Hitler Youth was not compulsory, but it proved attractive to many young people with its regime of camps, sporting activities and marches. By 1936 there were over 5 million members and competition from other organisations was limited. Youth clubs connected with other political parties or with churches were shut down. In 1936 the Hitler Youth Law made membership compulsory, although some young people were still reluctant to join. By 1939, as the table shows, the vast majority of young Germans were part of the organisation.

SOURCE B

DIE
NSDAP
SICHERT DIE
VOLKS-
GEMEINSCHAFT
VOLKSGENOSSEN
BRAUCHT IHR RAT UND HILFE
SO WENDET EUCH AN DIE
ORTSGRUPPE

A Nazi poster showing an ideal German family.

Education

Not surprisingly, the Nazis used schools to indoctrinate the young. They laid down what was to be taught and placed special emphasis on the subjects that they considered suitable in producing 'ideal Nazis'. So subjects like History (to show how successful the Nazis had been) and Biology (to explain Nazi racial beliefs) became much more important. The amount of time given to physical education trebled in the 1930s. Other subjects, such as Race Studies and Ideology, also appeared on the timetable as Nazi beliefs were taught as accepted facts.

Education for boys and girls was different. A greater emphasis was placed on domestic science and other subjects suitable for motherhood in girls' schools, whereas the importance of military training was emphasised in boys' schools.

In the classroom, Nazi ideas were promoted by using textbooks that had been rewritten to conform to Nazi beliefs, and by ensuring that lessons were taught by teachers who supported the party. A mixture of propaganda and intimidation led to 97 per cent of teachers becoming members of the National Socialist Teachers' League, founded to encourage teachers into the 'correct' way of thinking.

Examples used in class exercises further encouraged support for Nazi views. Geography lessons emphasised the harshness of the Treaty of Versailles, Physics lessons concentrated on weapon making, and even Maths lessons for young children were sometimes about bombing Jewish ghettos. Of course, a major message that was continually repeated in schools was the supremacy of the Aryan (Germanic/North European) race and the inferiority of blacks, eastern Europeans and, in particular, Jews.

How successful were Nazi policies towards women and the family?

As you will have realised from the way girls were treated, the Nazis had very strong views about the place of women in society. It was their duty to remain at home as child-bearers and as supporters of their husbands. They were not equal. Employment opportunities for women declined, and under the Nazis there were fewer women teachers, doctors and civil servants. They were banned from being judges and removed from jury service because they were said to be incapable of thinking without emotion. As a shortage of workers developed, particularly in the war years, more women were encouraged to work, but they were never allowed to play a part in the armed forces, as women did with such distinction in Britain.

As far as the Nazis were concerned, women should be encouraged to have as many children as possible. Hitler was alarmed at the falling birth rate in Germany, so contraception was discouraged and mothers with eight children or more were awarded a golden Mother Cross (with silver for six children and bronze for four). Motherhood and family life were also prominent in Nazi propaganda. Posters and broadcasts emphasised the qualities of 'traditional' German women. In some cities, women were banned from smoking because it was 'unladylike' and make-up and the latest fashions were discouraged. Ideal German women had flat heels, no make-up and plaited hair.

Of course, many German women objected to their role as second-class citizens, and some joined illegal opposition political parties to campaign for better status. But in the 1930s women were not considered to be the equal of men in most countries. Nazi beliefs about women were not necessarily unusual, just more extreme than elsewhere.

SOURCE C

We do not consider it correct for the woman to interfere in the world of a man. We consider it natural that these two worlds remain distinct. What the man gives in courage on the battlefield, the woman gives in self-sacrifice. Every child that a woman brings into the world is a battle; a battle waged for the existence of her people.

From Hitler's 'Address to Women' at the Nuremberg rally in 1934.

QUESTIONS

1 a What was the purpose of the Hitler Youth?
  b How effective was it?

2 Which subjects did Nazi education emphasise?

3 What were the Nazis' views on
  a women at work
  b the role of women in society?

Did most people in Germany benefit from Nazi rule?

When Hitler came to power, the German economy was in ruins as a result of the world depression that set in after the Wall Street Crash. Unemployment stood at 6 million and Hitler took steps to bring this figure down. After all, he had promised in 1933 to beat unemployment within four years.

A number of methods were used to win the battle against unemployment. Hitler's re-armament policy led to increased production in the iron and steel industry, and in companies making weapons. Obviously more workers were needed for this. Hitler also 'mopped up' unemployed men by putting them into the army. It was estimated that Germany's army had 750,000 more soldiers in 1938 than in 1933. The Nazis also helped create jobs by spending money on public works. For example, a network of motorways (autobahns) across Germany was begun (Source D). Between 1933 and 1938, over 3000 kilometres of Autobahns were built. Help was also given to private firms to build houses. These measures helped reduce unemployment to only 218,000 by July 1938.

SOURCE D

Hitler begins the construction of the first German Autobahn in 1934.

But things were not quite as rosy as they looked. Unemployment fell in all European countries as the Depression came to an end, so perhaps the achievements of the Nazis were not so great. Also there was no improvement in the level of wages. People's average working week rose from 45 hours in 1928 to 50 in 1939 and over 60 towards the end of the war. Yet wages were lower in 1938 than they had been in 1928.

German workers also lost the right to have their own trade unions. Instead the government set up the German Labour Front. Two other organisations, 'Beauty of Labour' and 'Strength Through Joy', were set up to promote better working conditions and to give rewards for good work, but there is no doubt that under the Nazis German workers worked harder and for less reward. There was also a shortage of consumer goods for Germans to buy as the German economy became increasingly linked to preparing for war.

So by 1939 the Nazis had reduced unemployment and brought political stability to Germany. But this was achieved at a very heavy cost. Hitler's totalitarian regime had abolished many of the rights that citizens in other countries took for granted. In Nazi Germany there were no opposition political parties and no free trade unions. The media were censored, workers had longer hours for less pay, and freedom of speech was stifled. Education, the churches, the courts, local government and even youth clubs were rigorously controlled by the Nazi regime. Yet none of this compares with the treatment handed out to minority groups in Germany, particularly the Jews.

Why did the Nazis persecute many groups in German society?

Hitler and the Nazis believed that the German people were the master race. The Germanic racial group (the Aryans) was superior to all other groups. The ideal Aryan was tall with blond hair and blue eyes, and Hitler was frequently photographed with men and women who fitted this model. Pride in one's racial background is a natural and common phenomenon, but the Nazis took this belief to extreme lengths. Race farms were set up, where carefully selected women were mated with ideal males in a form of selective breeding to produce 'super-Germans'. Not only did they believe that their race was best, but they believed that others were inferior human beings. Jews, eastern Europeans and blacks were *Untermenschen* (lowlife) who were not worthy of respect.

Even before Hitler came to power, he had set out his racial views in *Mein Kampf* and in speeches and Nazi literature. The Jews were not only an inferior race, but they had also joined with the communists to undermine Germany's efforts in the First World War. Since 1918, according to Hitler, the Jews had continued trying to ruin the German economy. At first, few people accepted Hitler's views on race. After all, many German Jews had fought with great bravery for their country in the war. But as Nazi propaganda continually reinforced the message, more and more people seemed prepared to accept the Jews as a scapegoat for all that had gone wrong in Germany between 1918 and 1933.

Once in power, Hitler wasted little time in putting his anti-Semitic policies into action.

SOURCE E

All human culture, all the results of art, science and technology that we see before us today, are almost exclusively the creation of the Aryan.

Adolf Hitler writing in *Mein Kampf*, 1924.

QUESTIONS

1. What steps did Hitler take to reduce unemployment in Germany?
2. In what ways were German workers worse off under Nazi rule?
3. What was Hitler's attitude towards racial equality in Germany?

Persecution begins

On 1 April 1933 the SA organised a boycott of Jewish shops throughout Germany. Sometimes Stormtroopers stood outside shops and physically prevented people entering. In the same year, Jews were banned from having jobs in the German civil service or in medicine, teaching and journalism.

In 1935 Jews were banned from public places such as swimming pools, restaurants, parks and cinemas, but much more serious were the Nuremberg Laws passed in the same year. There were two of these laws. The Reich Citizen Law deprived Jews of the German citizenship, while the Law for the Protection of German Blood and Honour outlawed marriages and sexual relations between Jews and non-Jews. These were followed by persecution as hundreds of Jews were arrested and sent to concentration camps.

Large numbers of Jews decided to emigrate from Germany – in the 1930s, half the German Jewish population left the country. Many others felt that they could not leave their homeland and hoped that things would not get worse. But in 1938 they did. A Jewish student shot dead a German diplomat in the embassy in Paris. The authorities in Germany reacted by ordering widespread attacks on Jewish homes, businesses and synagogues. In this *Kristallnacht* (Night of Broken Glass), 8000 Jewish homes and shops were attacked, and synagogues were burned to the ground. Over a hundred Jews were killed and thousands were sent to concentration camps. When he heard of the cost to German insurance companies of all the damage, one leading Nazi is reputed to have said, 'We should have smashed fewer windows and more heads.'

SOURCE F

The front of a Jewish shop in September 1938.

SOURCE G

My grandmother was 90 years old. She went to a shop to buy some butter. In the door of the shop was a Stormtrooper with a gun. He said, 'You don't want to buy from a Jew.' My mother shook her stick and said, 'I will buy my butter where I buy it every day.' But she was the only customer that day. No one else dared. They were too scared of the man with the gun.

A Berlin woman remembers an incident in 1933.

Kristallnacht was followed by a new set of anti-Semitic laws. The Jewish community had to pay a fine of one billion marks for the murder of the diplomat in Paris. Jews were no longer allowed to run businesses and Jewish children were banned from school. It seemed that things could get no worse, and few people could have imagined what was in store for Jews across Europe (see pages 130–1).

Other minorities

The Nazis also persecuted other minorities. Homosexuality was despised by the Nazis, as it was not in keeping with their ideal of Aryan masculinity. From 1936 homosexuals were forced to go on a national register and were placed under police supervision with a night curfew. Many were castrated and up to 15,000 homosexuals were sent to concentration camps during the 1930s. Some were later used in medical experiments.

People of eastern European descent also received harsh treatment at the hands of the Nazis, who considered them work-shy vagrants. They too lost their citizenship in the Nuremberg Laws and had to live on specially designated sites. If they refused, they were sent to concentration camps. Many people labelled 'gypsies' were sterilised. During the Second World War, they suffered the same fate as the Jews.

In 1933 the Nazis passed a law to say that all mentally disabled people should be compulsorily sterilised. In 1939 a euthanasia programme was introduced against mentally and physically disabled Germans. Some 70,000 adults and 5000 children were put to death by lethal injection, gassing or starvation. Disabled people simply did not fit in with Nazi views of the master race. Nazi propaganda was used to persuade people that euthanasia for the disabled was a good thing.

Even tramps and beggars were dealt with severely. Up to half a million of them were rounded up and put into labour camps. Many of them were sterilised.

SOURCE H

A caricature of Jews from the front page of a newspaper in 1935. The Jewish butcher is making sausages from rats.

SOURCE I

Are you, German people, determined, if the Führer so commands, to work ten, twelve, if need be fourteen hours a day and to give your utmost for victory? The nation is ready for anything. The Führer has commanded and we shall obey him.

A speech by Goebbels in 1943. He asked the audience ten questions and each was answered with loud shouts of agreement.

How did the coming of war change life in Germany?

In the first few years of the war, the German blitzkrieg tactics brought outstanding victories and western Europe was quickly overrun. At home, Nazi propaganda films celebrated victory over the French, and the German people rejoiced at the revenge they had gained for their harsh treatment in the Treaty of Versailles. Victory had been won with such ease that there had been little cost to Germany. In fact the spoils of war – raw materials, captured land, slave workers – opened up the prospect of Germany becoming a very rich and powerful country. It was true that food and clothes rationing had been introduced at the end of 1939, but this seemed a small price to pay.

In 1941, Hitler launched his attack on Soviet Russia. At first, the Germans made rapid advances and drove deep into the Soviet Union. By the end of 1941, however, the advance had ground to a halt in the Russian winter. Soon the campaign became a bleeding sore in which the Germans lost nearly 200,000 men. Setbacks soon occurred elsewhere, too, as the German army suffered defeats in North Africa.

Suddenly the German people began to realise how difficult war was when you were not winning. Supplies were needed for the armed forces and sacrifices had to be made at home. Goebbels stepped up his propaganda campaign to raise morale and ask for sacrifices. When a call went out for warm clothing for the troops in the Soviet Union, the German people donated 1.5 million fur coats. In 1942 Albert Speer was made armaments minister and told to organise the country for 'total war'. German factories were forced to work longer hours and food rations were cut. More and more women were drafted into the factories to keep production up.

SOURCE J

BE CAREFUL TO FIX THEM SO THAT THEY CAN TURN BOTH WAYS
LOW
DEFENCE OF THE NAZI HOME FRONT

A cartoon in a British newspaper in August 1943.

While these sacrifices were being made, another factor entered the equation. From 1942 the Allies began bombing raids on German cities. They intended to knock out important factories and disrupt production of goods for the war. However, they were quite prepared to cause civilian casualties too, since this was considered an acceptable way to break the morale of the German people and force surrender.

'Thousand bomber' raids poured bombs on to German cities and killed more than half a million civilians. In one raid alone, on Dresden in February 1945, 135,000 Germans died. By April 1945 Berlin was in ruins and its people were starving.

These raids were often followed by pamphlet drops, which encouraged the German people to give in. By 1945, with the German armies in retreat, shortages of basic foods, more than 3 million civilians dead and many major cities reduced to rubble, most Germans were happy to end the war. The problem was that the Führer, who was seen less and less frequently, was determined to fight on. So the German people had to endure four more months of fighting. It was no wonder that opposition to Nazi rule grew dramatically in the last year of the war.

QUESTIONS

1 In what ways did the war bring benefits to the Nazis in the years 1939–41?

2 In what ways were those benefits reversed as the war developed?

SOURCE K

Victims of the Dresden bombing, February 1945.

Case Study: The 'Final Solution'

Life for Jews under the Nazis became increasingly difficult during the 1930s. Their civil rights were withdrawn and thousands of them were sent to concentration camps to carry out forced labour.

During the Second World War the Nazis took control of much of Europe and millions of Jews came under their control. Many of them were herded into ghettos in the cities, where conditions were so bad that thousands starved to death. Others were sent to concentration camps to join other victims of the Nazi regime.

In 1941 the Germans invaded the Soviet Union. As the German army advanced, it was followed by 3000 men in the *Einsatzgruppen*. This was a group of four death squads whose job it was to kill communist officials and Jews in the occupied territories. By the end of 1941 some half a million Jews had been shot or poisoned by exhaust fumes from specially built vans.

The setting up of the extermination camps

In January 1942 at the Wannsee Conference in Berlin, a 'Final Solution' to the 'Jewish problem' was found. The Jewish people of Europe were to be rounded up and sent to extermination camps where they would be put to death. By the summer of 1942 six concentration camps had been converted into extermination camps and in the next four years almost six million Jews were slaughtered in what has become known as the Holocaust.

Various methods were used to carry out the killing. At first, shooting was common, but it proved too slow. So huge chambers were built, disguised as showers. Up to 2000 Jews at a time were led into the showers, supposedly for 'delousing'. Then gas was released and within three minutes everyone was dead. Useful by-products like gold teeth, hair and glasses were removed from the bodies before they were burned in huge ovens. In some of the camps, medical experiments were carried out on Jews to find out the limits of human endurance. For example, some Jews had major surgery carried out on them without anaesthetics.

The need for secrecy

The Germans did not publicise what they did and Himmler, the leader of the SS in charge of the camps, ordered that the work should be kept secret. Propaganda films showing good conditions in the camps and talking or 'resettlement' of the Jews gave the impression that they were being treated well. This helped the round-up of Jews to be sent to the camps run more smoothly and with less opposition. But word spread amongst the Jewish community about what was really happening. Soon Jewish people reacted with horror to names such as Auschwitz, Dachau and Belsen.

The Allied governments were in a very difficult position. They were aware that something terrible was happening, but not the scale of it. But in any case, there was little that they could do. At the time, many Jews hoped that the Allies would bomb the extermination camps, but the Allies did not consider this a practical, or humane, thing to do.

Number of Jews killed in death camps and by the Einsatzgruppen.

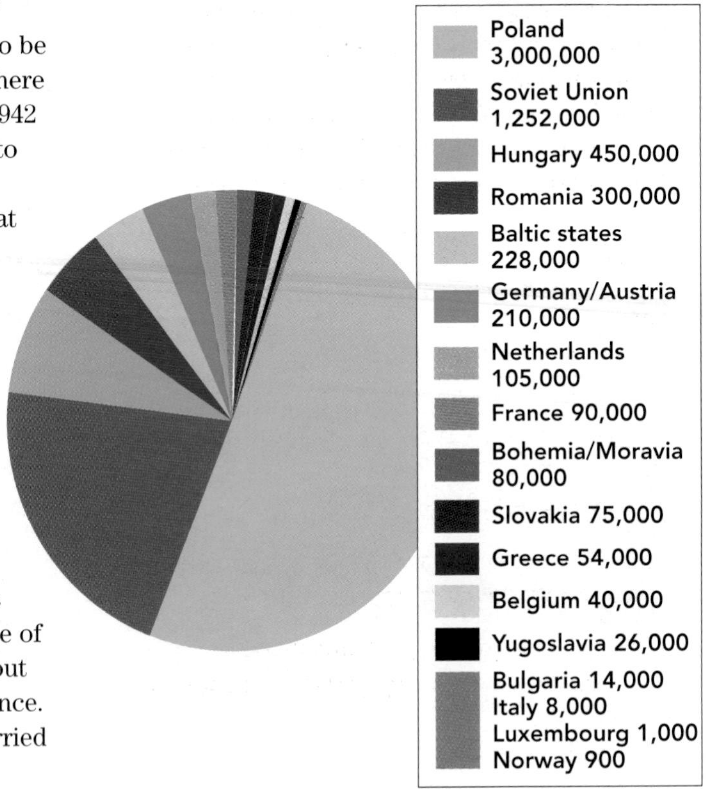

As defeat loomed for Germany, an attempt was made to cover up what had happened. To speed the process of killing, the Germans had built railway lines running directly into the camps. These were pulled up, but there was no disguising what had been done – especially as the Allied soldiers found thousands of Jews in the camps, abandoned to die of starvation or diseases such as tuberculosis.

The Nuremberg Trials

After the war, the treatment of the Jews was a major factor in putting 21 senior Nazis on trial in Nuremberg for war crimes. Two of them (Himmler and Goering) committed suicide and eleven others were hanged. Rudolf Hoess, the commandant at Auschwitz concentration camp, went into hiding but was captured in 1946. He was put on trial in Poland for crimes against humanity. Two million Jews had died at the camp and horrifying medical experiments had been carried out on inmates. Yet at his trial Hoess talked of how he was an ordinary family man who did not like what he was doing, but merely obeyed orders. He was found guilty and condemned to death. He was hanged on 7 April 1947 at Auschwitz. Goebbels committed suicide in Hitler's bunker during the final Soviet assaults on Berlin in May 1945.

The case of Anthony Sawoniuk, a former British Rail worker, tried for war crimes in Britain in 1999. The trial cost over £1 million. Sawoniuk was found guilty of 18 murders and sentenced to life imprisonment.

The Case of Anthony Sawoniuk

Anthony Sawoniuk was put on trial in Britain in February 1999 charged with murdering 16 Jewish women and 4 Jewish men in 1942. Sawoniuk was a policeman in Belarus when the Germans massacred 3000 Jews on the Yom Kippur holiday in 1942. It is alleged that Sawoniuk took part in rounding up and killing those Jews who escaped.

78-year-old Sawoniuk told the court that he was deaf in one ear, diabetic and had heart disease and brain damage. He also said that during the five weeks of accusations by witnesses for the prosecution he had been desperate to get into the witness box to put his side of the case. The judge in the case told the jury that they should not try to achieve justice for the victims of the Holocaust and that 'There can be no trial in our history that has been more emotive than this.'

QUESTIONS

1 What was the role of the Einsatzgruppen?

2 Why did the Nazis convert concentration camps to death camps?

3 Why do you think the Nazis made propaganda films showing good conditions in the camps?

4 Some people say that there is no longer any point trying to convict those accused of killing Jews in the war.
a Why do you think they say this?
b Do you agree?

Use the case of Anthony Sawoniuk to explain your answer.

Paper 1-type assessment: Germany 1918-45

SOURCE A

"In these three years I have restored honor and freedom to the German people!"

A cartoon from an American newspaper in February 1936.

SOURCE B

We didn't know much about Nazi ideals. Nevertheless we were politically programmed to obey orders, to cultivate the soldierly virtue of standing to attention and saying 'Yes, Sir', and to stop thinking when the word 'Fatherland' was uttered and Germany's honour and greatness was mentioned.

A member of the Hitler Youth commenting after the war.

QUESTIONS

When answering these questions make sure you answer ALL three parts.

Remember that you should always explain your answer as fully as you can and support it with specific detail where possible.

Section C Questions

1 Study the sources carefully and then answer the three questions which follow.

a Study Source A. Is this an accurate portrayal of how the Nazis governed Germany? Use the source and your own knowledge to explain your answer. (7)

b Study Source B. How far does this source explain why the Nazis had the support of the German people? Use the source and your own knowledge to explain your answer. (7)

c Study Source C. Do you think that the cartoonist supported or opposed the Nazi Party? Use the source and your own knowledge to explain your answer. (6)

2a Describe the problems faced by the governments of the Weimar Republic in the years 1919–22. (4)

b Explain why Germany was restored to prosperity in the period 1924–29. (6)

c Explain how the following together contributed to the rise of the Nazi Party up to 1933:

i the economic depression from 1929

ii the Nazi Party's use of propaganda

iii the weaknesses of the Weimar Republic. (10)

3a What happened on the 'Night of the Long Knives'? (4)

b Explain why the Nazis persecuted many groups in German society. (6)

c Explain how the following together contributed to the success of the Nazis in maintaining themselves in power in the period 1933-39:

i the Enabling Law

ii the economic policies of the Nazis

iii Nazi policies towards the young. (10)

SOURCE C

A cartoon from a British newspaper in 1934 commenting on the 'Night of the Long Knives'.

4 The USA 1919–41

The USA emerged from the First World War as the richest country in the world. During the 1920s it experienced a consumer boom as its industries poured out more and more products for Americans to buy. Goods like motor cars, radios and washing machines became available to many ordinary people. Americans had more money to spend, and more leisure time in which to spend it. This was the 'Jazz Age' or the 'Roaring Twenties', a time to party and have fun.

However, many Americans did not share in the growing prosperity. It has been estimated that as much as half of the population actually lived below the poverty line. It was also true that American society had a nasty, intolerant side, and blacks and immigrants faced discrimination in housing, education and employment. Many people in rural areas, particularly agricultural workers, lived in poverty, as agriculture faced a crisis of over-production and falling prices. This was a period when the banning of the sale of alcohol brought about a rapid growth in organised crime.

In any case, over-production and the Wall Street Crash of October 1929 brought the party to an end. There was simply a limit to how much people could buy. The collapse of the stock market led to widespread unemployment and thousands of businesses went bust. President Hoover hoped that his policy of 'rugged individualism' would help deal with the effects of the Depression. He was wrong and lost the 1932 presidential election to Franklin Roosevelt, who promised a 'New Deal' to the American people. The New Deal involved spending huge amounts of government money in an attempt to create jobs. It partly worked. After 1933 unemployment did come down, but even Roosevelt found it impossible to get all Americans back to work until the Second World War broke out and production was stepped up to supply war goods.

This topic is examined in Paper 1 of the examination. Paper 1-type exercises are included at the end of the chapter. Mark schemes, sample answers and comments can be found in the accompanying Teacher's Resource Pack.

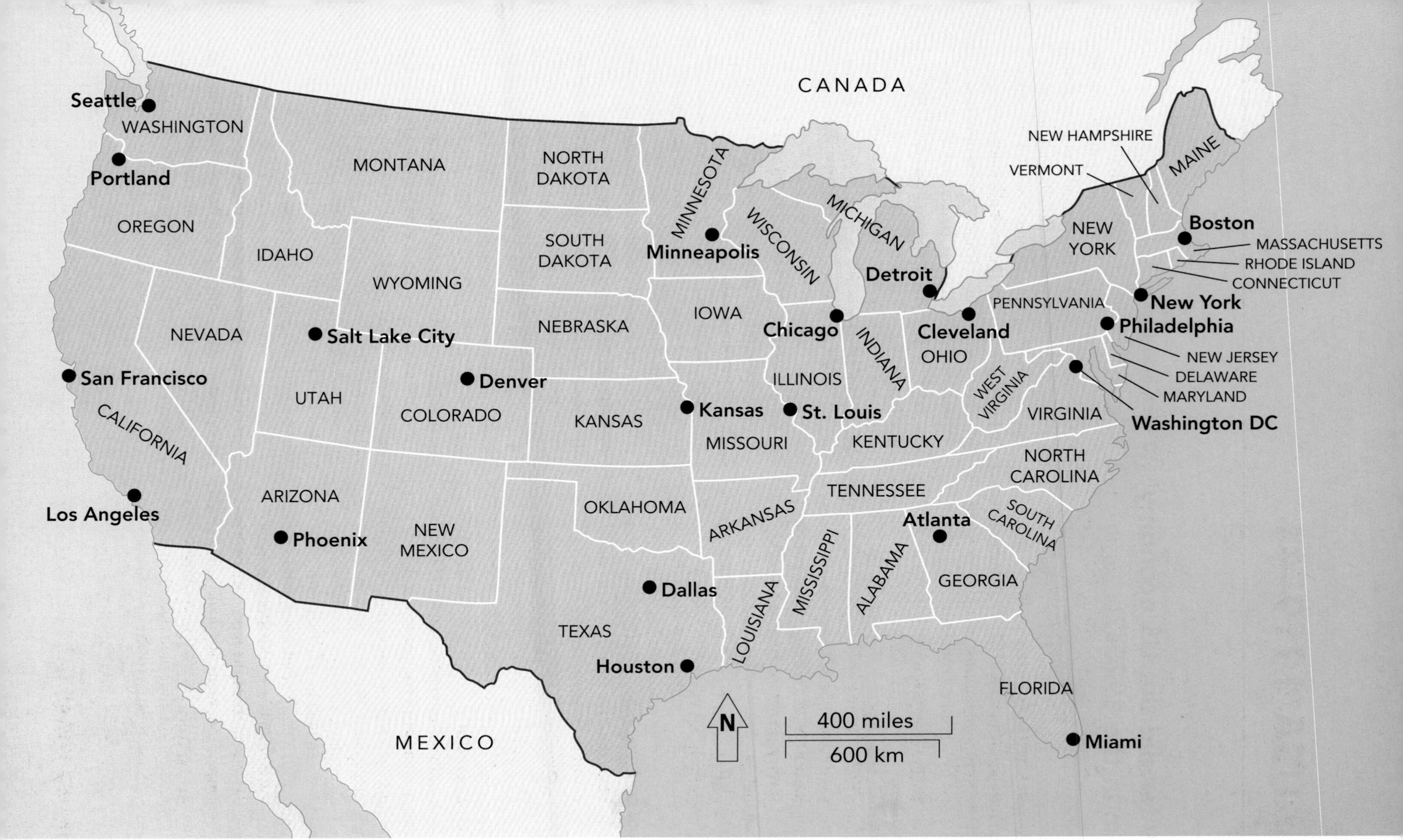

A map of the USA showing states and major cities

The USA 1919–41

How far did the US economy boom in the 1920s?

The First World War left the USA as the greatest economic power in the world. Having joined the war late, and being distant from the fighting, it had not suffered the financial and physical damage that affected the European nations. Its industries had been boosted by wartime production, and it was owed enormous sums by its Allies, to whom it had made war loans. The party of big business – the Republicans – was in power throughout the 1920s, and followed policies that stimulated the economy still more. Taxes were cut, so people had more to spend, and tariffs (taxes on trade) were put on imports of foreign goods in order to protect American industry from foreign competition. It is no wonder that the 1920s were boom years in the USA. And yet this was not a boom in which everyone shared. Agriculture was depressed, and some groups, notably many blacks, continued to suffer in poverty. By the end of the decade, there were clear signs that the boom was coming to an end.

On what factors was the economic boom based?

1 The USA's wealth

By the start of the twentieth century, the USA was the world's leading industrial nation. It was rich in raw materials such as coal, iron ore and oil, and had much fertile land. Its population, made up mainly of immigrants, was hard working and ambitious. It was a land of freedom and opportunity, with a strong culture of self-help. The First World War confirmed the USA's economic dominance. It also marked the moment at which the USA changed from being rural and agricultural to urban and industrial. By 1920 government figures showed for the first time that more than half the population lived in towns and cities.

2 New industries

The total production of American industry increased by around 50 per cent during the 1920s. This boom was fuelled by demand from consumers for a whole range of new products that industry was inventing and producing. It was in the 1920s that electrical goods like washing machines, refrigerators, vacuum cleaners and radios first became widely available. The chemical industry also created new materials, such as rayon (an artificial fibre) and types of plastic resin, from which many new products could be made. Most significant of all was the growth of the motor car industry (see page 138).

3 Rising wages and stable prices

People could afford to buy the new goods. The real value of incomes rose by around a quarter during the 1920s. At the same time, prices were steady or, in the case of some consumer products, actually falling. A major reason for this was the widespread adoption of the assembly-line techniques pioneered by Henry Ford. Mass production enabled manufacturers both to increase production and to make goods more cheaply.

4 Government policies

Throughout the 1920s, under three successive presidents, control of the American economy was in the hands of Andrew Mellon, Secretary of the Treasury. He believed that government should play as little part in economic life as possible, and his policy was to give big business what it wanted. His presidents agreed with him. One, Calvin Coolidge, president from 1923 to 1929, famously said, 'The business of America is business.'

Businessmen believed that, if taxes were low, people and companies would have more money to invest. These investments would help industry expand still more. Accordingly, time and again, throughout the 1920s, Mellon cut taxes.

The other main demand of business was for protection against foreign competition. It argued that cheap foreign imports would destroy American jobs. The government responded by increasing tariffs. The Fordney–McCumber Tariff Act of 1922 raised tariffs higher than ever before. The problem with tariffs is that, if every country uses them, international trade is damaged. For most of the 1920s this did not matter too much to American industry, which had a huge home market in which to sell its goods. But by the end of the decade, home demand was beginning to fall, and other nations had imposed their own tariffs against American goods, so industry found it hard to export its surplus production.

5 Hire purchase

The consumer boom was encouraged by the easy availability of credit. Pioneered by the car companies, hire purchase enabled consumers to buy the goods they wanted with a small deposit, and then pay off the rest of the price in weekly or monthly instalments.

Another marketing tool that reached its peak of popularity during the 1920s was the mail-order catalogue. This, in a huge area like the USA, gave people in every part of the country the chance to benefit from the consumer boom. There was no need for a local shop – the Sears, Roebuck catalogue meant that the latest fashions were available to you by post.

SOURCE A

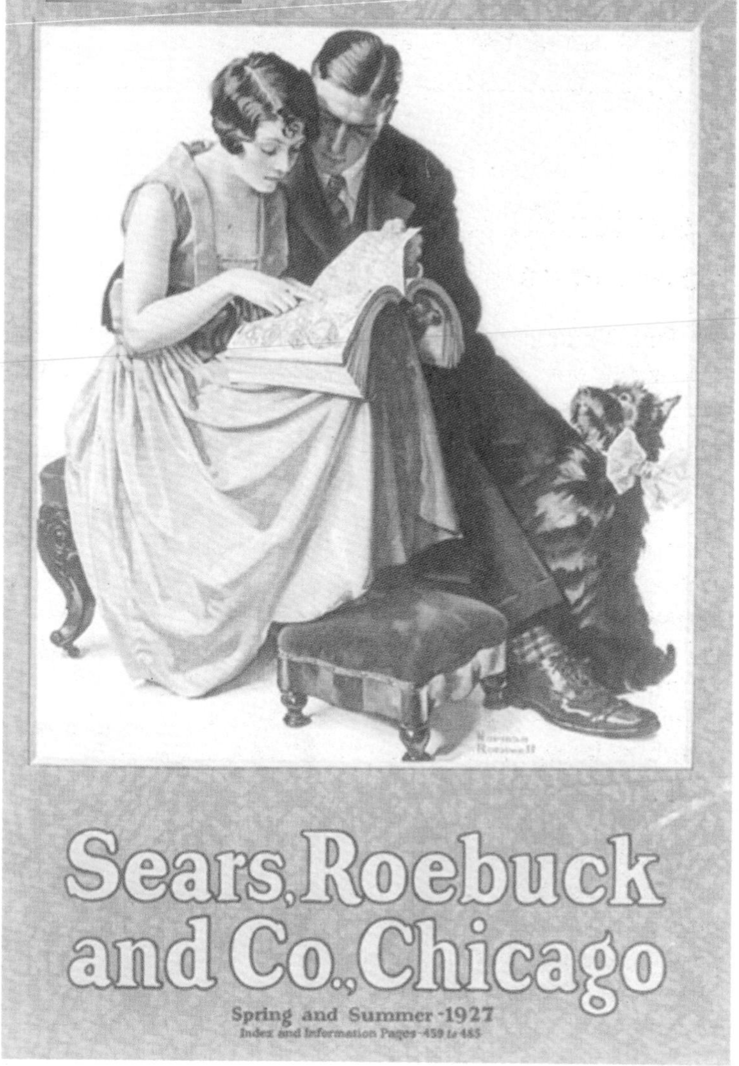

The front cover of the Sears, Roebuck catalogue, spring and summer 1927.

6 Weak unions

The Republican governments, like businessmen, were hostile towards trade unions. Employers were allowed to use violence to break strikes, and to refuse to employ union members. Unions were excluded altogether from the car industry until the 1930s. The effect of this was to permit employers to hold down wages and to keep hours of work long, at a time when profits were rising fast. It was a rare employer who showed the enlightened attitude of Henry Ford in paying wages above the going rate, and cutting hours of work.

Henry Ford and the automobile industry

One industry symbolises the 1920s boom more than any other – automobile manufacture. The industry had begun in the early years of the century, but it was in the 1920s that the price of cars dropped to the point at which ordinary people could hope to own one. The greatest figure in the car industry was Henry Ford. The Ford Motor Company was started in 1903. By 1908 Ford had developed the first version of the 'Model T' – the 'universal car' as Ford called it – specifically intended to be a car for the masses and not just for the privileged few. From 1913 Ford's factory was organised on assembly-line principles. Unlike traditional manufacture, in which a worker would carry out a whole range of tasks in making a product, the assembly line brought the work to the worker, who would carry out just one task – say, bolting in a seat – before the line moved the work on to the next man. This was the first use of the assembly line in modern manufacturing, and it produced a revolution in industry. Huge numbers of identical, standardised cars could be built more quickly and cheaply than ever before. Ford could cut the price of the Model T, so more people could afford one. The original price of $850 fell to just $260 by 1924 – not surprising when the man-hours needed to assemble one fell from $12\frac{1}{2}$ to $1\frac{1}{2}$ in the same period. Up to 1926 the Model T was the USA's best-selling car. By the time production finished in 1927, 15 million had been made.

As early as 1920 car manufacture was the USA's most valuable industry, and by 1929 it employed more workers than any other – half a million. It is impossible to guess how many jobs were created by 'spin-offs' from the motor industry, not just in firms making components, but also in the oil industry, in road construction and in services such as hotels and restaurants, which developed across the country to serve the newly mobile population. In 1929 nearly $4\frac{1}{2}$ million cars were manufactured, mostly by the three great firms that dominated the industry – Ford, General Motors and Chrysler. By this time, around 27 million motor vehicles were registered in the USA.

SOURCE B

BOSS OF THE ROAD
THE LATEST AND BEST
$850
THIS new light touring car fills the demand for an automobile between a runabout and a heavy touring car. It is positively the most perfect machine on the market, having overcome all drawbacks such as smell, noise, jolt, etc., common to all other makes of Auto Carriages. It is so simple that a boy of 15 can run it.
The FORDMOBILE with detachable tonneau
For beauty of finish it is unequaled, and we promise IMMEDIATE DELIVERY. We haven't space enough to enter into its mechanical detail, but if you are interested in the NEWEST and MOST ADVANCED AUTO manufactured to-day write us for particulars.
FORD MOTOR COMPANY
691 MACK AVENUE,
DETROIT, MICH.

An advertisement for an early Model T Ford.

The social consequences of the motor car

Mass ownership of cars had many social effects, some obvious – traffic jams and road accidents became a part of life – some less predictable but just as important, such as the growth of suburbs. The USA is a huge country; to move around it people had previously been dependent on public transport such as railways, or on horse-drawn wagons and coaches. Now they could go where they wanted.

SOURCE C

It's obvious that the automobile was faster than the horse and carriage. What is less obvious is that a car like the Model T was cheaper than a horse and carriage. A car consumes fuel only when it is moving; a horse has to be fed year-round ... Mobility and freedom, and at a lower cost. This was a product which sold itself.

The Model T was designed specifically to be mass-produced. Simplicity was the watchword. There were no doors, for example, and no side windows; there was no speedometer or windshield wipers, and no choice of body colours (for the first twelve years all Model Ts were black) ... The car was designed with the owner's needs in mind. The first buyers were generally farmers and small town folk (city people could travel on streetcars [trams] and buses), and the 20-horsepower engine and the rugged mechanics were designed to cope with bad country roads, just as the simple mechanical systems could be easily repaired by the driver himself. Sales of this revolutionary car rocketed. In 1914, only six years after it was introduced, a quarter of a million were sold; when production was finally halted in 1927, 15 million had rolled off the assembly line.

A description of the Model T Ford taken from a modern American history book.

Isolated rural communities were brought into contact with the outside world. Farmers could drive to the nearest town for their supplies, and young people could drive into town for entertainment. City dwellers could now escape into the country, or drive further afield for holidays. Many people in the USA were able to move anywhere to look for work, and were no longer tied to their home area.

Why did some industries prosper while others did not?

The boom of the 1920s was created by the development and growth of new industries – most importantly, cars, electrical goods and chemicals. The growth of national wealth meant that people had money to spend on goods that were new or that would previously have been seen as luxuries. Increasing wealth was visible in other ways. The construction industry boomed, with government money poured into road building. Skyscrapers changed the face of cities.

However, traditional industries, such as textiles, coalmining and shipbuilding, either grew less quickly or even declined. These were already mature industries with developed markets, in which consumer demand could grow only to a limited degree. They had less scope for expansion than the new industries. The textile industry of the north-east faced competition from factories in other parts of the country, such as the south, where labour was much cheaper, or from the new artificial fibres, and many factories had to close. Coal was another industry under pressure. Greater use of electricity and oil for heating meant that demand for coal fell. The least profitable mines were forced to shut down. However, these were the exceptions. In general, American industry prospered throughout the 1920s.

QUESTIONS

1 What was the economic boom of the 1920s?
2 What factors helped create the boom of the 1920s?
3 Why was Henry Ford so important to American industry?

SOURCE D

Construction workers on the Empire State Building, New York. Completed in 1931, this was the highest building in the world at that time.

Why did agriculture not share in the prosperity?

Not everyone prospered during the boom years. For the USA's farmers the 1920s were years of hardship and falling prices. Having benefited from high prices paid for their produce during wartime, farmers were ill-prepared to cope with the basic problem affecting agriculture – over-production. American agriculture was simply too successful: it produced more than the country could eat or use, and because of international competition and tariffs, it proved impossible to deal with the surplus by exporting it. Prices collapsed and, with them, farmers' incomes. In a poor state like South Carolina, farmers were earning only a third of the average wage of all other workers. Many farmers borrowed money in the hope that prices would recover. They never did, so sooner or later these farmers had to leave the land and forfeit their farms to the bank. In 1920 one-third of the USA's population was in farming families, but by 1929 this proportion was down to one-quarter.

Rural America saw little sign, then, of increasing prosperity. Farms enjoyed few of the basic amenities that in the rest of the USA were becoming standard. Less than 10 per cent had electric light or mains water supplies. The situation was especially bad in the south, where farms had traditionally been dependent on single crops, usually cotton or tobacco. Not only was the price of these at rock-bottom, but the crops were regularly decimated by pests such as the boll-weevil. Agricultural workers in the south, who were generally blacks, were either paid starvation wages or employed as sharecroppers – a system in which they were paid no cash at all, but instead received a proportion of the crop to sell. In practice, this made them almost entirely dependent on their employer, who provided housing and made loans to the workers against their share of the crop.

SOURCE E

Child workers in the cotton fields in the 1920s.

Did all Americans benefit from the boom?

The USA became much richer during the 1920s, but it would be wrong to think that this wealth was shared out equally. It has been estimated that, in 1929, 60 per cent of all American families lived below the poverty line. Many of these were in rural areas, but the poor were numerous in the big cities too. Those who benefited from the boom were the rich and the middle classes. In 1929 one-third of all income was earned by only 5 per cent of the workforce. Throughout the decade the poor remained poor, or in rural areas became even poorer.

Neither did the boom affect all areas of the country equally. The west and the north-east, where most of the country's industries were located, felt most benefit, and the south, which was almost entirely agricultural, did the worst. However, even some agricultural areas did better than others. Fruit farmers, for instance, were able to benefit from growing demand for fresh produce, and were among the best-paid groups in the country. Wheat farmers of the Great Plains, by contrast, suffered a decade of low prices caused by falling demand and stiff international competition.

The USA's black population suffered discrimination of all kinds, not least in employment. Historically, most blacks had lived in the south, but during the First World War many families had moved to cities in the north, attracted by jobs available in the factories. Once the war finished, competition for jobs increased, and many whites resented the black newcomers. During 1919 there were race riots in many cities. But whatever problems urban blacks in the north had to cope with, those who stayed in the south faced more, working as agricultural labourers and living in conditions of extreme poverty. And even their situation was marginally superior to that of the Native Americans, who, as a government report of 1928 admitted, were on reservations where the land was generally so poor that it was impossible to scrape a living from it.

So, despite the boom and the undoubted benefits that it brought to many people, by the end of the 1920s the USA was still a deeply divided society with enormous differences between rich and poor, white and black, city and country.

QUESTIONS

1 How far did the American people benefit from the economic boom?

2 Why did some sectors of the American economy do badly in the 1920s?

How far did US society change in the 1920s?

What were the 'Roaring Twenties'?

The popular image of the USA in the 1920s is of life as one long, crazy party, with jazz music playing on the radio, young, fashionable women known as flappers wildly dancing the Charleston, large quantities of illegal alcohol being consumed, and everyone behaving in as scandalous a manner as possible. These were the 'Roaring Twenties', and there is an element of truth in the image. In the aftermath of the war, people were determined to have fun. They had more money, and they had the leisure time in which to spend it. Women were freer than ever before to live their own lives: the flappers drank, smoked, dated and wore outrageous new fashions. The older generation could scarcely believe what was happening. The entertainment industry boomed. The 1920s were golden years for Hollywood films, with the first 'talkie' released in 1927. This was also the 'Jazz Age' with its crazes for new music and new dances.

But American society had another, much less permissive side to it. Throughout the 1920s, prohibition, which made making and selling alcohol illegal, was in force. Not everyone wanted to join the party. Neither was everyone allowed to. These were also years of violent racism and intolerance, with minorities excluded from any chance of sharing in the good times.

The movies

The movie industry had begun before the First World War, but its popularity soared during the 1920s. Audiences more than doubled during the decade, and 95 million people a week were going to the cinema by 1929. Hollywood, in California, was the centre of the film industry. Here great movie companies like MGM, Warner Brothers and Paramount had their studios, and produced the films that captivated the American public. Comedies, romances, westerns, historical epics – all kinds of films poured off the Hollywood production line. The studios encouraged the 'star system', which made actors like Charlie Chaplin, Clara Bow, Rudolf Valentino and Mary Pickford into household names. Such was the interest in the stars that when the heart-throb Valentino died in 1926, thousands of fans attended his funeral and several committed suicide.

However, many people were worried by the impact of the movies, particularly on the morals of the young. As early as 1922 the Hays Office was established by the studios to set strict rules about what could be shown on screen. These rules were particularly tight on how relationships between the sexes were portrayed. Yet no matter how harmless the films might be, they were bound to portray the greater social freedom of the age. Simply showing how young women could live independent lives, working in the big city, could be seen as shocking by the older generation who were used to more conservative times.

SOURCE A

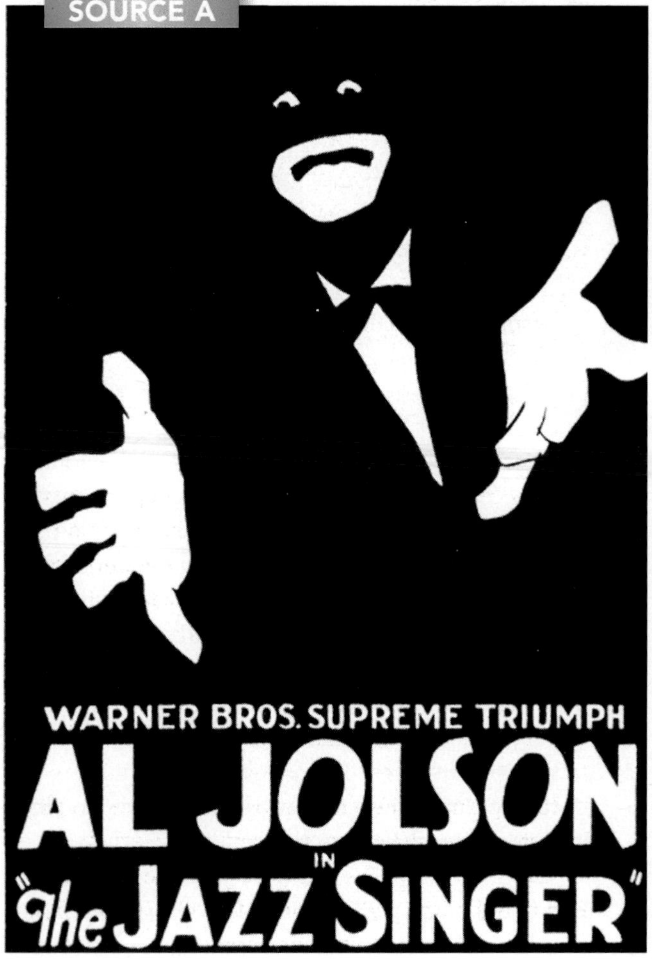
WARNER BROS. SUPREME TRIUMPH
AL JOLSON
IN
"The JAZZ SINGER"

A poster for the film *The Jazz Singer*, 1927.

SOURCE B

Babe Ruth in action.

The success of the cinema lay in the opportunity for escapism that it provided. The film companies appreciated this, and made a visit to the cinema a fantastic experience. Ornate and fanciful 'picture palaces' were built, often in the style of real oriental or classical palaces. The glamorous atmosphere was as much a part of the entertainment as the film itself.

In 1927 perhaps the most important change in the history of the film industry occurred. Warner Brothers released *The Jazz Singer*, starring Al Jolson – the first 'talkie' film. Prior to this, all films had been silent, with words shown as captions on the screen. The 'talkies' destroyed the careers of many actors and actresses who looked good, but had unattractive voices.

Sport

Sport was another form of mass entertainment that flourished as workers began to enjoy greater prosperity and to have more leisure time. Baseball was the most popular sport of the urban working classes, with great players like 'Babe' Ruth of the New York Yankees becoming national heroes. In 1927 he set a record for hitting home runs – 60 in a season – which lasted until 1961. By 1930 he was earning $80,000 a year – an immense amount for that time.

The most famous boxer of the time was Jack Dempsey, world heavyweight champion from 1919 to 1926. His courage and punching power made him a tremendous favourite with the fans. However, his most famous fight was one he lost. Fighting in 1927 to regain his title from Gene Tunney, he knocked Tunney down in the seventh round, but failed to retreat to a neutral corner. By the time the referee started to count, Tunney had already had several seconds in which to recover. He got up when the referee reached nine, and went on to win the infamous 'fight of the long count'.

One of the true sporting heroes of the time was the golfer Bobby Jones. He was the greatest golfer in the world, but he also set the highest standards of sportsmanship. On one occasion, he hit his ball into some trees and, while looking for it, accidentally trod on it. Nobody else saw this happen, but he immediately told his playing partner and accepted a penalty of one shot. Later, someone tried to congratulate him for his honesty. 'You might as well praise a man for not robbing a bank' was Jones's reply.

SOURCE C

A Chicago night club in the 1920s.

QUESTIONS

1 What do you understand by the 'Roaring Twenties'?

2 What entertainment was available to Americans in the 1920s?

3 Why was there fear of immigrants, even though most Americans came from immigrant families themselves?

Music

Another name by which the 1920s are known is the 'Jazz Age'. Jazz was a new form of music that evolved from earlier forms of black music, such as the blues and ragtime. Its spread was assisted by the migration during the war of southern blacks into northern cities. Famous night clubs like the Cotton Club in Harlem, New York, provided opportunities for some of the greatest performers, such as Duke Ellington, Louis Armstrong and Bessie Smith, to perform and achieve national reputations. The craze for jazz music was further encouraged by the development of radio as a form of mass entertainment.

Part of the appeal of jazz was the sense of excitement and danger it gave to whites, who were, for the first time, exposed to black music. In particular, jazz was the music of the illegal pubs and drinking clubs, known as 'speakeasies' (see page 150). Ironically, however, in many of the clubs where jazz was played, the only black people allowed were the musicians. Even the Cotton Club was owned and run by white people.

One spin-off from the popularity of jazz was the dance crazes. The drinkers and party-goers were always on the watch for a new dance to try. The most famous of these crazes was for the Charleston, the dance that will always be associated with the flappers, but there were others too, such as the Black Bottom. What linked these dances was their sexual suggestiveness, and their ability to scandalise the older generation.

Radio

The music of the 1920s was, more often than not, played on the radio. Sales of records actually fell as the popularity of radio increased. At the start of the decade, few people possessed a radio, but by the end they were everywhere. In 1920, $2 million worth of radios were purchased, but in 1929 the figure was $600 million. During these years, radio services developed. The first local station started up in 1920, and the first national network (the National Broadcasting Company) went on the air in 1926. All the stations were commercial, so the usual diet of dance-band music was frequently interrupted by advertisements.

How widespread was intolerance in US society?

Immigration

Most of the USA's population was descended from immigrants – unless, of course, they were immigrants themselves. During the nineteenth century, as the interior of the USA was opened up for settlement, people from Europe poured in. However, by the early twentieth century, Americans were beginning to feel that their country was full up, and that there was little room left for new immigrants. The First World War heightened this feeling, as well as stirring up fear and hatred of foreigners, and Germans in particular. Many Americans looked at the crowded slums of the big cities, teeming with immigrants from dozens of countries, many of whom spoke little if any English, and decided that enough was enough. Mass immigration had to be ended. This duly happened when Congress passed the Johnson–Reid Act of 1924, which fixed a quota of 150,000 immigrants a year – almost all of whom would be from Europe because Asian immigration was halted entirely.

The Red Scare

There was another motive for limiting immigration – the fear that immigrants might be bringing socialist ideas with them. The Russian Revolution of 1917 convinced many Americans that communism was about to take over the world. Serious strikes in a number of major industries during 1919 were taken as evidence that communist agitators were already at work in the USA. Attorney-General Palmer responded by ordering a round-up of several thousand suspected socialists, and deporting those who were recent immigrants. A wave of anti-communist hysteria – known as the 'Red Scare' – swept the country. This reached its height when prominent politicians began to receive bombs in their mail, and finally Palmer's house in Washington was blown up. The most famous victims of the Red Scare, however, were not politicians, but two Italian immigrant anarchists, Sacco and Vanzetti.

The Sacco and Vanzetti case

In April 1920 a robbery took place at a shoe factory in the state of Massachusetts. The robbers stole $16,000 and shot two of the staff dead. A month later, two poorly educated Italians, Sacco and Vanzetti, were arrested and charged with the murders. There was little firm evidence against them, although when arrested they were both carrying firearms. From the start it was clear that the police had suspected them as much for their radical political beliefs, and for the fact that they were immigrants, as for the likelihood of them being guilty of the crime. Their trial was a farce. A biased judge made it clear that he wanted them found guilty. Evidence was tampered with by both the prosecution and the defence. Throughout the trial the pair maintained their innocence, but it made no difference. They were convicted and sentenced to death. The American public, whipped up by the Red Scare, demanded a scapegoat for the bomb outrages that had culminated in September 1920 with an explosion in New York which killed 30 people.

For the next six years, Sacco and Vanzetti struggled to prove their innocence and gain a retrial. An international campaign was fought for their release. Another man was found who confessed to the murders. But the authorities refused to budge. Sacco and Vanzetti died in the electric chair in August 1927.

SOURCE D

A painting of Sacco and Vanzetti.

QUESTION

Look at Source D.
Do you think the artist was hostile or sympathetic towards Sacco and Vanzetti? Explain your answer.

Segregation and discrimination against blacks

In the south, black people were kept in a permanent state of poverty and disadvantage by a range of official restrictions known as the 'Jim Crow' laws. These ensured that black people were segregated (kept apart) from white people. They lived in separate areas, went to separate schools, and were not allowed to use facilities reserved for white people. Most black people in the south were dependent on agriculture and suffered badly from the farming depression of the 1920s. Their misery was made worse by the violence that many suffered at the hands of white people, who were determined to demonstrate their social dominance. They lived in permanent fear of white lynch mobs, who could murder black people for no reason and with little chance of anyone being arrested. The politicians, police and judges were all white, and could be relied upon to turn a blind eye to violence against black people. In the early 1920s there were around 50 lynchings a year, and few perpetrators were ever brought to justice.

SOURCE E

A black family and their home in Virginia, in the 1920s.

Black people in the northern cities did not face this kind of official discrimination and violence, but were still affected badly by the racism of American society. They lived in the poorest housing, found it hardest to get jobs, were paid the lowest wages, and were most dependent on government relief. White people regarded them as inferior, and from time to time the antagonism between white people and black people blew up into race riots. Ten per cent of the USA's population was black, but to a great extent they were excluded from the opportunities and freedoms that other Americans took for granted.

The Ku Klux Klan

In the mid-nineteenth century, after the American Civil War, a terrorist organisation was started in the south to try and preserve white supremacy over the newly freed black slaves. The members of this organisation dressed in white robes and wore pointed hoods to conceal their identity. They struck terror into the black community with their night-time raids and crosses of fire. The organisation was the Ku Klux Klan. In time it died out, although persecution of black people continued in other ways.

In 1915 the Klan was started again in Georgia by William Simmons. He kept the original Klan's ideas and costume, but added a whole new list of targets for the Klan's hatred: Catholics, Jews, foreigners, homosexuals and anyone of liberal views. In Simmons' eyes, the Klan

SOURCE F

Klansmen marching through a town in New Jersey.

stood for the preservation of true American values – the values of white, Protestant, rural America. Most other Americans simply regarded the Klan as violent bigots.

The new Klan grew slowly at first, but benefiting from the anti-foreigner atmosphere generated by the war, it began to recruit members from outside its traditional homeland of the Deep South. By 1925 it had reached a peak of 5 million members, which brought it considerable influence in national and state politics. Although it was a secretive organisation, its members became confident enough to parade openly through many cities, including Washington. The Klan had a strong appeal to white people who felt threatened and left behind by the social and economic changes of the 1920s. Its extreme, racist, conservative views were not dissimilar to those later put forward by European parties like the Fascists and the Nazis, which also thrived in the uncertainty and insecurity created by the First World War. Although the amount of racist violence actually declined during the 1920s, the threat posed by the Klan was very real, and a number of appalling murders were carried out by its members.

By the end of the 1920s, membership of the Klan had gone into decline. Its reputation was undermined by a number of scandals, notably the conviction of the Klan leader in the state of Indiana for the rape and murder of a woman on a train. Its influence rapidly waned, although it continued to pose a threat to black people in small towns in the south.

QUESTIONS

1. What discrimination did black Americans suffer during the 1920s?
2. Why do you think some white people joined the Ku Klux Klan?

SOURCE G

Q: [Darrow] Do you think the sun was made on the fourth day?
A: [Bryan] Yes.
Q: And they had morning and evening without the sun?
A: I am simply saying it is a period.
Q: The creation might have been going on a long time?
A: It might have continued for millions of years.

An extract from Darrow's cross-examination of Bryan. He is asking about the story of creation in the Bible.

SOURCE H

The main participants in the 'Monkey Trial' of 1925.

The Scopes trial, 1925

This sensational case illustrated how wide a gulf existed by the mid-1920s between traditional, small-town America and the modern values and outlook of the big cities. A Biology teacher in the town of Dayton, Tennessee, had been giving lessons on Darwin's theory of evolution. Although Darwin's ideas were not as widely accepted then as they are now, this event would not normally have grabbed the world's attention, However, in 1925, the state of Tennessee had passed a law forbidding the teaching of evolution, which it considered to be against the account of creation given in the Bible. The teacher, Johnny Scopes, was arrested and put on trial.

It was obvious that the real issue at stake was not whether Scopes was 'guilty' – he had been teaching evolution – but whether the religious beliefs and social values of rural America could be maintained against the advance of science. Two renowned lawyers were brought in to argue the case. For the defence, the American Civil Liberties Union hired the country's most famous counsel, Clarence Darrow. The prosecution was led by William Jennings Bryan, a fading giant of politics who had run unsuccessfully for president three times, but who, in his declining years, had become a religious fundamentalist and associated himself with the anti-evolution campaign.

The world's press flocked to the small courtroom in which the case was tried. They called it the 'Monkey Trial' because of Darwin's assertion that human beings evolved from apes. Scopes was bound to lose; Darrow's purpose was not to win the case, but rather to demonstrate the threat that such laws posed to freedom of thought and speech. In the turning point of the trial, Darrow called Bryan as a witness. He destroyed Bryan's case by questioning him in detail about the story of creation in the Bible, and forcing him to admit that he did not believe every word as literal truth.

The strain of giving evidence in the hot courtroom, under Darrow's relentless questioning, proved too much for Bryan. He was taken ill and died five days later.

The judge duly found Scopes guilty and fined him $100. However, even this small victory for the anti-evolutionists did not last long. The Tennessee Supreme Court overturned the verdict a year later, and the law was never used again.

QUESTIONS

1 Read Source G. Explain why Darrow asked these questions. Do you think he got the answers he wanted?

2 a Why do you think people in the southern states of the USA were so opposed to Darwin's theories?
b Why was the 'Monkey Trial' so important?

Why was prohibition introduced?

Many people in the USA thought alcohol was harmful and wanted it banned, or prohibited. After the First World War they got their way. In 1919 Congress (the American parliament) passed the 18th Amendment to the Constitution, which introduced prohibition on the manufacture, sale and transport of alcohol (although, interestingly, it was not made illegal to drink it). The Volstead Act, passed the same year, gave the federal government the power to enforce prohibition, and with effect from January 1920, the USA became 'dry'. What was known as the 'Noble Experiment' had begun. But why had it been introduced?

1 It already existed

Many individual states already had their own prohibition laws. There were thirteen totally 'dry' states by 1919, but a majority of other states had also introduced some kind of control on the sale and manufacture of alcohol. The 18th Amendment simply made prohibition nationwide.

2 Moral reasons

Those who opposed alcohol argued that it caused a variety of social problems, such as violence, poverty, crime and sexual promiscuity. If alcohol were banned, they believed that the USA would be a better, healthier, more moral place in which to live.

3 Campaigners

Many organisations led campaigns against alcohol. The most famous was the Anti-Saloon League of America, which was founded in 1893. These organisations launched an effective propaganda campaign, and put pressure on politicians to support their cause. As they had the support of many of the churches, they were very effective in making it seem that any politician who failed to support them was in favour of crime and immorality. Not many politicians were brave enough to put votes at risk in this way. The pressure was greatest in rural areas. In many ways, prohibition was another indication of the struggle between traditional and modern values, and between the country areas and the cities, which affected the USA in the 1920s. As one prohibition campaigner put it: 'Our nation can only be saved by turning the pure stream of country sentiment and township morals to flush out the cesspools of cities and so save civilisation from pollution.'

4 The First World War

Many of the USA's brewers were of German descent. When the USA joined the war in 1917, there was a lot of anti-German feeling, and campaigners were able to argue that it would be patriotic to close the brewers down. After all, they were using up grain that could otherwise have been sent to Europe to help feed the USA's allies.

SOURCE I

Daddy's in There---
WHISKEY
And Our Shoes and Stockings and Clothes and Food Are in There, Too, and They'll Never Come Out.
—Chicago American.
WANTED--A FATHER; A LITTLE BOY'S PLEA
JULIA H. JOHNSON

An Anti-Saloon League poster.

QUESTIONS

Look at Source I.

1. a Explain the message of the cartoon.
   b How effective do you think the cartoon would be as Anti-Saloon League propaganda? Explain your answer, referring to details of the cartoon.
2. What other reasons did prohibitionists have for wanting alcohol banned?

What were the effects of prohibition?

Prohibition had almost exactly the opposite effect from that intended. Once it was banned, alcohol became more attractive, and consumption increased. In many cities, the law was ignored. Illegal bars, known as 'speakeasies', opened in their thousands. But if the manufacture of alcohol was illegal, where was it all coming from?

1 Moonshine

The first reaction of those determined to beat prohibition was to make their own alcohol. These concoctions were known as 'moonshine', but unfortunately the end result could be poisonous. Several hundred people a year died from this during the 1920s. Despite the efforts of government prohibition agents, it was impossible to stop this illegal production. Throughout the country there were many thousands of illegal distilleries and breweries, and there could never be enough agents to close them all down.

2 Smuggling

It proved impossible for the USA to seal its thousands of miles of frontiers, let alone its coastline, to prevent alcohol coming into the country. Famous 'rum-runners' like William McCoy made fortunes by smuggling alcohol from the West Indies and Canada. In four years, McCoy is thought to have smuggled $70 million worth of whiskey.

3 Organised crime

The enormous profits to be made from alcohol inevitably attracted the attention of gangsters, who were able to take control of many cities by bribing local policemen, judges and politicians. This meant the criminals could operate with little fear of arrest. The most notorious city was Chicago, where Mayor 'Big Bill' Thompson was known to be a close associate of the gangster Al Capone. Competition between gangs led to constant violence. In Chicago alone, between 1927 and 1931, over 200 gang members were murdered, with nobody convicted for these crimes.

The boost to organised crime was easily the most significant long-term consequence of prohibition. The profits made during the prohibition period were so vast that the Mafia was able to extend its power, first into other areas of criminal activity, such as prostitution, labour rackets and illegal gambling, then later into a whole range of what appeared to be legitimate businesses.

Al Capone

In 1925, Al Capone became the boss of the Mafia in Chicago. He took over from his friend, Johnny Torrio, who had been injured during an attack. Capone soon showed an unparalleled talent for ruthless violence against all his competitors. He was implicated in dozens of murders. The violence reached its peak in 1929 with the St Valentine's Day Massacre, in which seven members of a rival gang were machine-gunned to death. At the end of the 1920s, Capone was earning $100 million a year. The web of corruption and bribery that he used to protect himself worked well in Chicago, but was not effective against federal government agents who, in 1931, were able to have him arrested and imprisoned for eleven years on tax-dodging charges. This was enough to put an end to his career as the USA's most feared criminal.

	1921	1925	1929
Illegal distilleries seized	9,746	12,023	15,794
Gallons of distilled spirits seized	414,000	1,103,000	1,186,000
Number of arrests	34,175	62,747	66,878

The fight against alcohol production in the USA, 1921–9.

QUESTION

Look at the table.
Do the statistics demonstrate that the fight against alcohol was successful?
Explain your answer.

SOURCE J

The murder of Frank Yale, liquor boss of New York, who was killed on Capone's orders in 1928.

SOURCE K

By 1929, only one organisation still challenged Capone's control of Chicago's underworld: George 'Bugs' Moran's North Side gang. Capone chose St Valentine's Day to put a bloody end to the rivalry.

The scheme relied on killers masquerading as cops. On 14 February, a Cadillac disguised as a police car pulled up in front of a garage that served as Moran's headquarters. Four men got out – two dressed as patrolmen, two as plain clothes detectives. Inside the garage the phoney plainclothesmen lined up six gangsters against a wall. Suddenly they opened fire with sub-machine guns; the other two assassins used shotguns to finish off anyone still twitching.

One of Moran's men miraculously survived for a few hours. When a real policeman asked who had shot him he followed gangster code. 'No one,' he said. But Moran, who'd escaped by chance (arriving late, he had seen the police 'raid' in progress and decided to wait it out in a coffee shop) was less prudent. Pressed for a comment by a reporter, he shouted, 'Only Capone kills like that!' His prestige as a mobster ruined, Moran soon left the rackets.

A historian's account of the St Valentine's Day Massacre.

QUESTIONS

1 How did people try to avoid the prohibition laws?

2 Why do you think prohibition failed?

Why was prohibition repealed?

As time passed, it became obvious to almost everyone that prohibition was not working, and was doing enormous damage. However, it took a long time before politicians were able to admit this openly. Al Smith, Democratic candidate in the presidential election of 1928, was a well-known 'wet' (that is, he wanted prohibition repealed), yet he lost the election heavily to the 'dry' Republican, Herbert Hoover. Nonetheless, some states went ahead and repealed their own prohibition laws, leaving it up to the federal government to enforce prohibition if it could.

The Depression made an important difference. With millions out of work, it seemed nonsense that the government was spending large amounts of money on enforcing an unpopular and ineffective law. The money could surely be spent more wisely on helping the poor. Opponents of prohibition were also able to argue that, by making alcohol legal again, an enormous number of jobs would be created, and tax revenues could again be raised on its sale.

Hoover was the one president who made a serious effort to enforce prohibition. In the presidential election campaign of 1932 he faced an opponent, Franklin Roosevelt, who promised a repeal of the 18th Amendment. By this time, public opinion was firmly in favour of repeal. Roosevelt won, and one of his earliest actions was to introduce the 21st Amendment to the Constitution, repealing prohibition. On 5 December 1933 this was approved, and the 'Noble Experiment' came to an end.

How far did the roles of women change during the 1920s?

The writer of Source M obviously thought there was something new and shocking about the way young American women were behaving in the early 1920s. Her description fits well the popular image of the flapper – the outrageous, promiscuous party-girls of Scott Fitzgerald's novels. But how much truth was there in this image?

There is little doubt that the First World War brought about important changes in behaviour and social attitudes. In 1920 women gained the right to vote. During the 1920s, more and more women went out to work. They became financially independent to a degree unknown in previous generations. They no longer had to live at home. Contraception became generally available. Being less dependent on men, women could make their own decisions about how to live. The divorce rate rose quickly. Certainly, there were changes that anyone could see. Women looked different. They cut their hair short in the new 'bobbed' style, they wore make-up, they went out on their own without a chaperon, they smoked in public. The new fashions were much simpler and freer than before the war, and skirts became much shorter.

Older people found all this threatening and improper. However, it is important not to make too much of these changes. Most women were not flappers. They were too busy at work, or raising families, to go out to parties. More important than fashion in changing their lives was the greater availability of labour-saving devices like washing machines and vacuum cleaners, which began to free them from domestic chores. As ever, change had a greater impact on city life than it did on those who lived in the country. There, traditional values of decency and respectability still acted as a powerful restraint on how people behaved.

QUESTION

Would you agree that the lives of American women changed a lot in the 1920s?

SOURCE L

Women's fashions of the 1920s.

SOURCE M

Think of the modern young American girl in every town and city of this great country. She is the loveliest physical creature since the age of the Greeks, and has the brightest mentality – if it were only used.

Do they ever think, these beautiful young girls? Do they ever ask whence they have come, whither they are going? It would seem not. Their aim appears to be to allure men, and to secure money. What can a man with a mind find to hold him in one of these lovely, brainless, unbalanced, cigarette-smoking morsels of undisciplined sex whom he meets continually? Has the American girl no modesty, no self-respect, no reserve, no dignity?

An extract from an article in *Cosmopolitan* magazine, written by a female English journalist in 1921.

What were the causes and consequences of the Wall Street Crash?

In 1928, when Herbert Hoover was elected president, the USA was still enjoying the benefits of the economic boom. During the election campaign, Hoover praised the economic achievements of the Republican governments of the 1920s and predicted the end of poverty in the USA (see Source A). This was one of the worst predictions in history.

In October 1929 the Wall Street stock market in New York crashed. Panic selling of shares ruined hundreds of thousands of investors as prices slumped. The effect on the American economy was profound. The wave of bankruptcies that followed the crash destroyed all confidence in American business. In the Great Depression that followed, up to 13 million people were made unemployed. The desperation of the people, and the failure of the government to do anything effective to help them, led directly to the victory of Franklin Delano Roosevelt in the 1932 presidential election.

How far was speculation responsible for the Wall Street Crash?

Wall Street is in New York, at the heart of the financial district of the city. On Wall Street is the American stock market. This is where people can buy and sell shares in businesses. Companies issue shares to raise money. Speculators buy the shares, hoping to make money. Owning shares means you own part of the company. The more shares you have, the more of the company you own. If the company does well, it shares its profits out among its shareholders by giving them a dividend, and the price of its shares rises. Investors can then sell their shares at a profit. Of course, the opposite can happen too. The price of the shares will fall if the company does badly, and the investors might lose some or all of their money.

During the 1920s, the Wall Street stock market was a good place for speculators to put their money. \$100 invested in typical shares in 1920 would have been worth around \$325 by 1929. This rise in value reflected the general prosperity and industrial growth of the 1920s boom. Investors had become used to the idea that speculation in shares was a safe bet, and that prices would almost always go up. Like Hoover, they assumed that the good years would go on for ever.

SOURCE A

> We in America are nearer to the final triumph over poverty than ever before in any land. We have not reached the goal but, given a chance to go forward with the policies of the last eight years, we shall soon, with the help of God, be in sight of the day when poverty will be banished from the nation.

Herbert Hoover, speaking during the presidential election campaign of 1928.

The role of speculators

Nowadays, tight rules govern the way stock markets are run, but in 1929 this was not the case. Wall Street attracted all kinds of shady financiers, who were looking for ways of making quick money. New corporations with imaginary assets could be set up, and misleading information issued to gullible investors. Nobody thought it mattered – the price of shares, even in dubious enterprises, always went up, so nobody lost money. A practice known as 'buying on the margin' pushed prices still higher. Here, for a small fraction of the price (generally around 10 per cent), a speculator could buy shares, wait until the price rose, then sell the shares, pay off what was owed and pocket the profit! It was a perfect way to make money with little effort or expense – as long as prices rose.

QUESTIONS

1 What is a stock market?

2 Why did Americans invest money in shares in the 1920s?

The banks were as much taken in by the lure of the stock market as were small investors. Indeed, the banks were only too ready to lend money for stocks to be bought 'on the margin'. As prices were forced ever upwards, few people stopped to ask whether the shares were actually worth the money. Shares are a stake in a real business, and the price of the shares should reflect the value of the business. But investors were ignoring this. The stock market was like a giant, speculative bubble, gently floating away from the reality of the American economy.

The state of the American economy

Although the economy did well during the 1920s, it did not grow at the same rate as the price of shares. By 1928 the growth of the economy was showing signs of slowing down. Foreign trade was declining, agriculture remained depressed, and home markets for consumer goods were becoming saturated. Above all, a slow realisation was dawning that the boom had been fuelled by debt. Banks had lent money too easily. Investors and businesses had been all too willing to take the money. But eventually debts have to be repaid. Everything depended on the economy continuing to prosper and, just as importantly, on everyone believing that it would continue to prosper.

What impact did the Crash have on the economy?

As the New York stock market opened on Thursday, 24 October 1929, dealers were nervous. The previous day had seen a lot of investors selling shares and prices dropping sharply. For a week or so, the market had been unstable. Now, on 'Black Thursday', it was about to collapse. Almost from the start of trading, prices moved downwards. Frustratingly, the 'ticker-tape' that transmitted current prices around the country was running almost an hour late, so it was impossible for investors to be sure of how prices were moving. During the morning, the market was engulfed by panic selling. Even with prices in free fall, nobody wanted to buy. With every passing minute, fortunes were being lost. More and more investors, desperate to cut their losses, gave orders to sell their stock. Complete panic was avoided only when representatives of the USA's biggest banks started to buy shares, thus bolstering up the market. Temporarily, investors recovered their nerve – surely the banks would not throw their money away if anything was seriously wrong? By the end of the day, prices had recovered somewhat – but that was little consolation to the thousands who had been ruined during the day by selling at a loss.

Over the weekend, a kind of nervous calm was restored. Everyone was praying that 'Black Thursday' would not be repeated. In fact, the Crash had barely started. On Monday the 28th, prices fell sharply again. This time, ominously, the big banks made no move to support the market. Tuesday the 29th was the worst day of all. Over 16 million shares were traded during the day as prices slid downwards, out of control. The value of some of the USA's greatest companies was being slashed. $10,000 million were lost in a single day's trading. Thousands were bankrupted – small investors who had bought 'on the margin', firms that had bought and sold shares, banks that had lent money against the value of shares. Their money had simply disappeared.

October 1929 did not see the end of the collapse in share prices. The market continued to fall, bit by bit, until 1932, at which time the average value of shares was only one-fifth of what it was after the October 1929 crash. The bubble of speculation and greed had burst, with terrible consequences for both the USA and the rest of the world.

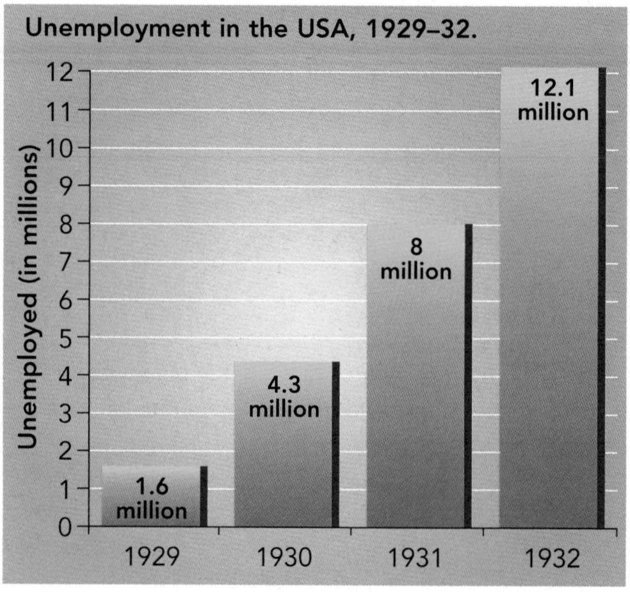

SOURCE B

> We seem to have stepped Alice-like through an economic looking glass into a world where everything shrivels. Bond prices, stock prices, commodity prices, employment – they all dwindle.

One writer sums up the plight of the USA after the stock market crash.

SOURCE C

A car for sale after the Wall Street Crash, October 1929.

The financial and economic effects of the Wall Street Crash

It would be too simple to say that the Wall Street Crash caused the Great Depression. What cannot be doubted is that it sparked the Depression off. The American economy went into a vicious downward spiral of bankruptcy, slumping production and unemployment, which devastated normal economic life, first in the USA and then, by the destruction of international trade, throughout the world. How did this occur?

Businesses need money. They have to buy raw materials, equipment and machinery. They must pay wages. They can raise money by selling goods, or by borrowing. The Crash made both of these much more difficult. Many people had lost a great deal of money and now had less to spend. So companies made fewer goods, and needed fewer workers and factories. For example, $4\frac{1}{2}$ million cars were sold in 1929, but only one million in 1932. As a result, unemployment rose rapidly.

Borrowing money was no easier. Who would want to lend money when so many businesses were failing? You would never get it back. In any case, it was often the banks themselves that were going broke – 5000 of them closed in the three years after the Crash. As money disappeared, industry shut down.

By 1932 a quarter of the working population was unemployed. As many as a third of the population were members of families in which the breadwinner was out of work. By 1933 production of manufactured goods was at barely 20 per cent of its 1929 level. The economy was ceasing to function.

The reaction of President Hoover

Hoover was notably unsuccessful in dealing with the effects of the Crash, and this failure saw him voted out of office in 1932. As a Republican, he believed that governments should stay out of business matters. Like most businessmen, when the Crash first occurred, Hoover assumed that all he needed to do was wait, and that eventually things would return to normal.

But it soon became obvious that doing nothing would not be enough. The USA was in the grip of a depression far more serious than any experienced before. Even Hoover eventually realised that government might have to play a role in dealing with it. He pleaded with employers to keep their nerve, and not to sack workers or cut their pay. He realised that this would just make matters worse. When this did not work, he set up the Reconstruction Finance Commission to make loans to businesses which were in trouble. He encouraged states and cities to launch public works programmes to make jobs for the unemployed. The Federal Farm Board purchased surplus crops in an attempt to hold up prices.

SOURCE D

Hungry unemployed people in New York queue for food on Christmas Day 1931.

These were all good ideas, but Hoover did not really believe in them and the programmes were not big enough to make a difference. Some of Hoover's measures actually made things worse. Under pressure from farmers and manufacturers, in 1930 he agreed the Hawley–Smoot tariff, which placed even higher taxes on imports. Naturally enough, other nations retaliated by doing the same, which made it even harder for the USA to export its surplus production. The damage done to world trade began to push the rest of the world into a depression.

Unfairly, Hoover's name came to be associated with the effects of the Depression. The name 'Hoovervilles' was given to the shanty towns built by the homeless unemployed, and 'Hoover blankets' were the newspapers that the destitute huddled under for warmth. Hoover's image was of being heartless and uncaring. It was not true, but he was undoubtedly the wrong man for the task of bringing about the USA's recovery.

What were the social consequences of the Crash?

The USA was supposed to be the land of opportunity, where a good life was available for all those willing to work hard. Now just finding

QUESTIONS

1 What happened on 'Black Thursday' (24 October 1929)?
2 Why did the price of shares keep falling, and not recover?
3 What effects did the Crash have on the American economy?
4 Why was Hoover ineffective in dealing with the effects of the Crash?

work was a problem. The numbers of unemployed increased by the day. Countless families lost their homes, or were split up, when parents lost their jobs. The USA was not a welfare state, and the unemployed were dependent on charity. Soon breadlines – queues of unemployed people lining up for handouts of food – became a feature of city life.

Hundreds of thousands of destitute people wandered the streets looking for food, work or somewhere to stay. Shanty towns constructed from scrap metal and tents sprang up on waste ground in the cities. By 1932 money to help the poor was running out. In June the city of Philadelphia had to cut off all relief funds to 50,000 families. The situation seemed hopeless.

The Bonus Marchers

A crisis point was reached in the summer of 1932. Since May, destitute veterans (ex-First World War servicemen) and their families had been arriving in Washington DC and demonstrating for the 'bonus' payment that had been promised to them by an Act passed in 1924. The bonus, around $500, was not payable until 1945, but the veterans wanted it now. In camps around the city, about 25,000 veterans gathered. The government was worried by their presence. In the desperate atmosphere of the time, it was possible to see the veterans as a revolutionary threat.

Hoover refused to meet the veterans, and by the summer the situation had reached a stalemate. The veterans showed no sign of moving or taking any other action, and the government was not going to give them the bonus. Hoover decided that the veterans would have to be evicted. He called in the army, which launched attacks on the marchers' camps, driving the veterans and their families out of the city.

Any remaining sympathy the American people might have had for Hoover was lost as he tried to explain away the action by claiming that most of the marchers were communists and criminals, and that more than half of them had never been in the armed forces (around 65 per cent had been, of whom nearly 70 per cent had served overseas).

SOURCE E

The troops reached Anacostia Field about eleven at night. Here bedlam had broken loose, when the news of the troops' coming was confirmed. Men and women were trying to gather what they could and flee. Some of them had had a whiff of gas over in the city and wanted no more of it. Men and women ran about wildly with packs and bundles on their shoulders.

They came with their gas bombs and their bayonets. The troops fired the shacks on the edge of the camp. Tanks and soldiers guarded the bridge back into the city so that no refugees could get into Washington. They might disturb the sleep of a few of the Government officials.

The jeers and cries of the evicted men and women rose over the crackling of the flames. The flames were mirrored in the drawn bayonets of the infantry as they advanced through the camp. There is no way of knowing whether, in the débâcle, a few homeless men perished or not.

On the evening after the crime against the Bonus Expeditionary Force had been done, General MacArthur said: 'That mob was motivated by a belief in revolution. In my opinion if the President had not acted he would have been faced with a very grave situation indeed.'

An eye-witness account of the attack on the Bonus Marchers.

QUESTION

Read Source E.
Do you think the writer would have agreed with General MacArthur that President Hoover was right to order action against the Bonus Marchers? Explain your answer with reference to the passage.

Why did Roosevelt win the election of 1932?

The Democrats' choice as candidate in the 1932 presidential election stood before the delegates at the nominating convention in Chicago to make his acceptance speech. He could not stand unaided – eleven years earlier he had been paralysed by polio, and now his legs were locked in place by metal braces. He was not the Democrats' first choice, but was simply a compromise when none of the other candidates could win enough support. He was, though, one of the great men of the twentieth century, as the USA was about to find out. The candidate was Franklin Delano Roosevelt.

Roosevelt's early life

Franklin D. Roosevelt came from a privileged background, the only son in a wealthy old Dutch family from New York state. Nothing in his early life indicated what he would eventually achieve. He was a fairly aimless student, both at school and at Harvard University. He worked for a law firm, but he was not much good at that either. He was the typical indulged rich boy, looking for a purpose in life. He found it in politics. A distant relative of ex-president Theodore Roosevelt, he had the social contacts that enabled him to make rapid progress in his chosen career. He also found that in politics his friendly, open and optimistic personality was a great asset in winning votes. Elected first as a state senator in New York in 1910, by 1913 he was Assistant Secretary to the Navy in Wilson's government, and in 1920 he ran as the Democrats' vice-presidential candidate. Unfortunately for him, 1920 was the year of the Republican landslide, which saw Harding elected president.

Then, in 1921, Roosevelt caught polio, which left his legs paralysed. For several years he fought to regain his health, but he was never again able to walk without help. At that time, physical disability was an almost impossible barrier to a career in politics, but Roosevelt showed the steely determination that lay beneath his apparently easy-going character. He was fortunate to be wealthy enough not to have to worry about making a living, and he could afford the best care available. But he refused to allow his illness to force him out of politics.

In 1928 he felt strong enough to stand for governor of New York state, and won by a narrow margin. This was the office he held when the Depression struck the USA. As governor, he took vigorous action to help the unemployed in his state, setting up the Temporary Relief Administration, which used public money on schemes to create employment – a forerunner of the ideas he would later implement as president. To many people, it seemed clear that Roosevelt's lengthy illness had given him a sympathy for the problems of ordinary people, which would make him act to relieve the suffering caused by the Depression. He had critics, who complained that he was inconsistent, or that his ideas were woolly and vague, but even they could not ignore his sheer energy and willingness to experiment.

SOURCE F

Roosevelt before his illness.

The presidential election, 1932

Roosevelt's opponent in the election was President Hoover, who by this time was extremely unpopular. Everyone knew what Hoover stood for. His policies to deal with the Depression were not working, and he seemed to believe that the only solution was to wait for the economy to cure itself. Even in the depths of the Depression, Hoover did not regard business as the responsibility of the government. So a vote for Hoover would be a vote for doing nothing. When Hoover went out campaigning, he often received a hostile reception. His train was frequently pelted with eggs and tomatoes, and demonstrators carried placards reading 'Hang Hoover'. He nearly caused a riot in one city when, speaking of the Bonus Marchers, he said, 'Thank goodness we still have a government which knows how to deal with a mob.'

The contrast between Hoover and Roosevelt was striking. Although it was not clear exactly what Roosevelt intended to do about the Depression, voters were clear that he would do something. Although Roosevelt's and Hoover's ideas were not all that different, their personalities and image were almost opposites. Roosevelt ran an energetic, optimistic campaign which, above all, offered the USA hope. At a time when millions of unemployed Americans were dependent on soup kitchens for their next meal, his words made them feel that at last someone was on their side. Even the middle classes who were still in work responded to Roosevelt, as they saw in him the only hope to save the USA from revolution.

When the results of the election were announced, Roosevelt had won a remarkable victory. He received 22.8 million votes against Hoover's 15.8 million. In 1932 there were 48 states in the USA, and 42 of them chose Roosevelt.

However, although he had been elected, he would not be president until his inauguration in four months' time. Meanwhile, Hoover would be a 'lame duck' president, still in office, but with no power or authority, and with the economic crisis becoming worse by the day.

SOURCE G

I pledge you, I pledge myself, to a New Deal for the American people.

From Roosevelt's acceptance speech to the Democratic Party, Chicago, 1932.

QUESTIONS

1 How did Roosevelt's early life prepare him for a career in politics?

2 Why did the Democrats choose Roosevelt as their candidate in the 1932 election?

3 Why did Roosevelt beat Hoover in the 1932 election?

SOURCE H

Roosevelt making a speech about the New Deal.

How successful was the New Deal?

Roosevelt had promised the American people a 'New Deal'. From the moment he came into office, he launched a programme of legislation that gave the government a central role in trying to cope with the effects of the Depression. By spending public money on a huge scale, Roosevelt attempted to create jobs and put the USA back to work. Most Americans supported these efforts – Roosevelt remained president until his death in 1945, winning further elections in 1936, 1940 and 1944.

However, many were worried that he had given government a role that went against American traditions. The Supreme Court declared some of his New Deal measures to be unconstitutional, and business bitterly resented government controls. The New Deal did not solve the problem of unemployment, although the numbers of unemployed did fall significantly. Instead it was the impact of the Second World War that finally brought back full employment.

What was the New Deal as introduced in 1933?

Roosevelt's inauguration as president took place on 4 March 1933. The USA was poised on the brink of economic disaster. On that very day, banks throughout the country had failed to open. Nobody trusted the banks any more because so many had gone bust. Had they opened, they would have collapsed because of the thousands of panicking depositors who wanted to draw out their money. In this feverish atmosphere, millions of Americans gathered around their radios to listen to Roosevelt's inauguration speech (Source B). His calm, confident voice immediately gave them reassurance.

SOURCE A

An American cartoon from 1933 entitled 'The new Chauffeur'.

SOURCE B

The only thing we have to fear is fear itself. Our greatest primary task is to put people back to work. This is no unsolvable problem if we face it wisely and courageously.

It can be accomplished in part by direct recruiting by the government itself, treating the task as we would treat the emergency of a war, but at the same time, through this employment, accomplishing greatly needed projects to stimulate and reorganise the use of our natural resources.

From Roosevelt's inauguration speech.

QUESTION

Look at Source A.
What is the message of the cartoon? Explain your answer, referring to details of the cartoon.

The inauguration speech was a summary of the 'New Deal', which in Roosevelt's first 'Hundred Days' in power would be brought into being. Between the inauguration and 16 June, when the session of Congress came to an end, a whole series of laws designed to deal with the impact of the Depression had been passed.

Helping the banks

If the banks stayed closed, the economy would cease to function. Very quickly, nobody would have any money to spend. If the banks opened, they might collapse. Roosevelt solved the immediate crisis by having the Emergency Banking Act passed. It forced all banks to stay closed for four days. Those whose finances were completely hopeless were ordered to close permanently. The rest were promised the backing of government grants so that the public could regain confidence in them. Roosevelt broadcast to the nation, appealing for the panic to end and for people with money to take it back to the banks. It worked, and the banks were saved.

Roosevelt did not just want to deal with the financial crisis. He also wanted to reform the harmful practices that had got the USA into the trouble it now faced. One of the causes of the Wall Street Crash had been the uncontrolled activities of disreputable financiers, who were willing to resort to any trick or shady deal to make money out of the stock market. Roosevelt was determined to bring Wall Street under control.

The Securities Act forced companies issuing new shares to provide full information about the company to the public. Directors of companies that failed to do this could be prosecuted. This was followed up in 1934 with the establishment of a Securities and Exchange Commission, which was given sweeping powers to control the activities of the stock market. In future, investors could have greater confidence that they would not be swindled out of their money. This was another important step in rebuilding confidence in American business.

Helping the farmers

Agriculture's most serious problem was over-production. While this continued, prices would remain low, and farmers would be unable to make a decent living. Roosevelt's solution was to pay farmers for not producing! The Agricultural Adjustment Act gave the government the power to influence prices by destroying surplus produce, and giving farmers compensation for lost production. In the short term, cotton farmers were told to plough their crop into the ground, and the government bought millions of piglets for slaughtering. The Agricultural Adjustment Administration (AAA) was established to put the Act into operation, and to try and reduce production in the longer term by reaching agreement with farmers on sensible amounts to be produced in future years.

SOURCE C

An American cartoon about the AAA, 1933.

QUESTION

Look at Source C.
Do you think the cartoonist supported Roosevelt's plans for agriculture? Explain your answer, using details of the cartoon.

Helping the unemployed

Within three weeks of the inauguration, Roosevelt had taken an important first step in helping the unemployed. By setting up the Civilian Conservation Corps (CCC), the government provided work for unemployed young men on a whole range of environmental projects in the countryside. Being in the CCC was a bit like being in the army – it even had a uniform – and as pay rates were very low, the work could be criticised as forced labour. But the CCC carried out many useful projects, such as strengthening river banks, fish farming, fighting forest fires and controlling mosquitoes to prevent malaria. Its members eventually planted around 200 million trees, which helped to reduce soil erosion and provided shelter belts for crops. During the 1930s, for around 3 million young men under the age of 25, the CCC provided their first experience of work.

Next, in an attempt to help the destitute, the Federal Emergency Relief Administration (FERA) was set up. This could make grants of federal money to state and local governments to help them give relief to the unemployed. This was really only an emergency measure. Roosevelt, like most Americans, did not believe that the right way to help the unemployed was to give them the 'dole'. He wanted to put them to work, but the USA's plight in 1933 was so serious that people had first to be saved from the threat of starvation.

Helping industry

The National Industrial Recovery Act set up two important agencies. The National Recovery Administration (NRA) tried to create a partnership between the government and industry that would do away with employment evils like child labour, long hours and low pay. The idea was that each industry would agree an employment code with the government. The code would guarantee workers fair wages and conditions in return for fair prices that could be charged for the goods. Those employers that agreed a code were allowed to display the NRA's logo of a blue eagle. The government rewarded these firms by favouring them when contracts were awarded.

The Act also created an agency called the Public Works Administration (PWA). This aimed to use unemployed, skilled industrial workers on large-scale public construction projects, such as building roads and bridges. Over the next few years, PWA workers would construct many of the USA's public buildings, including schools, hospitals, city halls and court houses.

Another feature of the Act was that workers were given the right to collective bargaining of wages. This gave an enormous boost to trade unions, which could now organise in industries where previously they had been excluded.

QUESTION

Study Source D.
What does the poster tell you about the NRA and its aims? Explain your answer, referring to details of the poster.

SOURCE D

An American poster about the NRA.

Helping home-owners

Many home-owners who had been affected by the Depression faced the threat of losing their homes if they could not keep up their mortgage repayments. This would be bad both for the family evicted from their home, and for the bank which would not recover its money. To prevent this happening the government set up the Home-Owners' Loan Corporation (HOLC), which gave low-interest loans to home-owners. Such loans would enable home-owners to adjust mortgage repayments in order to cope with temporary unemployment. Similar help was given to farmers through the Farm Credit Administration.

Help to depressed areas

The valley of the Tennessee River was a particularly depressed region, where agriculture was badly hit by frequent floods and the soil erosion that these caused. Half the population of the area was dependent on government relief for survival. In 1932 barely 2 per cent of farms in the valley were served by electricity. The Tennessee Valley Authority (TVA) was set up to regenerate the area by encouraging industry and helping agriculture. It planned to tame the Tennessee River by constructing a series of dams, which in turn would be used to generate hydroelectricity, as well as encouraging leisure activities on the newly created lakes. People in the valley would benefit from the availability of electricity, and the Tennessee River would become navigable, which would bring more commerce to the area.

The 'alphabet agencies'

One of the most striking features of the frantic activity of the Hundred Days was the creation of a number of new government organisations, set up to carry out the work of the New Deal. Americans had to get used to a range of previously unknown acronyms: AAA, TVA, CCC and so on. In the years to come, the New Deal would create even more of what soon became known as the 'alphabet agencies'.

The end of prohibition

Another of the measures taken during the Hundred Days was the ending of prohibition. This process was started by the Beer Act of March 1933, which made legal again the manufacture and sale of beer and light wines. The process was completed when the 21st Amendment to the Constitution was ratified at the end of the year.

The 'fireside chats'

Roosevelt was one of the first politicians to realise fully the potential of radio as a means of communication. During the banking crisis, he started his 'fireside chats', broadcasting to the nation very much as if he were talking to a group of friends in his own living room. He was a natural radio performer. He communicated complex issues in simple language, without ever patronising his audience. He gave the impression of being caring, approachable and informal. These fireside chats were extremely important both for keeping Americans in touch with what the government was doing, and for creating a sense that the whole nation was united in facing its problems together.

SOURCE E

The Norris Dam, constructed by the TVA.

QUESTIONS

1 What were the Hundred Days?

2 What steps did Roosevelt take to deal with the problems of the Depression?

3 Why did he take these measures?

How far did the character of the New Deal change after 1933?

By 1935 the first phase of the New Deal had been carried out. However, with a presidential election to face in 1936, Roosevelt had several problems. The Supreme Court was beginning to challenge some of the New Deal laws, and radical opponents of the New Deal were criticising him for not taking enough action to help the poor. Roosevelt's response was to introduce another phase of reform, which some historians have called the 'Second New Deal'.

To continue providing work for the unemployed, a new agency, the Works Progress Administration (WPA), was set up. Its aim was to find emergency, short-term employment for unskilled workers, mainly in construction projects. However, it also sponsored community arts projects. In its eight years of existence, the WPA found work for around eight million people.

One of the casualties of the Supreme Court's hostility to the New Deal was the Public Works Administration, whose codes were found to be an infringement of the rights of individual states, and therefore unlawful. However the Wagner Act of 1935 tried to restore some protection to workers by confirming their right to join trade unions, and forbidding employers from preventing the organisation of unions.

Under pressure from critics, in 1935 Roosevelt introduced the Social Security Act. This set up a national insurance scheme, which provided old age pensions, unemployment benefits, and financial support for the handicapped. It was funded by contributions paid by workers, employers and government.

The AAA also had to close because of the Supreme Court. However, the government continued to find ways of helping the farmers. The Resettlement Administration (RA) helped poor farmers by purchasing equipment for them, and even resettled some of the poorest on land purchased by the RA. Grants were also given to farmers for soil conservation schemes.

SOURCE F

An American cartoon showing Roosevelt trying to restore American prosperity.

QUESTION

Look at Source F.
This cartoon is a judgement on the Hundred Days. How favourable is it towards Roosevelt? Explain your answer, using details of the cartoon.

The presidential election, 1936

Roosevelt's enormous popularity guaranteed him victory in the 1936 election. The Republicans' unfortunate candidate, Alf Landon, never had a chance and went down to an even heavier defeat than Hoover had suffered in 1932. It seemed as if Roosevelt had overwhelming support for carrying on the New Deal. Instead, he was drawn into a quarrel with the Supreme Court, after which the spirit of reform was never really recovered. By 1936 almost all of the great achievements of the New Deal were in place. From now on a combination of determined opposition, misjudgements by Roosevelt, a return to Depression and the approach of world war meant that no more significant reforms would be made.

Why did the New Deal encounter opposition?

The political opponents of Roosevelt were, naturally enough, consistent critics of the New Deal. Their most basic objection was that Roosevelt allowed government to become involved in economic life in an unprecedented manner. New Deal laws tried to create jobs, fix prices, dictate working conditions and control levels of production – all activities that opponents felt were none of the government's business. They also saw these measures as a threat to the traditional freedom of Americans to live without interference from government. It was also true that Roosevelt's measures cost money and some Americans resented paying higher taxes to fund employment schemes which they thought were a waste of time.

Most ordinary Americans were simply too grateful to Roosevelt for trying to cope with the country's problems to worry about whether the freedom of the rich to make money was being limited. However, the New Deal was clearly sympathetic in its aims towards the poor, the unemployed, the exploited and the working class, so Roosevelt's opponents found it easy to criticise him for steering the USA along the road to socialism.

SOURCE G

TRYING TO CHANGE THE UMPIRING
LISTEN - I DON'T LIKE YOUR "DECISIONS" FROM NOW ON, YOU'RE GOING TO HAVE TO WORK WITH SOMEONE WHO CAN SEE THINGS MY WAY!
THE SUPREME COURT
PRESIDENT ROOSEVELT
MORE NEW DEAL LAWS
NEW DEAL ACTS DECLARED UNCONSTITUTIONAL
N.R.A. - "OUT"
A.A.A. - "OUT"
ORIGINAL FARM MORTGAGE MORATORIUM - "OUT"
A.A.A. TAX REFUNDS - "OUT"
REGULATION OF "HOT OIL" SHIPMENTS - "OUT"

An American cartoon of 1937, commenting on Roosevelt's clash with the Supreme Court.

QUESTION

Study Source G.
How far does this cartoon support Roosevelt in his clash with the Supreme Court? Explain your answer, using details of the cartoon.

Opposition from the Supreme Court

The Supreme Court is the highest court of law in the USA. One of its functions is to judge whether laws passed by Congress are consistent with the terms of the American Constitution. If the court finds them unconstitutional, the laws cannot stand. From the start of the New Deal, it was clear that Roosevelt would have problems with the court. As the nine judges were mainly conservative by nature and politics, there was always the chance that they would declare against a piece of New Deal legislation. This eventually happened in 1935 when the court found the National Industrial Recovery Act unconstitutional. Subsequently, it also found against the Agricultural Adjustment Act. The possibility of the court dismantling the whole New Deal appalled Roosevelt. To him it seemed as if the court was prepared to put legal quibbles before the wishes of the country.

After his re-election in 1936, Roosevelt determined to reform the Supreme Court so that it could no longer block his plans. His idea was to increase the number of judges from nine to fifteen. Under normal circumstances, he would have had to wait for one of the judges to die or retire before getting the chance to appoint a replacement. Naturally enough, presidents always nominate judges who are sympathetic to their own political views. Now Roosevelt planned to appoint six at once!

It was clear to everyone that this would give him control over the court. Even many of his friends were very uneasy about this. In fact, the plan was one of Roosevelt's biggest mistakes. Americans believe that one of the ways their constitution protects their freedom is by ensuring that politicians cannot interfere in the work of judges. Roosevelt's plan to 'pack' the court with his own allies produced a storm of criticism, and made him look like a dictator. It was obvious that Congress would never approve, and eventually he was forced to back down and withdraw the plan.

However, in a way, Roosevelt still won his battle with the court. He had made the judges realise that they could not use their power just to impose their own political views on the country. From then on, they were much more cautious in the way they interpreted their duties.

Radical critics of the New Deal

Ironically, Roosevelt was also criticised for not doing enough to help the poor and oppressed. These radical critics claimed that the effect of the New Deal was not to change American society, but to enable capitalism to survive.

1 Father Coughlin

Coughlin was known as the 'radio priest'. Based in Detroit, he built up an enormous national audience for his broadcasts. At first he supported the New Deal, but he rapidly became disillusioned with Roosevelt. Coughlin formed the National Union for Social Justice, which at its peak had over seven million members.

His ideas were confused and incoherent, but his basic message was that the New Deal was not providing social justice. To people whose lives had been shattered by the effects of the Depression his simplistic and extreme ideas had much appeal, although as the years went by it became ever clearer that Coughlin had much in common with the European fascists. For him the New Deal was the 'Jew Deal', and he did not hesitate to preach a gospel of hate to his gullible listeners.

2 Dr Francis Townsend

Townsend and Coughlin were two of the founders of the Union Party, which opposed Roosevelt in the 1936 election. Townsend achieved fame as the author of the 'Townsend Plan' – a scheme by which all those over 60 would receive a monthly pension of $200 in return for a promise to retire from work and to spend all the pension each month. 'Townsend Clubs' were organised to campaign for the plan. These were influential in pushing the government into passing the Social Security Act of 1935 which, among other measures, introduced old age pensions.

QUESTIONS

1 Explain why Roosevelt was opposed by the rich and 'big business'.

2 What problems did Roosevelt experience with the Supreme Court?

3 Huey Long

Unlike Townsend and Coughlin, Huey Long was a professional politician who, for a short while, posed a real threat to Roosevelt. Elected Governor of Louisiana in 1928 as spokesman for the poor and underprivileged of the state, he used every trick in the political book, as well as some criminal ones, to boost his personal power. He became a virtual dictator in Louisiana, intimidating and bribing his opponents into silence. Yet however disreputable his methods, nobody could doubt his effectiveness. Public services in the state improved rapidly, and his popularity soared.

Long became a fierce critic of Roosevelt, whom he blamed for being too cautious and not doing enough to help those in need. Long's 'Share Our Wealth' scheme promised to confiscate the fortunes of millionaires and to hand out the proceeds so that all American families could buy a home, a car and a radio. The government would buy up all agricultural surpluses and sell them as cheap food. The state would provide a range of benefits such as free education and old age pensions. Once Long became a senator for Louisiana in 1930 he became a national figure, and by 1934 he was clearly preparing himself to be a rival to Roosevelt for the presidency. Had he not been assassinated in September 1935, he might well have stood against Roosevelt in the 1936 election.

SOURCE H

Huey Long (on the left) and his bodyguards, 1935.

Why did unemployment persist despite the New Deal?

As we have seen, one of the main aims of the New Deal was to put the USA back to work. Various agencies took part, such as the PWA, the CCC and the WPA. Literally millions of Americans were found work on government-sponsored projects.

QUESTIONS

1. Look at Source H.
   Why did Huey Long need bodyguards?
2. What objections did Roosevelt's radical critics have to the New Deal?

However, there was a limit to the effectiveness of these schemes. Critics suggested that they did not provide 'real jobs' – the moment government ceased to pay, the jobs would disappear. And although the USA benefited enormously from much of the work carried out – new roads, schools, hospitals, conservation schemes and so on – there was also a concern that many of the tasks were just making work for the sake of it. The greatest worry, though, was that unemployment would not go away. The government could reduce it, but they could not solve it. True, the numbers of unemployed fell year by year (at least until the return of the Depression in 1937–8), but by 1936 there were still 9 million people out of work. The effort that the government was making was huge, but it was not enough.

SOURCE I

Hired thugs beat up a union organiser attempting to hand out leaflets to Ford motor workers.

The New Deal and workers

Roosevelt believed that it was important to create a new relationship of trust and co-operation between workers and employers. He was sympathetic to the cause of workers' rights, and tried to improve working conditions. The National Recovery Administration codes did a lot to regulate conditions in many industries, and when the Supreme Court declared these unconstitutional, the Wagner Act recovered some of the lost ground, establishing workers' rights to join unions and to bargain collectively for their wages. During the 1930s, union membership rose steadily.

Nonetheless, the USA's employers deeply resented this aspect of the New Deal, and many did all they could to deny workers their rights. Many large companies hired thugs to beat up union activists and to intimidate workers who went on strike.

During 1937 there were many violent strikes in the steel and auto industries. During a strike by steelworkers in Chicago, ten demonstrators were shot dead by police, and ninety wounded, in what became known as the 'Memorial Day Massacre'. Workers used 'sit-down strikes' – occupying their factories to make sure the machinery could not be kept running. However, without the backing of the New Deal laws, these workers would almost certainly have been defeated by the employers. As it was, during 1937 there were around 4700 strikes, and about 80 per cent of them were settled in favour of the workers.

QUESTION

Look at Source I.
Does this source prove that the New Deal failed to protect workers? Explain your answer.

The New Deal and farmers

The New Deal did much to improve the lives of American farmers. Measures were taken to restrict production, raise prices, encourage soil conservation, and provide loans to purchase equipment and to help indebted farmers to save themselves from eviction. These were all effective, but they benefited large-scale farmers the most. By the mid-1930s farmers' incomes were rising, but small farmers, farm labourers and sharecroppers saw little of the benefit. There was still much poverty in rural America, and particularly in the south.

In 1934–5 a long-term drought hit the prairie states, and in many areas the soil was turning to dust. With no rain, previously fertile areas were becoming deserts. Parts of Kansas, Oklahoma, Texas and Colorado became known as the 'Dustbowl'. The farmers in these areas had little choice but to pack up their belongings and leave the land. Many of them, known as 'Okies' (after the state of Oklahoma), made their way west to look for work in California.

The plight of the Okies was famously described by John Steinbeck in his novel *The Grapes of Wrath*, and illustrated in pictures taken by photographers commissioned by the Farm Security Administration– a New Deal agency. As migrants they suffered great hardship, and were often treated with suspicion and contempt in the areas through which they passed.

The New Deal and the poor

One of the most valid criticisms of the New Deal is that it did not go far enough in dealing with poverty, or in helping the poorest people to improve their position in American society. Emergency relief prevented people from starving, jobs were provided for as many of the unemployed as possible, and the Social Security Act of 1935 began to set up a system of national insurance. However, although around 30 per cent of all black families were dependent on emergency relief for survival, no New Deal laws specifically attempted to assist black people.

Roosevelt felt dependent on the support of Democrats from the south, who were determined that no concessions should be made to improve the status of black Americans. Reluctance to deal with the race issue gave ammunition to Roosevelt's critics, who claimed that he was less interested in social justice than in preserving the USA's existing social structure.

SOURCE J

Dust storm damage in Oklahoma, 1936.

QUESTIONS

1 How far was the New Deal effective in helping American farmers?

2 What were the 'Dustbowl' and the 'Okies'?

3 How far was the New Deal effective in helping black Americans?

SOURCE K

A migrant mother in California, 1936.

The slump of 1937–8

The limitations of the New Deal were exposed by events in 1937. Although conservative critics always tried to portray Roosevelt as a socialist spendthrift, in reality he believed just as strongly as the Republicans in balancing the budget. In early 1937 it seemed that the economy was recovering well. Roosevelt decided to take the opportunity of cutting the amount spent on New Deal programmes. Without the stimulus of government spending, the economy promptly plunged back into depression. Industrial production fell by a third, and unemployment jumped by nearly 3 million. By early 1938, Roosevelt had acknowledged his mistake and increased spending again, but even by 1940 employment had not recovered to the level of early 1937.

Did the fact that the New Deal did not solve unemployment mean that it was a failure?

Judgements on the New Deal have been remarkably varied, although no one denies its importance. It did not solve unemployment, but it did reduce it. It did not solve the problems of the Depression, but it did much to protect Americans from its worst effects. On the next page you can read the opinions of several modern historians on why the New Deal was important. Once you have read them, decide whether you think the New Deal was a failure or not.

SOURCE L

WORLD'S HIGHEST STANDARD OF LIVING
There's no way like the American Way

Black people queuing for food handouts, 1937.

QUESTION

Look at Source L. Why do you think the photographer chose to take this picture?

SOURCE M

Roosevelt came in on a promise to do something that has balked governments of every ideological brand before or since – to guarantee full employment in peacetime – he didn't make it. In 1938 there were still 10 million unemployed. In the next four years the number did indeed shrink, but this was not Roosevelt's doing, but Hitler's. The stacks of the steel mills barely began to belch smoke again until the first war orders came in from the British and the French.

SOURCE N

If the New Deal is judged by economic success alone, then the verdict must be a mixed one. But, generally speaking, the economy had by 1937 recovered to the level reached before the Depression started in 1929. [However,] the New Deal established a far more important role for the Federal government in a whole range of areas previously considered to be outside its scope. Roosevelt quite deliberately extended the powers of central government in order to achieve a fairer society that offered its citizens greater security.

SOURCE O

Unquestionably the most important [achievement] was the preservation of American democracy, the American constitution, and American capitalism. By his gallantry, energy, eloquence and warmth of heart, Roosevelt not only transformed the prestige of his office but galvanised an entire generation with faith in their country, their leader and their political system.

QUESTIONS

1 For each of Sources M–Q , say whether or not it considers the New Deal a failure.

2 Why do you think these judgements differ from each other?

3 Use these sources and your own knowledge of the New Deal to explain whether or not you think it failed.

SOURCE P

Important advances had been made in working conditions, relief of poverty, and the running of business, but there had been no economic miracle. To have achieved such an economic miracle would have required policies of government spending on a scale beyond Roosevelt's dreams or nightmares. Instead, his policies were often hesitant or contradictory, perhaps due to his lack of interest in, and understanding of, economics.

SOURCE Q

The New Deal, while not infusing into American society any brand-new set of values or ideas, did make possible a vigorous dialogue about the values of existing society, about their shortcomings, and about how to improve them. By the end of the 1930s America's social conscience was more sensitive than it had ever been before, and the old catchwords like 'rugged individualism' were coming to be dismissed more and more widely as another name for selfishness.

Paper 1-type assessment: The New Deal

SOURCE A

An American cartoon of 1933 commenting on the cost of Roosevelt's New Deal.

SOURCE B

A resident of Park Avenue (a rich area of New York) was sentenced to a term of imprisonment for threatening violence to the person of President Roosevelt. This episode was significant as an example of the fanatical hatred of the President which today obsesses thousands of men and women amongst the American upper class.

From an article in an American magazine, published in 1936.

QUESTIONS

Section C Questions

1 Study the sources carefully and then answer the three questions which follow.

a Study Source A. Do you think that the cartoonist supported or opposed the New Deal? Use the source and your own knowledge to explain your answer. (6)

b Study Source B. Explain why many Americans opposed President Roosevelt in 1936. Use the source and your own knowledge to explain your answer. (7)

c Study Source C. Why do you think this photograph was taken? Use the source and your own knowledge to explain your answer. (7)

SOURCE C

President Roosevelt visiting a Civilian Conservation Corps camp in Virginia in 1933.

QUESTIONS

When answering these questions make sure you answer ALL three parts.

Remember that you should always explain your answer as fully as you can and support it with specific detail where possible.

Section C Questions

2a What happened in the 'Red Scare' in America in the years 1919-20? (4)

b Explain why not all Americans were able to be part of the prosperity of the 1920s. (6)

c 'The Wall Street Crash occurred in America only because of unwise speculation by investors in shares.' Do you agree with this statement ? Explain your answer. (10)

3a What was 'The New Deal'? (4)

b Explain why the New Deal aroused such strong feelings amongst the American people. (6)

c Was the New Deal a failure or a success? Explain your answer. (10)

5 Russia, 1905–41

In 1905 Russia was a backward country with a mainly rural economy run by an absolute monarch, Tsar Nicholas II. But industry was growing fast, creating new cities and an industrial working class. In the poor conditions and social misery of these cities, revolutionary groups, committed to overthrowing the Tsar's regime, could flourish.

In 1905 the growth of opposition, combined with a Russian defeat in the war against Japan led to a revolution against the Tsar's rule. Nicholas was forced to make reforms, including the introduction of a Duma (parliament).

But the Tsar soon regained his authority. His secret police broke up the revolutionary groups and many of their leaders were forced to flee into exile.

Although Nicholas appeared to have restored his control, the impact of the First World War showed that this was only a temporary state of affairs. After early successes the Russian armies suffered terrible defeats. Back home there was rapid inflation and shortages of basic necessities, such as food. In March 1917 the Tsar was forced to accept that he had lost the support of his people. He abdicated and was replaced by a 'Provisional Government'. This government lasted only a few months before it too was overthrown.

From November 1917 the Bolsheviks (later called communists) governed Russia. Under Lenin the Bolsheviks defeated their opponents in civil war and began building a new communist Soviet Union. On Lenin's death in 1924, Stalin emerged as the new leader. He made himself a feared and ruthless dictator who crushed all opposition, even turning against his colleagues in the Communist Party. Stalin was determined to modernise the Soviet Union. By brutally enforcing collectivisation of agriculture, he gained control of the countryside, and his Five-Year Plans saw massive government investment in heavy industry. By the time of the Second World War, the Soviet Union had been transformed into one of the world's great industrial powers, but at great cost.

This topic is examined in Paper 1 of the examination. Paper 1-type exercises are included at the end of the chapter. Mark schemes, sample answers and comments can be found in the accompanying Teacher's Resource Pack.

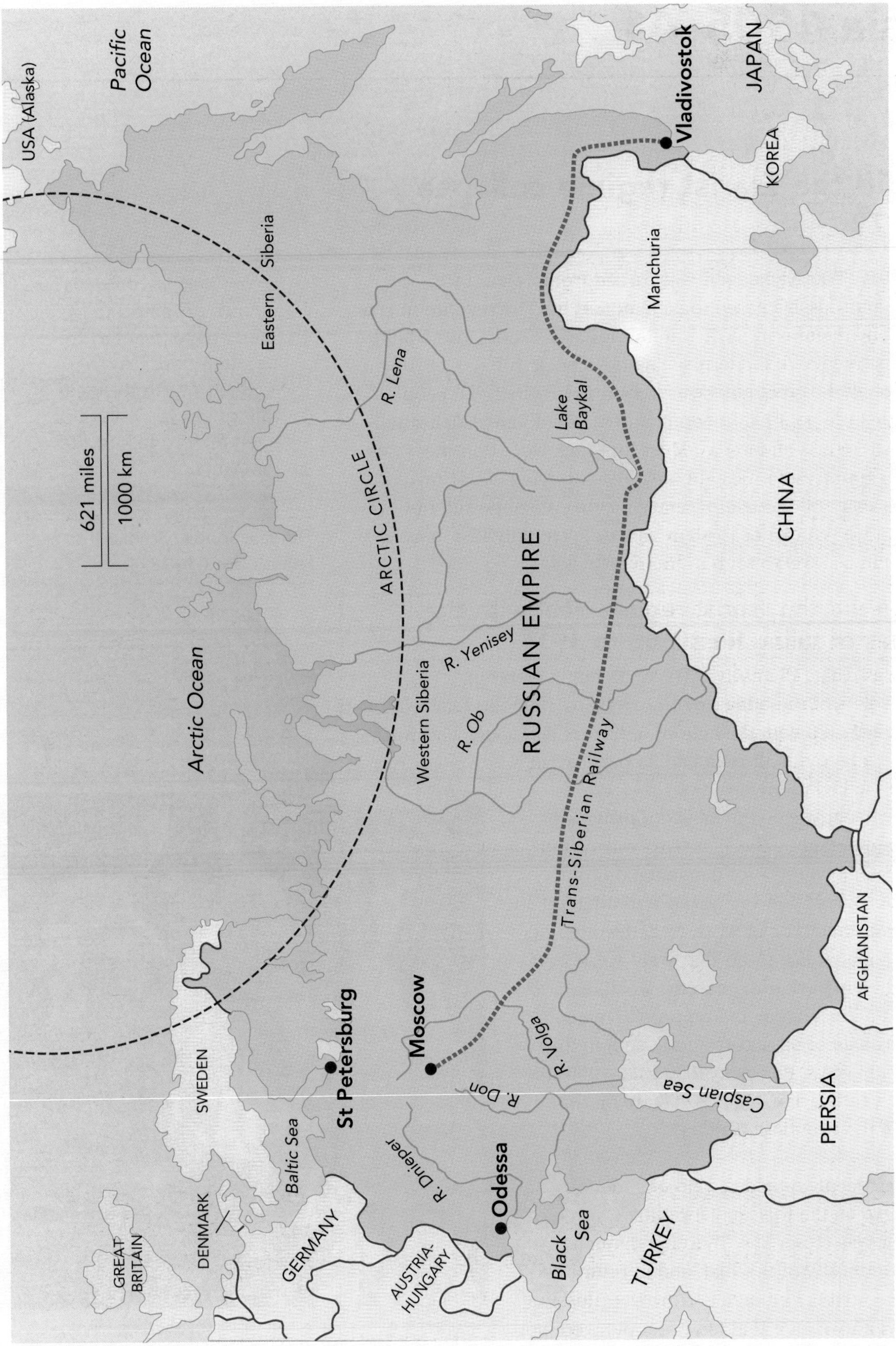

A map of the Russian Empire.

Russia 1905–41

Why did the Tsarist regime collapse in 1917?

In March 1917, Tsar Nicholas II was forced from power by a revolution, and Russia ceased to be a monarchy. The revolution was sparked off by the pressures of war, but it had its roots in the failure of the Tsarist regime to modernise itself. Nicholas ruled over the most backward of all the great powers – a country in which the people enjoyed very little political freedom, and in which industrialisation was only just getting under way. Most Russians were poor peasants living in the countryside. Despite only just surviving a first revolution in 1905, the Tsar still thought of himself as the absolute ruler of his country, and his reluctance to share power eventually lost him the support of almost every group in Russian society.

SOURCE A

What is going to happen to me and all of Russia? I am not prepared to be a Tsar. I never wanted to become one. I know nothing of the business of ruling. I have no idea of even how to talk to the ministers.

The reaction of Nicholas II to his father's death in 1894.

How well did the Tsarist regime deal with the difficulties of ruling Russia up to 1914?

Russian kings called themselves 'Tsar', meaning emperor.
Unlike the rulers of the other great powers, by 1900 the Tsar still ruled the country himself, with the help of ministers he chose, who were answerable only to him. Russia had no parliament, and the people had no right to vote in elections. Local government was in the hands of provincial governors appointed by the Tsar. This was a very personal system, where a lot depended on the ability of the Tsar. If he were strong and talented, Russia's government might work well, despite the size of the country. But if the Tsar were weak, Russia might slip back into anarchy. Most Tsars therefore ruled in a harsh and repressive manner, crushing any sign of dissent from the people they ruled. In many ways, Russia in 1900 was still in the Middle Ages, rather than a modern state on the threshold of the twentieth century.

SOURCE B

Nicholas II and his family. This picture was taken shortly before the First World War.

Russia was a deeply religious, Christian country. The link between the Russian Orthodox Church and the Tsar was close. The Church did much to uphold the authority of the Tsar, and in return had considerable political influence. However, Russia's size and diversity meant that many people were not members of the Orthodox Church. There were countless religious sects, not to mention the other

Christian churches and the different religions of the many nationalities that lived within the Russian Empire.

SOURCE C

Russian peasants in their village, mid-1890s.

When Tsar Nicholas II came to the throne in 1894, he seemed to have much to offer. He was hard working, sincere and devoted to his family. However, he also had significant weaknesses. He was indecisive and found it hard to concentrate on governing the country. Worst of all, he was not able to respond to the great pressures for change that were building up in Russian society. Instead, he wanted to turn the clock back to an imaginary golden age when the Tsar's power was unchallenged. Just when Russia needed a flexible and imaginative leader, it got a Tsar who saw any modernisation as a threat to his own position.

Russian society before the First World War

Russia was not so much a country as an empire stretching from Europe to the Far East, from the frozen Arctic in the north to the Mediterranean climate of the Black Sea coast in the south. It was inhabited by a bewildering variety of different nationalities. Less than half of the population was Russian, so Tsars faced constant demands for independence from Finns, Poles, Ukrainians and many other national groups. The country's sheer size meant that the people had little sense of national identity. There was strong loyalty to the Tsar, but most people identified with their own region, town or village rather than with the Russian Empire. By 1900 there were a few railways, but for most people travel outside their own immediate neighbourhood was unthinkable.

The countryside

Russia was a rural society in which most people were poor. Most of the population were peasants, who lived off the land. Until the mid-nineteenth century, most peasants were subject to a form of slavery known as serfdom. Their lives were totally controlled by the landowner whose land they lived on. Then, in 1861, the serfs were freed and allowed to have some land, but they had to pay for it. Often they did not receive enough land to make a decent living. The village elders retained control over the lives of individual peasants, who were not free to leave the village without permission. Peasants were allocated strips of land in fields as they had been for centuries. This was very inefficient and made it difficult for new methods to be introduced.

Although Russia could usually produce enough food for its people, bad harvests sometimes brought famine. By the end of the nineteenth century, there was a growing realisation that agriculture needed modernising. The population was growing fast and there was not enough land to go round.

QUESTION

Read Source A.
Do you find Nicholas's reaction to his father's death surprising? Explain your answer.

Landowners

Although there was poverty in the Russian countryside, there was also great wealth. The great landowners held on to large estates when the serfs were freed, and they were the most important and influential members of rural society. They provided local government in the villages, and acted as a link between the common people and the wishes of the Tsar. However, their position was becoming less secure. Tensions were increasing between them and the peasants, who wanted the land for themselves. Many landowners ran their estates inefficiently and frittered away their wealth. But the better landowners realised that they had to run agriculture more efficiently. These landowners dominated the local councils, called *zemstvos*, which began to press the Tsar for reforms.

The cities

By 1900 the process of industrialisation had begun. Towns and cities grew as people moved from the countryside to look for work in the factories. Russia now had an industrial working class – people who would previously have been peasants, but who now lived and worked in the cities. After Witte became Minister of Finance in 1892, the government encouraged the development of industry, and during the 1890s the Russian economy grew faster than that of any other country in Europe. This growth continued, more slowly, right up to the outbreak of war in 1914. A whole range of industries – mining, iron and steel, textiles, oil, food processing, railways – came into being. Foreign investment flooded in to take advantage of the boom. Within a single generation, Russia became a significant industrial power.

However, the pace of development created problems. Living and working conditions in the industrial cities were appalling. The

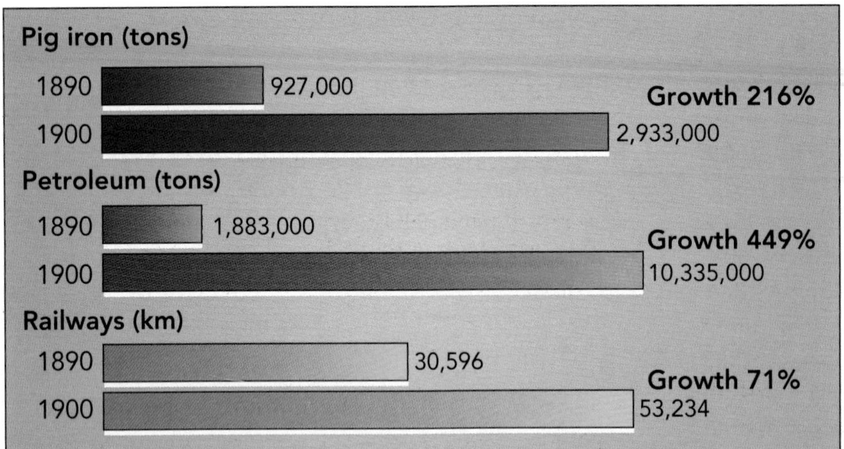

Growth of industrial production, 1890–1900.

SOURCE D

The peasants were of two kinds and it seemed to me that they were two completely different breeds.

Some were well bred, important looking, with greasy hair, fat paunches and shiny faces. They were dressed in embroidered shirts and caftans of fine cloth. These were the ones who were later called kulaks. They felled trees for new homes in the thick woods that had until recently been grandfather's. The Peasants' Bank gave them credit. In their houses there were geraniums on the window sills, and the smell of rich buns cooking. Their sons grew into energetic and ambitious men.

Other peasants wore sandals, dressed in rags, bowed fawningly, never came further than the door, and had faces that had lost all human expression. They were undersized, and often lay in the ditches near the state-owned wine shop. Their children did not grow because they were underfed. Their wives always seemed to be in the final months of pregnancy, and in their homes broken windows were stopped up with rags. Calves and hens were kept in the corners. There was a sour stench.

A Russian writer remembers the peasants on her grandfather's estate around 1900.

SOURCE E

A boarding house for industrial workers, Moscow 1911.

government did little to protect workers from exploitation. There were few controls on child labour, industrial injuries were common, and employers paid starvation wages. In these circumstances, dissatisfaction and unrest increased among the workers. The cities turned into breeding grounds for revolutionary ideas.

Opposition to the Tsar

Russia had a tradition of revolutionary violence against the monarchy. This was not surprising in a country where opposition to Tsarist rule was illegal. In 1881 revolutionaries had assassinated Tsar Alexander II. The rapid social and economic changes of the late nineteenth century gave great opportunities for revolutionary groups to spread their ideas among the working people.

The most important of Russia's revolutionaries were Marxists. These were followers of Karl Marx (1818–83), the German socialist, who in his book *Das Kapital* had described how capitalism would collapse and be replaced by communism. Although they claimed to be struggling to bring about a workers' revolution, these revolutionaries came mainly from Russia's emerging middle classes. They were constantly harassed by the Tsar's secret police, and many spent years in exile, either in Siberia or abroad.

QUESTIONS

1 Read Source D.
How do you think the two different groups of peasants felt towards each other?

2 Look at the people in Source E.
- **a** What do you think these people had in common with the poor in the countryside?
- **b** How were their lives different from those of the poor in the countryside?

3 What were the main features of Tsarist rule over Russia?

4 How was Russia changing by the end of the nineteenth century?

The revolutionaries argued a lot among themselves. At a conference in London in 1903, the most important of the revolutionary groups, the Social Democratic Party, split into two factions. These were known as the Bolsheviks (who took their name from the Russian word for 'majority'), led by Lenin, and the Mensheviks (the 'minority', although they tended to attract more support in later years). The Bolsheviks believed in seizing power at the first opportunity, while the Mensheviks believed in co-operating with other groups to improve the lives of working people.

Other revolutionary groups had their own distinctive ideas. Unlike the Social Democrats, who believed that the revolution would happen through the struggles of the industrial workers, the Social Revolutionaries (SRs) believed that revolution in Russia would have to be based on the peasants and their struggle for land.

Repression

By the early years of the twentieth century, it was clear to many Russians that change was needed to deal with the country's problems. But the Tsar's response to this was more repression. The Okhrana, the secret police, were extremely effective in dealing with opposition groups. An extensive network of informers made sure the authorities knew about the revolutionaries' plans. Many opponents of the regime were tortured, imprisoned or even executed. Disturbances in the countryside were crushed by troops. However, Tsarist repression was not just a matter of violence towards the opposition. Newspapers were heavily censored, and even the activities of moderate organisations like the *zemstvos* were strictly controlled so that there was no criticism of the Tsar.

The Russo-Japanese War, 1904–5

In February 1904, war broke out between Russia and Japan over Manchuria, an area of northern China. Russia had built an important extension of the Trans-Siberian railway in the area. People thought that Russia would have little difficulty dealing with Japan, which was regarded as a second-class power. But the war showed the weaknesses of the Tsar's regime. Fighting in the Far East placed Russia at a severe disadvantage, and the Japanese quickly gained the upper hand. The Russian Baltic Fleet was ordered to sail half way round the world to take part in the fighting. In the North Sea, the Russian commanders opened fire on the British fishing fleet by mistake. When they finally faced the Japanese fleet at the battle of Tsushima in May 1905, the Russians were decisively defeated. The Tsar was forced to ask the Japanese for peace.

SOURCE F

A picture from the early twentieth century showing the structure of Russia's society before 1917. The workers at the bottom are commenting on each of the classes above them, from top to bottom. 'We work for them while they – dispose of our money – pray on our behalf – eat on our behalf – shoot at us.'

How did the Tsar survive the 1905 revolution?

Defeat in the war helped to spark off revolution in Russia. The Tsar was so shaken by events in Manchuria that he relaxed control at home. In November 1904 a national congress of *zemstvos* representatives met in St Petersburg and demanded political reform. Strikes broke out in several industries, with the workers demanding better conditions. The growing wave of discontent was finally turned into a revolution by the events of Bloody Sunday (9 January 1905).

A mass demonstration had been organised in St Petersburg. The plan was to march to the Winter Palace to present a petition to the Tsar, asking for better wages and working conditions. Father Gapon, a priest well known for his work with trade unions in the city, led the procession. The marchers were orderly and unarmed, but when they reached the palace they were fired on by troops. Soldiers also attacked marchers elsewhere in the city. Around 200 people were killed.

Bloody Sunday did great damage to the relationship between the Tsar and his people. The respect that he had previously enjoyed was lost. There were riots and strikes in towns throughout the country, and peasants turned against the landowners in the countryside. At first, the disturbances lacked leadership and co-ordination. Even so, the authorities found it impossible to restore control. In an attempt to calm the situation, the Tsar promised to allow a parliament (called the Duma) to meet, but refused to give it any real power. The offer was ignored.

As the strikes grew worse, it became clear that the Tsar might be overthrown. In June, there was a mutiny on board the Russian battleship *Potemkin*. 2000 people were massacred as troops opened fire on crowds supporting the mutineers in the port of Odessa. The mutiny showed that the Tsar was in danger of losing the support of his armed forces.

As the months passed, the opposition began to organise more effectively. Even middle-class professionals like doctors and teachers formed unions to demand reforms. Later a political party, the Constitutional Democrats, or cadets, was set up to pursue these aims. By August 1905 a Peasants' Union had been formed, which organised strikes of agricultural workers. Most important of all, however, was the emergence of organisations representing the industrial working classes.

SOURCE G

A French picture drawn shortly after Bloody Sunday in 1905.

SOURCE H

The Cossack [a mounted soldier] circled round him and, shrieking like a woman, waved his sabre in the air. Swooping down from his dancing horse, he slashed him across the face, cutting him open from the eyes to the chin. I remember the strangely enlarged eyes of the worker and the murderer's face, blushed from the cold and the excitement, his teeth clenched in a grin and the hairs of his moustache standing up on his lip. Brandishing his bloody sword, he let out another shriek and with a wheeze, spat at the dead man through his teeth.

The writer Maxim Gorky was in the crowd on Bloody Sunday. Here he describes the death of one of the demonstrators.

Stolypin

Peter Stolypin was the dominant political figure after the 1905 revolution. As Prime Minister until his assassination in 1911, he provided Russia with firm leadership and a sense of direction. His policies were a mixture of repression and reform. The Okhrana was given free rein to crush opposition. By 1907 almost all the revolutionary leaders were in prison or had been forced to flee the country. Stolypin's greatest challenge, however, was to deal with Russia's agricultural problems.

He encouraged peasants to take loans from the Peasant Bank to purchase land, and he made it possible for individuals to consolidate their strips of land into separate farms. By 1917 around one-third of all peasant households in European Russia lived on their own farms. However, most peasants were cautious and resisted these changes. Those peasants who showed initiative and wanted their own farms were often prevented by the conservatism of the rest of the village.

Throughout the year, workers had been setting up councils, called soviets, in their workplaces. Then, in October, the St Petersburg Soviet was set up. This was like an alternative city council, to which all the workplace soviets sent representatives. Similar soviets were organised in other cities. The St Petersburg Soviet was deeply influenced by revolutionary ideas and quickly organised a general strike, which brought the whole economy to a standstill. For a while, it seemed as if the soviet was the only organisation in the country with any authority. It published its own newspaper, organised food supplies, set up law courts and established an armed force.

The Tsar realised that he would have to make concessions. He issued the October Manifesto, promising to turn Russia into a constitutional monarchy and give people more freedom. An elected parliament (Duma) would have the power to make laws. In this way, the manifesto promised the middle classes what they had been demanding. They now became alarmed by the extremism of the workers and peasants, which threatened to undermine social order completely. By issuing the manifesto, the Tsar had succeeded in splitting the opposition.

In fact, the Tsar had acted in bad faith. As soon as circumstances permitted, he was determined to recover as much power as he could. First, he moved against the St Petersburg Soviet and arrested its leaders. Then, in December, an uprising organised by the Moscow Soviet was bloodily repressed. In little more than a month, the 1905 revolution had collapsed. Now the country waited to see what would become of Nicholas's promised reforms.

Attempts at reform before the First World War

The Tsar had survived, but only by making concessions. It was not possible to go back on all of these, however much the Tsar wanted to. Russia had changed and the Tsar's power was no longer absolute. Russia was now to have an elected parliament. What remained uncertain was how much power Nicholas would allow it.

The first Duma met in 1906. Most of the revolutionaries refused to take part in the elections, so the assembly was dominated by the Cadets. There were also around 200 peasant representatives. The Duma demanded further concessions from the Tsar, including the confiscation of all large estates (so the land could be distributed to the peasants), making government ministers responsible to the Duma, and the abolition of the Tsar's emergency powers, including

QUESTIONS

1 Why did revolution break out in Russia in 1905?

2 What were the soviets and why were they important?

3 How did the Tsar manage finally to defeat the 1905 revolution?

use of the death penalty. The Tsar simply dissolved the Duma. When some Duma members called on people to refuse to pay their taxes, they were arrested. A second Duma, which met in 1907, ended the same way. This time the revolutionaries did stand for election, which meant that the Duma was even less acceptable to Nicholas, so again was dissolved. By the time the third Duma met, later in 1907, the government had changed the rules so that more of its supporters, such as rich landowners, were elected. This produced a Duma more to the Tsar's liking. It was dominated by Octobrists – moderates who thought that the concessions in the October Manifesto were sufficient. Any opposition in the Duma was kept within limits acceptable to the Tsar.

It would be easy to conclude that Russia's experiment with parliamentary democracy was a sham. However, the existence of the Duma was evidence that the Tsar's position had changed. For the first time, people could share in Russia's political life. The Duma could debate important issues, people could read about them in the newspapers, the Tsar's ministers went to the Duma to answer questions – in short, there was more freedom and openness than before. Russia had begun to evolve towards a more modern, democratic system of government. Who knows where this might have led had it not been for the interruption of the First World War?

SOURCE I

Peter Stolypin in 1909.

How far was the Tsar weakened by the First World War?

When Germany declared war on Russia, on 1 August 1914, everybody expected the war to be short. Russia, like the other nations dragged into the war, was totally unprepared for lengthy hostilities. Once it became clear that the war would last months or even years, the Tsar's government soon proved incapable of responding to the challenge.

Like the war on the Western Front, fighting on the Eastern Front quickly became bogged down, with neither side capable of striking a decisive blow. A Russian advance into East Prussia in autumn 1914 was halted by the Germans at Tannenberg, where 100,000 Russians were killed. An offensive in 1916, organised by General Brusilov, made significant advances against the Austrians. However, with German help, the Austrians halted the Russian advance. This was the Russians' last success. Their armies eventually collapsed in 1917, but this was due more to poor leadership, inadequate supplies and political developments at home, than to defeat in the field.

SOURCE J

We impose on the government the obligation:

1 To grant ... civil liberty based on the principles of freedom of conscience, speech, assembly and association;
2 To include in the work of the Duma those classes which until now have been deprived of the right to vote, and to extend in the future the principle of universal franchise;
3 To establish the rule that no law shall acquire force without the approval of the Duma, and that the people's representatives shall have an effective opportunity to supervise the legality of the actions of the authorities.

The three articles of the October Manifesto.

Around 15 million peasants were drafted into the Russian army, but their removal from agricultural production had surprisingly little effect. Throughout the war, Russia produced ample food. As with other supplies, the problem was not so much production as transport. Russia's railway system was unable to keep the country and its armies supplied, and the incompetence of the Tsarist administration made matters worse. Almost from the start of the war, Russia's cities experienced food shortages. These became severe as the war continued, and were an important factor in the outbreak of revolution in 1917.

Russia was a poor country and could not afford a long war. The government was forced to borrow from other countries, and to print money. At the same time, its income from taxes was falling. In August 1914 the government prohibited the sale and manufacture of alcohol. Previously around a quarter of all its revenues had been raised from alcohol sales. The result was inflation – Russia's money lost value. As wages failed to keep up with price rises, workers became worse off.

Meanwhile, industry geared production to the war effort. The output of heavy industries, such as iron and steel, increased, as did that of armaments and clothing manufacturers with government contracts. Other industries suffered badly – many factories closed as consumers could not afford their goods. Job losses, higher prices and food shortages began to have an impact on the urban population. Among the working class, enthusiasm for the war quickly disappeared, to be replaced by discontent and waves of strikes. The strikers were disillusioned with the Tsar and wanted the war to end.

The discontent of the working class was matched among the middle class. When the Duma met in August 1915, a 'Progressive Bloc' of moderate politicians was formed to press the Tsar for a representative government that could unite the country and fight the war more effectively. The Tsar rejected the idea and dissolved the Duma after a month. Just as in 1905, war was creating a situation in which more and more of the Tsar's subjects were losing faith in his ability to rule the country.

SOURCE K

Russia, hard put to it for munitions and arms, was unable to equip masses of the trained men that it had ready, and it was the custom to have unarmed troops in the rear of any action, who could be used to fill gaps and take up the weapons of the dead. Men were flung into the firing line without rifles, armed only with a sword-bayonet in one hand and a bomb in the other. That meant fighting, desperate fighting, at the closest quarters. The Russians had to get at all cost within range to throw their bombs, and then they charged with cold steel.

An American historian, writing in 1922, describes the effects of supply shortages on the Russian army in 1915.

The Tsar blessing his troops, 1914.

SOURCE L

By 1916, the Tsar was alienated from almost all Russians apart from his immediate advisers. In 1915 he had taken over personal command of Russia's armies. In reality he was no more than a figurehead, but the task took him away from Petrograd (as St Petersburg had been renamed at the start of the war) and left government in the hands of Tsarina Alexandra and her favourite, Rasputin. It would be hard to imagine a more disastrous situation.

Rasputin

Rasputin was a Siberian peasant, who had a reputation as a mystic or holy man. He also claimed to be a healer, and it was in this capacity that he was introduced to the royal family in 1905. The Tsar's only son, Alexis, suffered from haemophilia – a condition that prevented his blood from clotting. The slightest accident could therefore be fatal to him. Rasputin seemed able to control the condition, and thereby gained the friendship of the Tsar and Tsarina. Despite stories of Rasputin's sexual adventures among the female nobility, the royal family stayed loyal to him.

Until the Tsar's departure for the front in 1915, Rasputin was not allowed any political influence. Once the Tsar was away, however, the Tsarina came increasingly to rely on Rasputin's advice. Ministers were appointed and sacked according to his whims. There were rumours that Rasputin was the Tsarina's lover, and that they were plotting to make peace with the Germans. The story sounded all the more plausible given the Tsarina's German background.

Eventually, a group of noblemen decided to kill Rasputin. One night in December 1916, Rasputin went to the home of Prince Yusupov for dinner. An initial attempt to poison him failed, and Rasputin was finally shot and killed. His body was dumped in one of the city's canals. The identity of the conspirators was common knowledge, but none received serious punishment. Too many people, including many close to the royal family, were involved in the plot. The murderers had killed Rasputin not because they wished to harm the Tsar, but because they were his friends. And by December 1916 the Tsar did not have many friends left.

A Russian cartoon showing Rasputin with the Tsar and Tsarina.

SOURCE M

QUESTIONS

1 Why were Russia's armies unsuccessful in the First World War?

2 How did the war affect Russia?

3 Look at Source M.
What is the cartoonist's opinion of the relationship between Rasputin and the royal family?

4 Why was Rasputin's influence over the royal family so harmful?

SOURCE N

Soldiers in Petrograd supporting the revolution, March 1917.

Why was the revolution of March 1917 successful?

By early 1917 all the ingredients for revolution existed in Russia. The Tsar had lost all support, the government was incompetent, the army faced defeat and its loyalty was suspect. Perhaps most important of all, workers in the capital, Petrograd, were struggling to survive on insufficient food and pay. Strikes were common. Yet when the revolution did take place, it came as a surprise and was unplanned.

In early March 1917 a particularly severe wave of strikes hit factories in Petrograd. By 10 March, industry had almost come to a halt. Unusually mild weather encouraged demonstrators on to the streets. At first the authorities were able to control the crowds peacefully, but finally the soldiers were ordered to fire on the demonstrators. They were reluctant to do this because many shared the grievances of the workers. The men of the Petrograd garrison had only recently been drafted into the army. Most were peasants. They, too, were hungry and cold, but they also deeply resented the harsh discipline of military life. By the 12th, many in the garrison had begun to mutiny. Government buildings were attacked and ransacked. Within a few hours, Petrograd was in the hands of rioting mobs.

Tsar Nicholas was unaware of how serious the situation had become. He was at his country estate outside Petrograd, receiving over-optimistic reports from his ministers. He made matters worse by ordering the dissolution of the Duma. This served only to persuade the middle classes to join the revolution. As the disorder continued, it seemed that only a Duma government could bring the disturbances to an end. Delegates of workers and soldiers began to pledge their support for a Duma government. Although the Duma had refused the Tsar's order to dissolve, its leaders were reluctant revolutionaries. Whether they liked it or not, however, they were emerging as Russia's new rulers.

The Petrograd Soviet re-emerged on 12 March. From the start, the soviet asserted its authority over the armed forces. Many of its members were soldiers who had mutinied against their officers. They wanted to make sure that they would not suffer reprisals. The soviet's famous Order Number One stated that soldiers did not need to obey any orders from the Duma that went against orders of the soviet. It set up soldiers' committees throughout the armed forces, which did much to undermine the authority of officers, and abolished the harsher aspects of military discipline. The government had lost command of its own armed forces.

SOURCE O

It is obvious that His Majesty and you do not realise what is going on here. One of the most terrible revolutions has broken out, which it will not be so easy to quell. The troops are completely demoralised; they not only disobey but murder their officers. Hatred of Her Majesty [the Tsarina] has reached extreme limits. I must inform you that what you propose is no longer adequate. Troops everywhere are joining the people and the Duma, and there is a definite, terrible demand for abdication.

A telephone conversation between one of the Duma's leaders and one of the Tsar's advisers in March 1917. The Tsar had just agreed to permit a new Duma government to be formed.

SOURCE P

The roof had already fallen in, the fire crackled between the walls, and red and yellow wisps like wool were creeping out of the windows, throwing a sheaf of paper ashes up into the black sky of the night. No one made any attempt to extinguish the fire. A tall stooping man in a shaggy sheepskin hat was walking about like a watchman. He stopped and asked in a dull voice, 'Well, it means that all justice is to be abolished, doesn't it? Punishments all done away with, is that it?' No one answered him.

The writer Maxim Gorky witnessed the events of the March revolution. Here he describes the burning of the Palace of Justice by the rioters.

On 15 March, Nicholas finally decided to abdicate. His generals advised him that the situation was hopeless and that any attempt to put down the revolution using troops from outside the capital would only make matters worse. As his son Alexis was so young, he chose to give the throne to his brother Michael. But the time for monarchy was past. The people had decided that Nicholas would be the last Tsar. When moderates in the Duma spoke in favour of a constitutional monarchy, they were openly jeered.

So, on 14 March, the Duma announced the formation of a Provisional Government, which would rule until elections could be held for a new Assembly. The first Prime Minister was Prince Lvov and the government had members from several parties, including a Social Revolutionary, Kerensky, as Minister of Justice. It immediately announced a series of reforms, which transformed Russia overnight into one of the freest countries in the world. There was freedom of the press, the vote for all adults over 21, abolition of the death penalty and full civil rights for all regardless of religion.

The revolution seemed to have triumphed, but worries remained. How would the new government cope with the real problems of Russian society – the war, the land question, food supplies? And how would it deal with the power of the Petrograd Soviet, which had better claims to represent those who had really made the revolution – the workers and soldiers of Petrograd?

QUESTIONS

1 Why did revolution break out in March 1917?

2 Why was the Tsar so easily overthrown?

3 Read Source O.
What does this source tell you about
a the Tsar
b the Duma
during the March revolution?

4 Read Source P.
What does this source tell you about the nature of the March revolution?

How did the Bolsheviks gain power, and how did they consolidate their rule?

In the four years after the overthrow of the Tsar in March 1917, Russia suffered further revolution, civil war and widespread devastation. The result was the emergence of the world's first communist state. Under the leadership of Lenin, the Bolsheviks overthrew the Provisional Government in the revolution of November 1917. They then defeated their enemies in a bloody civil war that lasted until 1920. How did a small revolutionary socialist party manage to seize and hold on to power, when the great majority of the Russian people did not support it?

The Russian calendar

Until February 1918, Russia used the old calendar, which was thirteen days behind the rest of Europe. Then the new Bolshevik government decided to bring Russia into line. This means that alternative dates exist for events before the changeover. This book uses the new dates, but you might come across the alternatives elsewhere. This makes a particular difference with the second revolution of 1917, which is known either as the October or the November revolution.

How effectively did the Provisional Government rule Russia in 1917?

The Provisional Government was intended to hold power only temporarily, until elections took place. Then a new assembly would decide Russia's future. But many important decisions could not wait for the elections.

- Russia was still at war. The strains this imposed had been a major reason for the Tsar's downfall. Would Russia make peace or fight on?
- In the countryside, the peasants were seizing landowners' estates and murdering those who resisted. Would the government approve land reforms to try and bring this anarchy to an end?
- The people in the cities did not have enough to eat. Would food supplies be restored?

The Provisional Government failed to deal with almost all the challenges it faced. It was a divided government, made up of members from several different parties. The middle-class Cadets wanted to restore order and create a parliamentary democracy. The socialists wanted to push the revolution further and transfer more land to the peasants. During its short life the government split several times as ministers quarrelled among themselves. In July, Kerensky replaced Lvov as Prime Minister. There were many other ministerial resignations and changes, which showed the government's divisions and weakened its authority.

The one major decision that the government did take was disastrous. It decided to continue the war. When Russia's armies were ordered to take the offensive in June, the soldiers' response was wholesale desertion and mutiny. Henceforth it was clear that Russia had lost the war against Germany. In many areas, the army ceased to offer any resistance to the German advance.

SOURCE A

The Provisional Government has no real power of any kind and its orders are carried out only to the extent that the soviet of workers' and soldiers' deputies permits it. The soviet controls the most essential levers of power, insofar as the troops, the railways, and the postal and telegraph services are in its hands. One can assert bluntly that the Provisional Government exists only as long as it is permitted to do so by the soviet.

From a letter written by a minister in the Provisional Government, March 1917.

QUESTION

Read Source A.
Does this source prove that the Provisional Government never had a chance of success?
Explain your answer.

Attempts were made to improve food supplies to the cities. Rationing was introduced, and the government established a monopoly over grain trading. But transport problems continued, and the peasants were reluctant to sell their grain for increasingly worthless money. As the winter of 1917 approached, Russia's cities faced food shortages again. Meanwhile, the government lacked the political will to deal with the land issue. Its policy was simply to leave the problem for the new Assembly.

The soviets

The re-establishment of the Petrograd Soviet was followed by the setting up of workers' and soldiers' soviets across Russia. The Petrograd Soviet co-ordinated the activities of the national soviet movement, and it soon became obvious that its authority over the working classes, coupled with the military force it possessed through its Order Number One, made it an alternative national government. Although at first it was prepared to work with the Provisional Government, it became increasingly hostile as it fell under the influence of revolutionary groups, particularly the Bolsheviks.

Proceedings of the Petrograd Soviet, to which there were often over a thousand delegates, were noisy, chaotic and unproductive. Its power was exercised through a small executive committee, which the Bolsheviks targeted for takeover. As the power of the Provisional Government ebbed away during 1917, so control of the soviet became more important. Whoever controlled the soviet could also control Russia.

QUESTIONS

1. What was the Provisional Government?
2. Why was it weak?
3. In what ways was the Petrograd Soviet more influential than the Provisional Government?

SOURCE B

A Russian soldier trying to stop colleagues from deserting in 1917.

The growing power of revolutionary groups

The Mensheviks and Social Revolutionaries (SRs) welcomed the March revolution because it offered the chance to improve the conditions of the workers and peasants. They were prepared to work with the Provisional Government, and some of them even served as ministers. The Bolsheviks, however, were more hostile, particularly after the return of Lenin (see page 192) from exile in April.

According to Lenin's *April Theses*, the Bolsheviks' must overthrow the government as soon as possible and seize power for themselves. They could then set up a socialist dictatorship. To bring this about, it was essential to gain control of the Petrograd Soviet. Some Bolsheviks disliked the idea of destroying the results of a revolution that had only just occurred, but they fell into line with Lenin's policy. The Bolsheviks' propaganda machine swung into action in support of the slogans 'All Power to the Soviets!' and 'Peace! Bread! Land!'

At first, the Bolsheviks were only a minority in the soviet. When an All-Russian Congress of Soviets was held in June, the Bolsheviks had fewer than half the delegates of either the Mensheviks or the Social Revolutionaries. However, the Bolsheviks were not tainted by co-operation with the Provisional Government, and as the weakness of the government became clearer, the Bolsheviks grew bolder.

The July Days

In July, demonstrations organised by the Bolsheviks turned into an uprising against the government. This took the Bolshevik leaders by surprise. Lenin was on holiday when the disturbances started, and could not make up his mind whether to try and seize power or not. Petrograd was entirely in the hands of rioting mobs, but without leadership they could achieve nothing. Lenin's hesitation gave the government time to move loyal troops into the city, and the 'July Days' came to a rapid end.

SOURCE C

Troops open fire on the crowds during the July Days.

The Kornilov affair

These developments were a setback to the Bolsheviks. Hundreds of them were arrested, and Lenin, whom the government had shrewdly accused of being a German spy, was forced into hiding in Finland. Yet they did no long-term damage to the Bolsheviks because the Provisional Government's fortunes continued to decline. In an attempt to restore discipline in the army, in July Kerensky appointed General Kornilov as commander-in-chief.

He promised Kornilov support in restoring the authority of officers over the ordinary soldiers. However, Kerensky soon began to have second thoughts, as this was bound to bring him into conflict with the soviets. On the other hand, Kornilov had powerful support among the middle and upper classes, who expected him to restore some control in Russia. On 8 September, Kornilov, assuming he had Kerensky's support, ordered his troops to occupy Petrograd, as a first step to breaking the power of the soviet. Kerensky had to choose whether to back this move or not. He lost his nerve and dismissed Kornilov from his command.

Kornilov decided to revolt against Kerensky's government, but he had no chance of success. His troops had no enthusiasm for overthrowing the soviet, and were easily persuaded by the Bolsheviks to abandon the attempt. The revolt collapsed with no fighting, but it revealed how totally the Provisional Government depended on the soviet for its survival. During the revolt, many Bolshevik leaders were released from gaol as part of the soviet's preparation to resist an attack by Kornilov's men. It was clear that the Bolsheviks had most influence over the soldiers and workers who would have done the fighting. These 'Red Guards' were practically the Bolsheviks' private army.

By late September, the soviets in most major cities, including Petrograd and Moscow, were in Bolshevik hands. Now it was just a matter of selecting the most favourable moment for a takeover of government. Under Trotsky, one of Lenin's closest colleagues, the Military Revolutionary Committee of the Petrograd Soviet was actively planning to seize power.

QUESTIONS

1 Why did the revolutionary groups become stronger after the March revolution?

2 What effect did
   a the July Days
   b the Kornilov affair have on the fortunes of the Bolsheviks?

3 Look at Source D. Why do you think the Provisional Government published this poster?

SOURCE D

A Provisional Government poster. It shows a Russian soldier backed by workers and soldiers in a heroic continuation of the war.

Why were the Bolsheviks able to seize power in November 1917?

By mid-October 1917, Lenin's main concern was to ensure that, when Kerensky's government collapsed, the Bolsheviks would take over. Moderate groups like the Mensheviks still had influence in the Petrograd Soviet. However, Lenin believed that if the Bolsheviks could seize power by force, the other groups would not have the courage to fight them. Lenin returned from hiding in Finland, and took control of the Bolsheviks' preparations. The decision was taken to stage an armed uprising, but no date was fixed.

Meanwhile, Kerensky seemed as out of touch with reality as the Tsar in his last days. He ordered the Petrograd garrison to the front, to take part in the fighting against the Germans. The soldiers had no

SOURCE E

A painting showing Lenin addressing a crowd at Finland station in 1917.

Lenin

Lenin was born Vladimir Ilich Ulyanov in 1870, but later changed his name to avoid arrest by the Tsarist police. Lenin's background was not working class, but he was attracted to radical politics from a young age, and was expelled from university for taking part in student protests. His brother was executed for his part in a plot to assassinate Tsar Alexander III.

Lenin spent some time in internal exile in Siberia, then left Russia for western Europe, where he developed the revolutionary ideas that were later known as Marxism-Leninism. Marx had taught that once industrial capitalism had developed, workers would be exploited by their bosses and would rise up in a class struggle against them. But Lenin believed that a party of determined revolutionaries could seize power and introduce communism. After the split of the Social Democrats in 1903, Lenin was one of the most important leaders of the Bolsheviks. He returned to Russia too late to take part in the revolution of 1905 and was forced back into exile in Switzerland, where he remained until 1917. Then, after the March revolution of 1917, the Germans helped him to return home. They hoped he would weaken Russia's war effort. Lenin was smuggled across Germany on a train, reaching Petrograd in April.

Lenin's great contributions to the Bolsheviks before 1917 were his intellectual leadership and his determination. He was a tireless propagandist, churning out dozens of books and articles, and founding *Pravda*, the Bolshevik Party newspaper. He was difficult and prickly towards those who disagreed with him. But nobody doubted his ability. His insistence on discipline and his refusal to compromise made the Bolsheviks the most formidable force in Russian revolutionary politics.

SOURCE F

The defenders of the Provisional Government: the Women's Battalion outside the Winter Palace.

desire to sacrifice themselves, so they mutinied and declared themselves loyal to the Bolsheviks. On 3 November, Trotsky's Military Revolutionary Committee announced that it had taken command of the garrison. Lenin was still worried that the working classes of Petrograd would not support a Bolshevik takeover.

During 6–7 November 1917, Red Guards occupied government buildings throughout the city. Most citizens of Petrograd did not even notice that a revolution was taking place. Kerensky fled the city and the rest of the Provisional Government barricaded themselves in the Winter Palace. The palace was guarded by a few thousand soldiers, including young cadets and around 200 women soldiers, but they gradually slipped away. Late in the evening of the 6th, guns opened fire on the palace. Finally, around 2 a.m. on 7 November, Bolsheviks entered the palace and arrested the ministers inside. This event was later transformed by Bolshevik propaganda into an epic assault against determined defenders.

Their determination and the weakness of the Provisional Government had enabled the Bolsheviks to seize power. On hearing of the Bolsheviks' takeover, the Mensheviks and SRs in the Petrograd Soviet reacted just as Lenin had hoped. They walked out in disgust, leaving the Bolsheviks in total control. The way was clear for Lenin to form a Bolshevik government. However, although the Bolsheviks controlled the capital, their authority was minimal in the rest of the country. In Moscow, loyalist troops fiercely resisted the takeover, and the city was not in Bolshevik hands for another ten days. Before long the Bolsheviks' enemies would begin to fight back, and then the true level of their support would become clear.

SOURCE G

We were under assault. Defence was useless. Victims would be sacrificed in vain. The door flew open. A soldier rushed in, his face excited, but determined. 'What does the Provisional Government command? Defend to the last man? We are ready if the Provisional Government so orders. All the entrances have been taken. Only these quarters are still guarded. What does the Provisional Government command?'

Surrender!' we shouted. 'Hurry! Go and tell them! We want no blood! We surrender!'

The soldier left. The whole scene, I believe, took no more than a minute.

A member of the Provisional Government describes the surrender of the Winter Palace to the Bolsheviks.

Bolshevik rule

The Bolsheviks had won support from working people with their slogan 'Peace, Bread, Land!' Once in power, Lenin moved quickly to put these policies into effect. On 8 November, two important decrees were issued. The Decree on Peace called for a fair and honourable end to the war. The Decree on Land announced that all landowners' estates would be confiscated, and the land made available to the peasants. Private ownership of land would be abolished. A huge redistribution of land to the poorer peasants began immediately.

Getting Russia out of the war was more difficult. The Germans would not give Lenin the fair and honourable peace that he wanted. The Russian armies had disintegrated; most of the soldiers had deserted and gone home. The Germans' peace terms were so harsh that most of the Bolsheviks wanted to reject them, but Lenin accepted them to save the revolution. By the Treaty of Brest-Litovsk, signed in March 1918, Russia lost huge areas on its western frontier – Finland, Poland, the Baltic States, the Ukraine and half of Belorussia. This was half of its territory in Europe, including some of its richest agricultural land. Half of Russia's grain and coal production was lost.

Meanwhile, Bolshevik power over the economy was increased. Although the Bolsheviks allowed small businesses to stay in private hands, workers' control of factories and mines was introduced. Banks and many of the larger factories, particularly in the textile and metal industries, were taken into state ownership. Under the combined pressures of state control, inflation and lack of consumer spending, production collapsed. The peasants also refused to release their grain for sale. The Bolsheviks quickly faced an economic crisis.

Unlike his predecessors, Lenin took the necessary steps to deal with his opponents. He closed down all opposition newspapers, and in December 1917 he set up a secret police force called the Cheka. At first, the Cheka concentrated on criminals and saboteurs, but before long any opponent of the Bolsheviks was at risk of murder, torture or imprisonment.

Lenin allowed the long-promised elections for a new parliament to go ahead. The Constituent Assembly finally met on 5 January 1918. Although the vast majority of Russians voted for socialist parties, the Bolsheviks gained only 24 per cent of the vote, against the SRs' 38 per cent. The Assembly met for only a day. When it would not accept Bolshevik control, it was dispersed by Bolshevik troops. Demonstrations in favour of the Assembly were met with bullets. From now on, Russia was ruled by the Bolshevik Party (renamed the Communist Party in March 1918). Whoever controlled the party controlled Russia.

QUESTIONS

1 What was the storming of the Winter Palace?

2 What changes did the Bolsheviks introduce when they came to power?

3 Look at Source H.
What did the cartoonist think of the Whites?

Why did the Bolsheviks win the civil war?

As the communist dictatorship emerged, its enemies began to organise resistance. The opposition included many different groups – monarchists, middle-class liberals, landowners, industrialists, army officers, Mensheviks and Social Revolutionaries, not to mention foreign powers hostile to the existence of a communist state. By comparison, the communists were a small group. They had strong support among industrial workers, but little or no party organisation in rural areas.

Before long, anti-communist armies, known as the Whites, were put together under the command of Tsarist generals: Yudenich in the north-west, Kolchak in Siberia, and Denikin, Alexeev and Kornilov in the south. Czech prisoners of war being transported out of the country on the Trans-Siberian Railway formed the Czech Legion and joined the Whites. The British landed troops in the far north at Archangel and Murmansk, and the French at Odessa in the south. The communists seemed to be surrounded.

However, the opponents of the communists had many different aims and ambitions. By contrast, the communists were united and single-minded. The Whites were also geographically split, unable to help each other or co-ordinate their efforts. The communists held a central position, which included Russia's two greatest cities – Moscow (the new capital) and Petrograd. They were also under a single command.

At first, the communist forces were weak. Then Trotsky created a Red Army that was capable of defeating the Whites. His ruthlessness, determination and charisma made him ideal for the task.

SOURCE H

A communist cartoon of 1919. The three dogs are labelled Denikin, Kolchak and Yudenich.

The Russian Civil War.

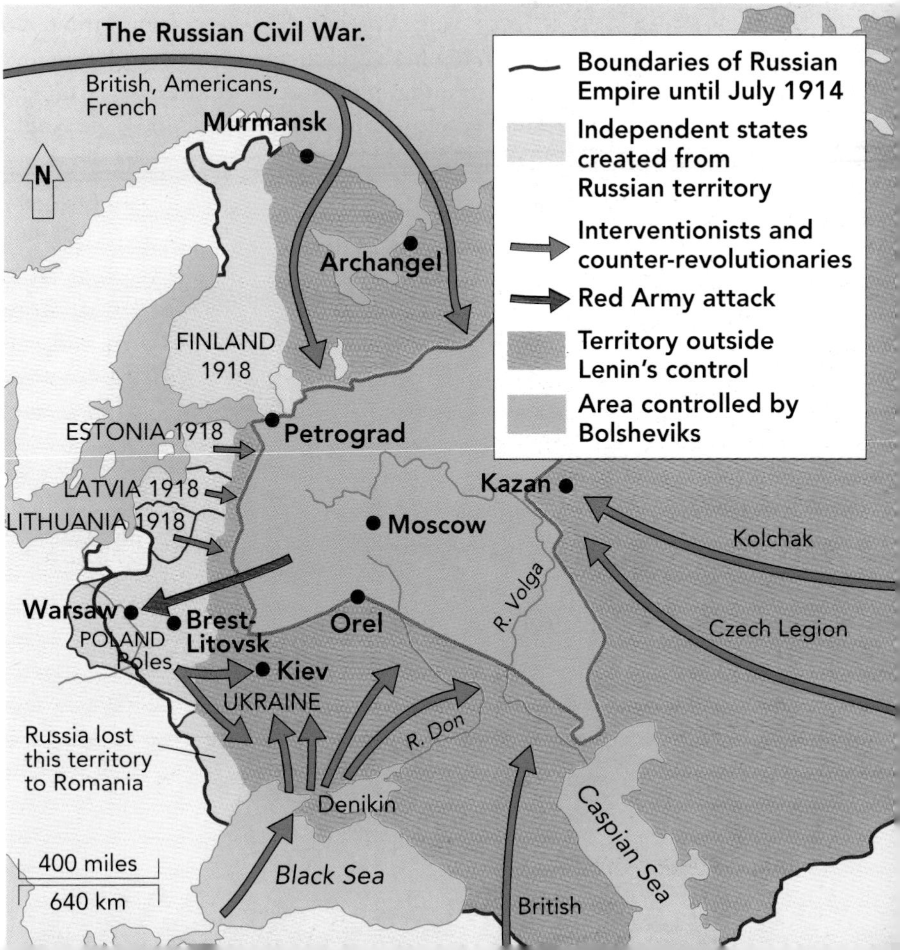

Although Trotsky had joined the Bolsheviks only in 1917, he had quickly established himself as Lenin's second-in-command and had organised the November revolution. Now he used his talents to ensure that the revolution would survive. Trotsky encouraged officers from the Tsar's old army to join the Reds, and took their families hostage to make sure they stayed loyal. He established fierce discipline, including summary executions for deserters. He travelled around by train to meet the troops and spur them to ever-greater efforts. By 1920 the Red Army comprised around 5 million men.

War Communism and the Red Terror

The Russian economy had to provide the army with the supplies it needed. To achieve this, War Communism was introduced. The state took over all aspects of the economy, nationalising more industry and controlling the production and distribution of all goods. Normal economic life came to an end. Once the army's needs were catered for, there was little spare for anyone else. Food supplies were so poor that Lenin sent Cheka units (the Bolshevik secret police) into the countryside to seize peasants' grain stores.

Then, following an assassination attempt on Lenin in August 1918, a 'Red Terror' was launched. The Cheka was unleashed on the regime's opponents. Mass executions were used to intimidate any possible opposition. Members of the middle and upper classes were automatically suspected of being disloyal to the communists. As many as three-quarters of a million people may have been murdered by the Cheka during the three years of civil war.

Among the victims were the ex-Tsar and his family. Exiled to Ekaterinburg in the Ural Mountains, the royal family posed an obvious threat to the communists, particularly if they fell into the hands of the Whites. When the Whites' advance brought them near to where the Tsar was held, it was decided to kill the whole family. On the night of 16–17 July 1918, the Tsar, his wife, their son and four daughters, with some of their servants, were taken into the cellar of the house where they were staying and shot. Their bodies were buried in a nearby forest, where they remained undiscovered until the fall of communism in 1991.

The end of the civil war

The fighting in the civil war was exceptionally bloody and vicious, with countless atrocities committed by both sides. The Whites enjoyed early successes, but were never able to co-ordinate their attacks or agree on a single commander. After Germany's defeat in November 1918, the Allies lost one of the main reasons for intervening in the civil war. Within a year, most of their troops had left Russia. Their intervention had allowed the Reds to portray the Whites as unpatriotic.

SOURCE I

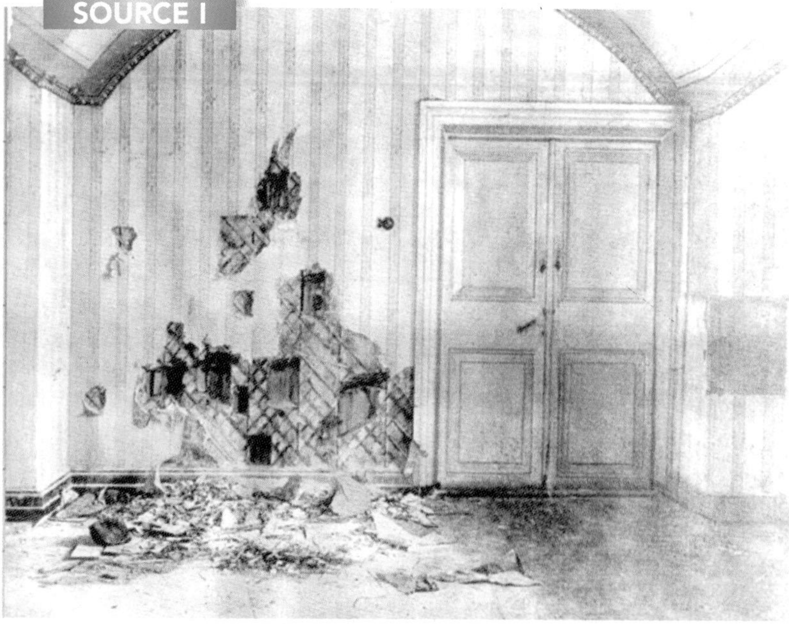

The cellar in which the Tsar and his family were murdered. The damage to the wall caused by the shots that killed the royal family can be seen clearly.

SOURCE J

My next visit to Moscow took place after the fall of Ekaterinburg to the Whites. Talking to a colleague, I asked in passing, 'Oh yes, and where is the Tsar?'
'It's all over,' he answered. 'He has been shot.'
'And where is the family?'
'And the family along with him.'
'All of them?' I asked, apparently with a touch of surprise.
'All of them,' he replied. 'What about it?' He was waiting to see my reaction. I made no reply.
'And who made the decision?' I asked.
'We decided it here. Lenin believed we shouldn't leave the Whites a live banner to rally around, especially under the present difficult circumstances.'

I did not ask any further questions and considered the matter closed. Actually the decision was not only convenient but necessary. The execution of the Tsar's family was needed not only in order to frighten, horrify and dishearten the enemy, but also in order to shake up our own ranks to show there was no turning back.

In 1935 Trotsky published his diaries. Here he describes how he heard of the Tsar's death.

In addition, the fear that a White victory would mean losing the gains of the revolution helped to keep the peasants on the communists' side. The Reds gradually took the upper hand and were finally victorious in 1920. Around half a million people had been killed.

The Russian people suffered terribly in the civil war. The economy collapsed, money became almost worthless, and people had to rely on the black market for food. In 1920, industrial production was less than 20 per cent of the 1913 level, and the harvest produced only 60 per cent of the normal amount of grain. During the civil war, famine and disease claimed 8 million lives and the communist regime became a cruel dictatorship. Even many of the communists' supporters were beginning to wonder if the ideals of the revolution were being forgotten.

The Kronstadt rising

In March 1921 the sailors at Kronstadt, the naval base near Petrograd, mutinied. They demanded an end to the communist dictatorship, and to the forced seizures of grain. The Kronstadt sailors had previously been supporters of the communists. Trotsky had called them 'the pride and glory of the Russian Revolution'. If they were prepared to mutiny, anyone could. On 16–17 March, 50,000 Red Army troops were sent to storm the Kronstadt fortress. 10,000 of them died in the attack, but finally the sailors were defeated. More than 2000 of those captured were executed without trial. A further 8000 of them fled to Finland. Thousands more were sent to labour camps. That spring, peasant revolts were crushed with similar ruthlessness, although the famine spreading through Russia's countryside did as much to break the peasants' resistance.

QUESTIONS

1. What advantages and disadvantages did the communists have in fighting the civil war?
2. What were 'War Communism' and the 'Red Terror'?
3. Read Source J. Do you trust Trotsky's account of how he found out about the Tsar's death?

How far was the New Economic Policy a success?

Against this background of economic crisis and political opposition, Lenin introduced the New Economic Policy (NEP). He realised that a real change of policy was needed if disaster was to be avoided. The peasants had to be given an incentive to produce more food, and to release their produce for sale. This could be done only if state control was relaxed and the peasants were allowed to make a profit on what they produced. In other words, capitalism and a free market had to be brought back. For many communists this was a bitter humiliation, but they realised that their survival depended on it.

Once peasants and shopkeepers could work for a profit, goods appeared for sale. New small businesses and market stalls sprang up in the towns. A whole new class of profiteers emerged, who did well out of the new freedom to trade. They were known as 'NEP men'. The government kept control of the country's largest industries, but elsewhere capitalism made a comeback. Many workers who had supported the revolution thought the NEP was a betrayal of socialism. Lenin saw it as the only way to get the country back on its feet. Communism could wait a little longer.

By 1926–7 production had returned to pre-1914 levels. The recovery happened as much in heavy industry as in agriculture, so it probably owed much to the years of stability and peace. But the introduction of the NEP was particularly significant in the countryside, where peasant disturbances became a thing of the past. Even so, progress was not quick enough for those of Lenin's colleagues who wanted to transform Russia into a modern, industrialised state.

Lenin's death

In May 1922 Lenin suffered a stroke, which was followed by two further strokes in December 1922 and March 1923. After these, he was no longer able to play an active role in political life. A struggle for the leadership began, which would not be finally resolved for several years. On 21 January 1924, Lenin died. The first phase of the communist transformation of Russia was over.

SOURCE L

A Soviet cartoon from 1927. A NEP man has become so wealthy that he has to fill a tax return in. Members of the aristocracy (who do not pay tax) are laughing at him.

SOURCE K

> First of all, the workers and peasants need freedom. They do not want to live by the decrees of the Bolsheviks.
>
> We demand the liberation of all arrested socialists and non-Party working men; abolition of martial law; freedom of speech, press and assembly for all those who labour; free elections of factory committees, trade unions and soviets.

Demands of demonstrators in Petrograd, February 1921.

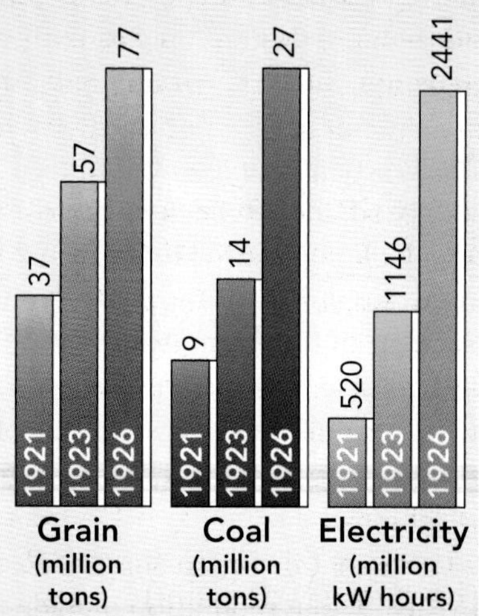

The increase of production under the NEP.

How did Stalin gain and hold on to power?

After Lenin's death, Stalin emerged as the dominant figure in the Communist Party. This did not happen immediately. A struggle for power between Stalin and Trotsky went on for several years before Stalin was finally able to triumph in the late 1920s.

Under Stalin, the Soviet Union (a shortened version of Union of Soviet Socialist Republics – USSR – as Russia became in 1922) underwent another period of revolutionary turmoil. He was determined that it would become a modern, industrialised nation. To achieve this he had to force the Soviet people into submission. Peasants lost their land and were made to work on collective farms. Ambitious Five-Year Plans were devised to build up heavy industry. Everything was sacrificed to the aim of higher production.

Any opposition, real or imagined, was ruthlessly crushed by the secret police. Finally, by the mid-1930s, Stalin was strong enough to turn on his rivals within the Communist Party itself. Show trials were held at which many of the most famous of the 'Old Bolsheviks' admitted imaginary crimes. They, and countless thousands of less well-known Soviet people, died in Stalin's Great Purges. Within little more than a decade, Stalin's fearsome dictatorship succeeded in making the Soviet Union one of the world's great industrial powers, but the human cost of this achievement was appalling.

Why did Stalin, and not Trotsky, emerge as Lenin's successor?

Lenin was only in his mid-fifties when he died. He had been the outstanding personality in the communist government, and he left no accepted successor. The most obvious candidate was Trotsky, who was certainly the best known of the communist leaders after Lenin. He was extremely able and could claim both to have organised the Bolshevik takeover in 1917 and to have saved the Bolshevik government by organising the Red Army during the Russian Civil War. He also had a reputation outside the Soviet Union, having been Commissar for Foreign Affairs. However, he never really had much chance of taking over. The most important reason for this was that the other communist leaders were determined to prevent it. Most of them disliked him. They found him arrogant, and they suspected his cleverness. They also mistrusted him for not joining the Bolsheviks until 1917. He had lost support by wanting to persist with War Communism when the NEP was introduced. Finally, in a country with a long and deep tradition of anti-Semitism, it was Trotsky's disadvantage to be Jewish.

Stalin was almost the complete opposite. If Trotsky was the hare, then Stalin was the tortoise. Although he had been a prominent Bolshevik for many years, he had no outstanding achievements to his

SOURCE A

He was very pale and shaken. He poured out a glass of water, gulped it down and said, 'You know, I have never seen anything like this! This was worse than anything! And why, why did Trotsky say this? Stalin will never forgive him!' Piatakov was so upset that he was unable to relate clearly what had happened. When Trotsky at last entered the dining room, Piatakov rushed at him asking, 'But why, why, have you said this?' With a wave of his hand Trotsky brushed the question aside. He was exhausted but calm. He had shouted at Stalin 'Grave-digger of the Revolution'. We understood that the breach could not be healed.

An account of the aftermath of the Politburo meeting in 1926 at which Trotsky was sacked. The author, a well-known communist, met Piatakov, a member of the Politburo, immediately after the meeting.

name. He came from a working-class background and had none of Trotsky's brilliance. He was an organiser and a loyal supporter of Lenin, who after 1917 rose steadily into positions of influence in both the Communist Party and the government. By 1924, Stalin was little known outside the Soviet Union, but during his time as Commissar for Nationalities, and then as General Secretary of the Communist Party, he had taken the chance to appoint his supporters into positions of influence.

Before his death, Lenin had begun to be concerned by Stalin's ambition, and relations between the two men deteriorated sharply. In the documents known as his political testament (or will), Lenin warned that Stalin had concentrated enormous power in his hands and suggested that he should be removed as General Secretary. Yet the other communist leaders were willing to ignore Lenin's doubts in their efforts to keep Trotsky out. They were worried by Trotsky's radicalism and his belief in 'permanent revolution', which they saw as opposition to the NEP. They preferred Stalin's belief in 'socialism in one country', which seemed to mean allowing the Soviet Union to move towards socialism more slowly.

In the aftermath of Lenin's death, Stalin with Zinoviev and Kamenev, two other communist leaders who had ambitions of their own, emerged and took power. Trotsky was accused of trying to split the Communist Party and take power for himself. He was unpopular enough that few were willing to defend him against these charges.

One by one, Trotsky was stripped of his positions of power. He ceased to be Commissar for War in January 1925, lost his place on the Politburo (the Soviet Union's cabinet) in 1926, and was removed from the Central Committee of the Communist Party in October 1927. Shortly afterwards he was expelled from the party and sent into internal exile. Finally, in 1929 he was forced out of the country and eventually into exile in Mexico.

No sooner had Stalin manoeuvred Trotsky out of power than he turned on Kamenev and Zinoviev, who were becoming worried about Stalin's ambition and the degree of control he had over the party. By 1926 they had joined Trotsky in a 'United Opposition' to Stalin's policies. However, they too found that Stalin could rely on his supporters to deal with those who challenged him. Both were sacked from their party and government posts, and although Stalin allowed them back into the party in 1928, their power was broken. By 1928 Stalin had emerged as the sole leader of the Soviet Union. However, the struggle for power had left him deeply suspicious of his colleagues.

SOURCE B

A Soviet cartoon from 1927. Kamenev, Trotsky and Zinoviev are portrayed as members of a family, showing their alleged closeness.

QUESTIONS

1 Read Source A.
Why do you think the writer was so sure that the split between Trotsky and Stalin would not be healed?

2 Look at Source B.
What was the opinion of the cartoonist about the struggle for power in the Soviet Union? Explain your answer, referring to details of the cartoon.

SOURCE C

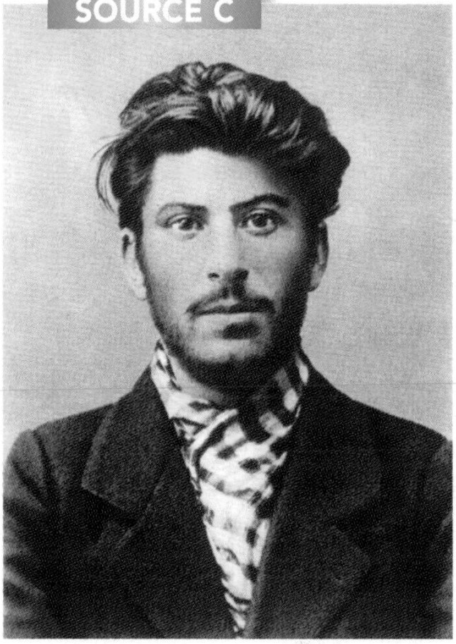

A police photograph of Stalin taken around 1900.

Stalin

Stalin was born in Georgia, in the far south of the Russian Empire. He was one of the few Bolshevik leaders from a working-class background. His father was a shoemaker. Stalin was born Josif Dzhugashvili, but used false names once he became a professional revolutionary. He finally settled on 'Stalin' ('man of steel') in 1913.

As a young man, Stalin trained as a priest at the seminary in Tbilisi, but he was expelled when he became involved with local revolutionaries. In his late teens he joined the Social Democratic Party and devoted himself to revolutionary activities, including bank raids to raise party funds. He was arrested several times and exiled to Siberia. When not in prison, he was constantly being sought by the secret police. It was a hard and secretive way of life, and it left Stalin with a taste for conspiracy and subterfuge.

Although Stalin played little part in the 1905 revolution, he gradually became well known in the Bolshevik Party. Lenin trusted him and made him editor of the party newspaper, *Pravda*. He was imprisoned during the First World War, and was only able to return to Petrograd from Siberia in February 1917. By then he was one of the leaders of the party, and he was prominent in organising the Bolsheviks during 1917. Once they took power, he held a succession of posts that enabled him to build a strong position. By the time of Lenin's death, he was well placed to deal with his rivals in the struggle for leadership.

Why did Stalin launch the 'purges'?

The struggle for power after Lenin's death demonstrated that the leaders of the Communist Party disagreed strongly with each other on a variety of issues. By the end of the 1920s, Stalin had got the better of Trotsky and his other rivals, but he was still concerned that sooner or later his enemies would attempt to overthrow him. This was particularly worrying to Stalin during the terrible violence that accompanied the collectivisation and industrialisation campaigns of the early 1930s.

Since it had come to power, the Communist Party had periodically 'purged' its membership, getting rid of those who were suspected of being disloyal. Now Stalin began to plan a purge of the top levels of the party, to deal with his rivals once and for all.

By 1934 Stalin believed that his opponents were planning to replace him with Kirov, the young and popular boss of the Leningrad section of the party. He secretly ordered Yagoda, head of the NKVD (the secret police), to have Kirov murdered. When this was done, Stalin used it as an excuse to turn on his enemies. Zinoviev, Kamenev and others were accused of being involved in the murder. They were arrested, put on trial and in January 1935 sentenced to long gaol terms.

This was not enough for Stalin. Later that year he accused Zinoviev and Kamenev – along with Trotsky, who was now living in exile – of being spies for foreign countries. When in 1936 the NKVD provided evidence that their supporters had been in contact with Trotsky, they were put on public trial on charges of terrorism. Despite being promised their lives if they confessed, when they did so, they were shot. This trial, in August 1936, marked the start of the 'Great Terror'. For two years the people of the Soviet Union were subjected to a campaign of state terror in which the secret police hunted Stalin's enemies, real and imagined, in all sectors of Soviet society. Literally nobody was safe.

The Great Terror

Stalin launched the terror by sacking Yagoda, whom he thought had shown insufficient enthusiasm for rooting out traitors among the 'Old Bolsheviks' – the other leading communists who had played a part in the struggles that brought the Communist Party to power. He replaced him with Yezhov, who showed none of Yagoda's restraint. Two further show trials of Old Bolsheviks followed during 1937–8, with a procession of senior party figures admitting a variety of imaginary crimes against the state. Those who were unwilling to confess were persuaded by torture and threats against their families. Almost all were found guilty and shot, although a few cheated Stalin's plans by committing suicide.

During 1937 Stalin turned against the generals of the Red Army. According to the confessions forced out of them, they were plotting to overthrow Stalin. So many senior officers were shot during the purges that when Germany attacked the Soviet Union in 1941, the Red Army was seriously short of competent leaders. This was a major factor in the initial success of the German invasion.

The secret police

Yezhov's NKVD was the instrument that Stalin used to crush any potential opposition. They arrested and shot hundreds of thousands of people in all walks of life. Even the official Soviet records admit that nearly 700,000 people were executed during the Great Terror of 1937–8. Stalin took a personal role in many of these murders. The NKVD prepared lists of victims for Stalin to authorise. He approved nearly 400 of these lists, containing around 40,000 names.

SOURCE D

An American cartoon about the Moscow show trials.

By 1938 the terror was beginning to have severe effects on the economy. The sheer numbers of managers, officials, supervisors, foremen, officers, scientists and engineers who had disappeared meant that many organisations were close to collapse. Stalin decided to end the Great Terror. As a final twist, however, he first turned against the NKVD. Many of its senior officers were shot and Yezhov was replaced by another of Stalin's cronies, Beria. At a party meeting the following year, Stalin personally denounced Yezhov. He was arrested and finally shot in 1940.

In 1940 Stalin's agents finally caught up with Trotsky, whom they had been hunting for years. In exile in Mexico, Trotsky was murdered with an ice pick by an NKVD agent. The death of Stalin's greatest enemy marked the true end of the Great Terror. Every one of Stalin's rivals was now dead.

What methods did Stalin use to control the Soviet Union?

The Soviet Union under Stalin was a totalitarian police state. No opposition was tolerated and any sign of independence or individualism was crushed. All Soviet people lived in fear of arrest by the secret police, the NKVD. There was no rule of law, no human rights. Once arrested, prisoners could be beaten, tortured or even murdered. Many of those arrested simply disappeared and nobody knew what had happened to them. Often people had no idea why they had been arrested. It was not necessary to have committed a crime – being suspected of disloyalty to Stalin's state was enough. In these circumstances, few dared to oppose him. The terror was at its worst towards the end of the 1930s, but it was a feature of Soviet life throughout Stalin's years as dictator.

Informers

The NKVD used an army of informers in schools, factories and farms – even children were encouraged to inform on their parents. A young peasant boy, Pavlik Morozov, who informed on his father for hoarding grain, was held up as an example to others. Russians ceased to talk freely with anyone they did not know well, and even then it was a risk. The poet Osip Mandelstam read his friends a poem in which he criticised Stalin. One of them informed on him, and he was sent into internal exile for three years.

SOURCE E

In school, Volodya began to notice that some classmates would become strangely sad and withdrawn. They stood alone in the play-yard; they were never called on in class; they sat silent and shrivelled at their desks. After some time they disappeared. Somehow everyone in the school knew not to talk about them. Volodya told his father about the vanishing students. His father explained that a new organisation of secret political police had been established – the NKVD. It was made up of people who were clever and more talented than those in the previous political police forces, and was uncovering spies, enemies and traitors who had not been discovered before. Those uncovered were being arrested and sent away, along with their families.

One day Volodya saw his father remove some books from a shelf and toss them into the garbage; the authors had been arrested. Another time his father took down a history of the Russian Civil War and proceeded to ink out the photographs of Trotsky and others. In school Volodya's teachers told the students to tear out the pictures of this or that person who had just been discovered to be an imperialist spy. Volodya thought it a good thing that all these spies and traitors were being uncovered; now the Soviet Union would live safely without enemies.

An account of the impact of terror on daily life in the Soviet Union.

QUESTIONS

1 Look at Source D.
Is this cartoon reliable evidence that those accused in the show trials were guilty? Explain your answer using details of the cartoon.

2 Read Source E.
What can you tell from this source about life in the Stalinist Soviet Union?

3 Why do you think senior communists pleaded guilty to spying for foreign countries?

Prison camps

Victims of the police state who were not executed for their 'crimes' were usually sent to labour camps. These were located in some of the most inhospitable and remote areas of the Soviet Union. The prisoners were used as slave labour on many of the prestige projects of the Five-Year Plans. Up to a quarter of a million convicts worked on the White Sea Canal, of whom nearly two-thirds did not survive the appallingly harsh conditions. When the canal was finished, it was too shallow to take the large ships for which it had been intended.

Inside the camps, conditions were brutal. Prisoners were expected to work in all weathers, even in the icy conditions of the Soviet winter. They were never given enough food. Camp guards had complete power over the inmates and routinely used violence against them. It has been estimated that around 3 million people were imprisoned in the camps by 1939. During Stalin's time in power, several million convicts probably died in the camps from hunger, cold and exhaustion.

Propaganda

In the Soviet Union under Stalin, people were not allowed to think for themselves. They were told what to think by the state. Education served the purposes of the Communist Party. Pupils were taught the communist version of history and even communist theories about science. Propaganda influenced almost every aspect of life. The mass media – radio, films, newspapers – were all controlled by the state and could only produce approved material. The state's messages were everywhere, at work, at school, on posters in the streets. Even artists were brought under state control. They were only allowed to produce work that reflected the glorious achievements of communism.

SOURCE F

NOUS SOMMES BIEN HEUREUX

This cartoon was published in France during the 1930s.

QUESTION

Study Source F.
What was the cartoonist's opinion of Stalin's rule over the Soviet Union?

The cult of personality

The most important propaganda message of all was that Stalin was the greatest genius of his time. The Soviet people were taught to believe that Stalin was all-powerful and all-knowing. They came to look upon him as a god. His image was everywhere – in photographs and paintings, and on statues – and writers competed to produce the most glowing tribute to his achievements. In a set of eight records made of one of his speeches, the last record consisted solely of applause! In a single speech, one local party leader managed to call Stalin 'Leader of Genius of the Proletarian Revolution', 'Supreme Genius of Humanity', 'Leader of Genius of the Toilers of the Whole World' and 'Inspirer and Organiser of the Victory of Socialism'.

The flood of pro-Stalin propaganda, never balanced by a single word of criticism, created a kind of hero worship known as the cult of personality. It helps to explain why one of the most evil dictators the world has known was revered by many of the Soviet people.

How complete was Stalin's control over the Soviet Union by 1941?

The events of the 1930s left Stalin as the unchallenged ruler of the Soviet Union. He had destroyed all opponents or potential opponents. He was the only member of Lenin's Politburo (cabinet) left alive by 1941. All the others had died, been killed or committed suicide. The Communist Party had been repeatedly purged at all levels. The armed forces had lost almost their entire officer class. The secret police itself had been purged. The combined effects of terror, propaganda and official perks for the privileged few ensured that the Soviet people stayed subservient. Rarely in history has one person held such absolute power over the lives of the people he ruled.

Nonetheless, there were limits even to Stalin's power. In a huge country like the Soviet Union, it was impossible for the government to control everything. Open opposition was rare, but local officials and managers would often fail to co-operate with orders that they did not like. This is part of the reason why Stalin tried to purge these groups so thoroughly in 1937–8.

The scale of the social and economic changes in the Soviet Union during the 1930s also made it difficult for the government to control all aspects of people's lives. Petty crime and hooliganism were common in the cities; divorce and abortions were also rising fast. There were plenty of signs that, in their private lives, people behaved as they wanted rather than as the government wished.

Stalin's state was totalitarian at an official level, dealing ruthlessly with any signs of opposition and murdering opponents of the regime. However, in practice, Stalin found it much harder to control the lives of millions of ordinary people.

SOURCE G

The cult of personality: Stalin as father figure. The little girl's father was later shot. He was one of the victims of the purges.

What was the impact of Stalin's economic policies?

Stalin was determined to modernise the Soviet Union. He worried that if the country did not build up its economic strength then sooner or later the capitalist powers would invade and destroy the achievements of communism. He believed the New Economic Policy was working too slowly. It would take decades to transform the Soviet Union into a modern economy. Stalin felt that something much quicker was needed.

Starting in 1928 he forced profound changes on agriculture and industry. Collectivisation was introduced in agriculture. The state took over agricultural production, forcing peasants to work together on huge collective farms. This change was fiercely resisted by the peasants, who wanted to farm their own land. It took much violence to force collectivisation through, and agriculture was left permanently weakened.

Industry was modernised through a series of Five-Year Plans. The state set targets and priorities for industry, and with massive investment and superhuman efforts from the Soviet Union's workers, within a decade the Soviet Union had become a major industrial power.

Why did Stalin introduce the Five-Year Plans?

Stalin saw his plan to industrialise the Soviet Union as a matter of life or death. If his plans failed, he believed the Soviet Union's enemies would crush it. The Soviet Union was still a rural, backward country. Stalin was determined that within ten years it would be transformed into one of the world's great industrial powers. To do this he used Five-Year Plans. Gosplan, the state planning bureau, was given the task of devising the plans. The idea was that the state would decide targets for industrial production, and would use central planning and direction of the nation's resources to achieve the priorities set out in each plan.

SOURCE A

The Dnieper Dam, built during the Five-Year Plans.

The first Five-Year Plan was launched in 1928. It focused on building up heavy industries like coal and steel. To encourage Soviet workers, a propaganda campaign urged them to complete the plan in just four years. The targets set were tough, but enormous increases in production were achieved. However, the successes of the first plan also brought social and economic problems. The Soviet Union's transport system could not cope with all the extra goods produced. Towns and cities had to grow rapidly to house the expanding industrial workforce. The demand for housing, food, clothing and transport was so great that the system came close to collapse. The increase in production was being paid for by a decline in living conditions. Rationing was introduced to make sure that industrial workers had enough to eat, and towards the end of the plan targets had to be cut as the frantic growth of industry slowed down.

The second Five-Year Plan (1933–7) concentrated on improvements in transport and in the production of machinery. More investment was allocated to consumer goods. However, this does not mean that heavy industry was neglected. By the time of the second plan, many of the big projects of the first plan were in operation, and this enabled three times as many new enterprises to be set up during the second plan as in the first. It was a time for consolidation and building on the gains of the first plan.

The third Five-Year Plan (1938–41) ran for only three and a half years before it was interrupted by war. More and more resources were transferred into defence-related industries. The success of the plan was also undermined by the purges, of which many of the Soviet Union's most important planners and managers became victims. Nonetheless, when war broke out in 1941, Germany was attacking the world's second greatest industrial power, rather than the backward, agricultural nation the Soviet Union had been only fifteen years earlier. This transformation had been brought about by the Five-Year Plans.

The modernisation of Soviet industry

During the 1930s the Soviet Union became an industrialised nation. New factories were built, enormous dams and canals were constructed (often using the inmates of prison camps as slave labour), whole new towns sprang up, and the mineral resources of new areas were developed. An endless barrage of propaganda urged workers to make ever-greater efforts. Workers who produced more than the targets set for them were praised and given rewards. A whole movement was started urging workers to follow the example of Alexei Stakhanov, a coal miner, who was claimed to have exceeded his work quota by 1400 per cent in cutting 102 tons of coal in 6 hours.

This frenzied atmosphere produced problems as well as successes. The emphasis on targets meant that factory managers were much more concerned with quantity than quality. There was also a great shortage of skilled workers, so managers had great trouble keeping essential staff. They had to resort to giving higher wages and other incentives to certain workers. However, most workers were treated much less well. There was tough discipline, with fines for those who were late or absent without permission. Often, in the rush to boost production, safety standards were ignored, and accidents were common.

How successful were the Five-Year Plans?

It is impossible to be precise about the Soviet Union's achievements during the Five-Year Plans. Statistics released by the Soviet government, both at the time and later in the communist era, were completely unreliable. Not only did the government lie for propaganda purposes, but it was also being lied to by thousands of its own party bureaucrats and industrial managers with an interest in boosting their production figures.

To confuse matters more, even western historians who have tried to estimate the Soviet Union's progress during the thirties have reached differing conclusions. Nobody disputes that the Soviet Union was rapidly modernising and industrialising during these years, but the real questions are exactly how much was achieved, and whether similar progress could have been made without using the enormous power of the state.

Why did Stalin introduce collectivisation?

By the end of the 1920s it was clear to Stalin that the NEP would not transform the Soviet Union into a modern industrial state. The biggest problem was agriculture. The land was farmed by peasants who used traditional, inefficient methods and were reluctant to change. The NEP had encouraged the peasants to produce more, but it was the peasants who profited from this, and not the state.

Stalin had two reasons for wanting change in the countryside:

- He needed to get his hands on the peasants' grain so that he could sell it for export. Using the foreign currency this would raise, he could buy vital equipment for industry.
- The industrial workers needed cheap food. If the peasants controlled grain sales, they would try to keep the price high. This meant that industrial workers would need to be paid more.

Stalin planned to set up collective farms, on which peasants would work together under government control. The collectives would be large, modern and efficient. The government would be able to keep as much of the produce as it needed, and pay the peasants for their labour.

Throughout the Soviet Union the peasants rebelled against collectivisation. Stalin responded by sending the army and the secret police into the countryside to terrorise the peasants. Stalin claimed that it was only the richer peasants (called 'kulaks') who were resisting, for their own selfish reasons. This was an attempt to stir up class hatred between different groups of peasants, but it showed Stalin's ignorance of peasant life. By the end of the 1920s there were few true kulaks left – most had already perished during the civil war. Most peasants in Soviet villages were now very similar in wealth and status.

The truth was that the great majority hated Stalin's collectivisation policy, and would never willingly co-operate with it. In the end, they were forced to. The soldiers simply seized all stocks of grain. If the peasants handed these over voluntarily, they starved. If they did not, and attempted to hide their stocks, they were shot. Rather than lose all they had, most peasants killed all their animals and ate them while they could. In no time at all, famine loomed.

SOURCE B

Peasants demonstrating against the kulaks. Their banner says 'We demand collectivisation and the extermination of the kulaks as a class.'

Faced by these terror tactics, about 14 million households had joined collectives by the beginning of 1930. Unknown millions of peasants were forced off the land and went to swell the ranks of industrial workers in the cities. The more unfortunate peasants were labelled as kulaks and sent off to labour camps. In the atmosphere of terror which gripped the countryside, many were prepared to accuse their neighbours of being kulaks to save their own skins.

When collectivisation was complete, Stalin could treat the peasants as slave labour. In the Ukraine during 1932–3, Stalin demanded targets higher than the total amount of grain produced. The targets were rigorously enforced, and the peasants left to die of starvation. Those who tried to save themselves or their families by stealing some food from the collective were executed. Nowadays it is accepted that Stalin deliberately caused this famine to crush the resistance of the peasants. Probably around 5 million died as a result.

How successful were Stalin's economic changes?

Stalin always claimed that it would have been impossible to modernise agriculture without collectivisation. Some modernisation occurred. Machine tractor stations were set up to help mechanise agriculture. Farms began to specialise in certain products, which made it easier for new ideas and techniques to be adopted. Collectivisation also served Stalin's purpose. He was able to gain control of the Soviet Union's agricultural produce, and sell it for the hard currency he desperately needed.

However, collectivisation dealt agriculture a devastating blow, and it did not quickly recover. Production remained low. Not until the mid-1950s did production reach the levels that had been achieved before the First World War.

Some historians have even begun to question whether collectivisation brought the benefits Stalin wanted. The direct costs of introducing machinery and the slump in production meant that the Soviet Union was on balance worse off because of Stalin's collectivisation policy. The appalling human cost may have been completely pointless.

SOURCE C

The collective farm policy was a terrible struggle. It was fearful. Four years it lasted. It was absolutely necessary for Russia, if we were to avoid periodic famines, to plough the land with tractors. We must mechanise our agriculture. Only collective farms with workshops could handle tractors. We took the greatest trouble explaining to the peasants. It was no use arguing with them. It was all very bad and difficult, but necessary.

Stalin talking to Winston Churchill in 1942.

By 1936 collectivisation was almost complete. However, Stalin's aim of treating the peasants like agricultural wage labourers had not quite been achieved. Even under collectivisation peasants needed an incentive to work. So most peasants now worked together on co-operative farms known as *kolkhoz*. These handed over to the state whatever produce was demanded, but if there was any profit left over, the peasants could share it. In addition, they were allowed small private plots of land for their own use, and could sell what they produced in the *kolkhoz* market. The number of peasants working on state farms (*sovkhoz*) for wages was much smaller.

QUESTIONS

1 What were the Five-Year Plans and why were they introduced?

2 Were the Five-Year Plans successful?

3 What was collectivisation?

4 What effects did it have on Russian agriculture?

5 Look at Source B.
Why do you think this photograph was taken?

6 Read Source C.
Do you believe what Stalin said to Churchill? Explain your answer.

How were the Soviet people affected by these changes?

1 Ethnic minorities

Under Stalin the non-Russian nationalities of the Soviet Union were at first allowed to preserve their own cultural traditions and identities. However, this tolerant approach was replaced after 1934 with a policy of Russification. Ethnic minority groups were now encouraged to see themselves as Soviet citizens rather than as separate nationalities. The Russian language was made a compulsory subject in the school curriculum. Russian was also made the official language of state organisations like the army. Russians were encouraged to migrate into non-Russian areas, and non-Russian graduates were deliberately found jobs inside Russia itself. In this way the concentration of national groups in their own regions was diminished.

During the purges, the leaders of ethnic minority groups were a particular target for persecution. In addition, the Soviet government's disapproval of religion had harmful effects on the Muslim central Asian nationalities of the Soviet Union. The government pressurised them to close Islamic schools and hospitals, and thousands of mosques were forced to close.

It seems ironic that Stalin, a Georgian himself, should have been so willing to undermine the cultures of the Soviet Union's national groups. However, his suspicion of anything different or individual made the nationalities an obvious target. His purpose was to make them forget their own traditions, language and culture, and to turn them into loyal Soviet citizens.

2 Women

The socialist revolution in the Soviet Union was supposed to give women the same freedoms as men. Soviet propaganda always showed women as equal partners in the struggle to build the communist state. In the early years after the revolution, abortion and divorce were made easy to obtain, but under Stalin more conservative social values were re-established. The state encouraged marriage and parenthood, and awarded medals to women who had more than ten children. Sexual promiscuity was frowned upon, and the automatic right to abortion was abolished.

In the world of work, Soviet women were given equality with men, and the distinctions between men's and women's work were much less marked in the Soviet Union than in other countries. The problem for Soviet women was that while they were given opportunities to work – indeed, were expected to work – traditional male attitudes in social and home life still held sway, with domestic chores regarded as the women's responsibility. Soviet society remained male-dominated, and it is noteworthy that not a single woman held high office during Stalin's years in power.

3 Social groups

Soviet society in the 1930s consisted of three major groups.

- **Peasants.** These were now working in socialist agriculture, typically on a *kolkhoz*. In general, they were resentful of what had been done to them and would have found it hard to survive without the private plots of land they were allocated. Agriculture remained in deep depression, and life in the countryside was grim.
- **Industrial workers.** By the end of the 1930s, life was beginning to improve. Wages were still lower than in 1928, but more people were working, so most families had a little more to spend. The chaos and disruption of the First Five-Year Plan gave way to a few years of greater stability. Housing was poor, but rationing came to an end, and a few more consumer goods became available. Free education and medicine were made available to more and more of the population.
- **The social elite.** The managers, scientists and party bosses had a much higher standard of living than the workers did. In fact, under Stalin, society became more traditional again, with no pretence of equality between the social groups. The elite was given privilege and status. Not only did they earn more, but they enjoyed all kinds of perks, like special shops and holidays in state-run resorts. Nowhere was this trend more obvious than in the armed forces, which went back to the use of traditional ranks and titles, and ornate uniforms for officers.

However, being a member of a social elite was no guarantee of safety – these were the groups so viciously purged in 1937–8. Indeed, class jealousy between the workers and the elites made it easier for Stalin to purge the bosses and officials without losing the support of the ordinary people, who often enjoyed the downfall and humiliation of those previously in authority over them.

SOURCE D

At the end of the twenties and in the thirties the authorities started to raise the living standards of those who had proved their usefulness. The resulting differentiation was very noticeable ... and a thin layer of privileged people gradually came into being, with country villas and cars. They realised only later how precarious it all was: in the period of the Great Purges they found they could be stripped of everything in a flash, and without any explanation. But in the meantime those who had been granted a share of the cake eagerly did everything demanded of them.

N. Mandelstam, the wife of the poet Osip Mandelstam, writing in 1971.

SOURCE E

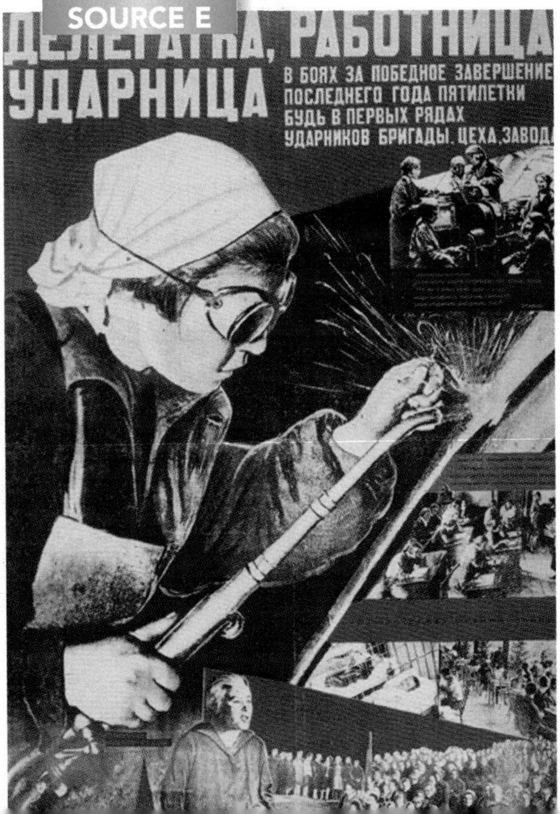

A Soviet propaganda picture from 1927 encouraging women to work.

QUESTIONS

1. Read Source D.
   Why do you think Stalin first allowed social elites to emerge, and then purged them?
2. Look at Source E.
   What was this picture saying about the role of women in Soviet society?

Paper 1-type assessment: Stalin's rule

SOURCE A

His fingers are fat as grubs
And words, final as lead weights, fall from
his lips

His cockroach whiskers leer
And his boot tops gleam

Around him a rabble of thin-necked leaders –
Fawning half-men for him to play with

They whinny, purr or whine
As he chatters and points a finger

One by one forging his laws, to be flung
Like horseshoes at the head, eye or groin

As every killing is a treat
For the broad chested Stalin

From a poem written about Stalin in the 1930s. The poet later died in one of Stalin's labour camps.

QUESTIONS

Section C Questions

Study the sources carefully and then answer the three questions which follow.

1a Study Source A. Why do you think people wrote poems like this in the Soviet Union in the 1930s? Use the source and your own knowledge to explain your answer. (6)

b Study Source B. Why do you think this poster was produced? Use the source and your own knowledge to explain your answer. (7)

c Study Source C. This source shows that Stalin treated the Soviet people badly. Why then did they continue to support him? Use the source and your own knowledge to explain your answer. (7)

SOURCE B

A Soviet poster of Stalin planning shelter belts to alter the climate.

SOURCE C

A French cartoon of the 1930s calling on people 'to visit the pyramids of the Soviet Union'.

QUESTIONS

When answering these questions make sure you answer ALL three parts.

Remember that you should always explain your answer as fully as you can and support it with specific detail where possible.

Section C Questions

2a What were the main weaknesses of the Tsar's government in early 1917? (4)

b Explain why the Provisional Government could not maintain itself in power in 1917. (6)

c 'The most important reason for the success of the Bolsheviks in the period 1917-22 was Trotsky's work in creating an effective Red Army.' Do you agree with this statement? Explain your answer. (10)

3a What were 'The Five Year Plans'? (4)

b Explain why Stalin introduced collectivisation into the Soviet Union. (6)

c Were Stalin's economic measures in the Soviet Union a failure or a success? Explain your answer. (10)

Core Part II:

International relations 1945–c.1989

6 International relations 1945–c.1989

As the Second World War drew to a close, the fragile alliance between the Soviet Union and the Western Allies (Britain, France and the USA) began to break up. The deep-rooted suspicion which East and West felt for each other led to the outbreak of Cold War in Europe. This was not a military war, but instead a war of words and of propaganda. The communist Soviet Union and its allies sought to discredit the capitalist USA and its allies. By the end of 1948 Europe had became divided by an 'iron curtain' separating the democratic, capitalist West from the communist East. The history of the next 40 years is the history of conflict between East and West, as each side sought to score diplomatic and tactical victories over the other. Although the United Nations had been formed to help maintain peace in the world, it was powerless to prevent increasingly sour relations between the USA and the Soviet Union.

The USA poured huge sums into western Europe to help bring about economic recovery and prevent the spread of communism. The Soviet Union resented American interference and took steps to assert its authority, as in the Berlin Blockade and the building of the Berlin Wall. It also ensured that those countries which were communist remained so – as Hungary and Czechoslovakia found to their cost. It would be wrong, however, to see the Cold War as a purely European conflict. The Americans were equally keen to stop the spread of communism outside Europe. Indeed, they went to war in both Korea and Vietnam to do so. In 1962 their determination to prevent the Soviet Union stationing nuclear missiles in Cuba almost brought about the world's first nuclear war.

The Cold War came to an end in 1989, because the Soviet Empire came to an end in the same year. Reforms introduced by Mikhail Gorbachev in the Soviet Union stimulated protest movements across eastern Europe. One by one, communist governments were overthrown and previously closed borders opened up. The communist control of eastern Europe had ended – and so had the Cold War.

This topic is examined in Paper 1 of the examination. Paper 1-type exercises are included at the end of each section. Mark schemes, sample answers and comments can be found in the accompanying Teacher's Resource Pack.

Who was to blame for the Cold War?

After 1941 the Soviet Union and the USA were allies in the Second World War. Their alliance, however, hid the deep-seated distrust that each country had for the other. As it became clear that Nazi Germany was close to defeat, the friendship between East and West came under pressure. By 1949 relationships had deteriorated to the point where a 'Cold War' had begun, as the two sides sought to extend their influence and win diplomatic victories over their opponents. Europe itself had been divided by what Winston Churchill called an 'iron curtain'. On either side of the curtain were the American-led western powers, later allied in the North Atlantic Treaty Organisation, and the Soviet-dominated eastern powers, later joined together in the Warsaw Pact. For the next 40 years, their bitter rivalry dominated European politics.

SOURCE A

WHAT, NO CHAIR FOR ME?

A cartoon from an English newspaper in September 1938. Stalin is complaining about his exclusion from the Munich talks.

Why did the USA–USSR alliance begin to break down in 1945?

From the end of 1941, the USA and the Soviet Union fought as allies against Nazi Germany, Japan and their allies. Yet in 1945 the alliance began to break down and the two superpowers soon became bitter enemies in a conflict that is known as the 'Cold War'. How did this happen?

In fact, the wartime alliance was close to breaking point even before the defeat of Germany and Japan. The main reason for this, and for the Cold War itself, was distrust. The USA and the Soviet Union simply did not trust each other enough to be on good terms.

Reasons for the distrust

1 Different political systems

Since 1917 the Soviet Union had been a communist state. Communists based their beliefs on the writings of the German philosopher Karl Marx. He believed that the government should control all aspects of citizens' lives and that individual rights were less important than what was good for the country as a whole. Industry and agriculture should be owned by the state and any profits made should be used for the common good. So in the communist Soviet Union, there were no wealthy businessmen using their capital to take risks and make personal fortunes. There was no such thing as private profit. Nor was there political freedom. There was only one party, the Communist Party, and in elections voters chose from different candidates in that party. There were also restrictions on freedom of speech, with newspapers and other media strictly controlled. Indeed, under Joseph Stalin, the Soviet Union was a country in which few citizens dared to criticise the government (see pages 201–5).

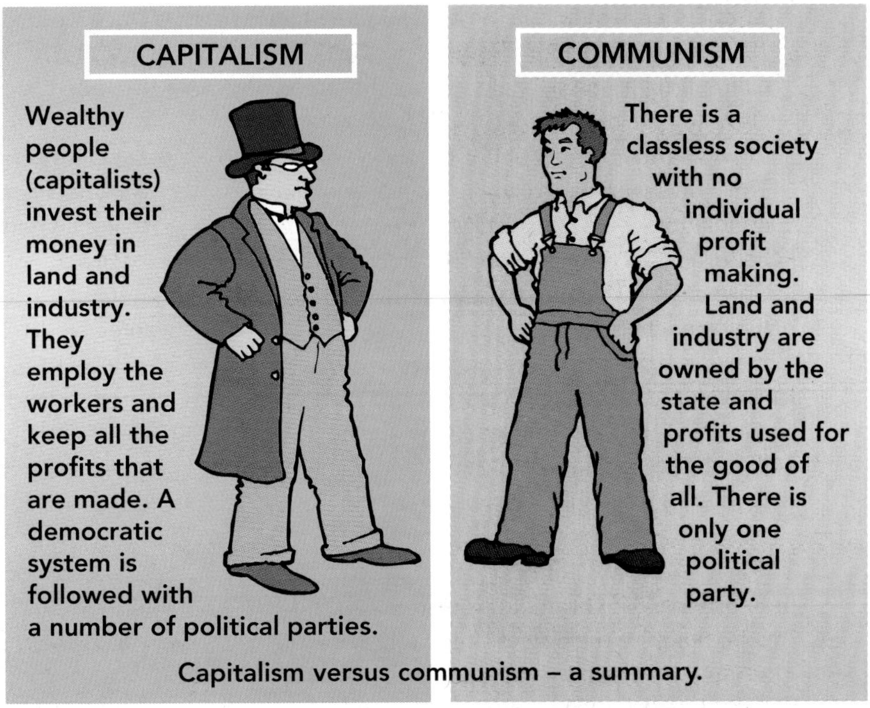

CAPITALISM
Wealthy people (capitalists) invest their money in land and industry. They employ the workers and keep all the profits that are made. A democratic system is followed with a number of political parties.
COMMUNISM
There is a classless society with no individual profit making. Land and industry are owned by the state and profits used for the good of all. There is only one political party.

Capitalism versus communism – a summary.

In contrast, the USA was a capitalist country. Industry and agriculture were in the hands of private individuals. Their major aim was to run their companies to make a personal profit. This would create jobs for individuals and provide wealth for the country as a whole through taxation. One of the major attractions for people emigrating to the USA in the early twentieth century was that it was seen as 'the land of opportunity', where immigrants such as Andrew Carnegie could acquire great personal wealth. Coupled with the right to make money was greater personal freedom than in the Soviet Union. There were free elections with a number of political parties and no control of the media by the government. Freedom of speech was considered a basic right of all American citizens.

2 A history of mistrust

Although having different political systems does not mean that countries have to become enemies, the basic mistrust that the Soviet Union and the USA had for each other made the breakdown of the wartime alliance inevitable. The problem was that both sides thought that their political system was the way that all governments should run their countries. The USA bitterly opposed communism and thought that the Soviet Union was trying to spread its beliefs across the world. It was joined in this thinking by capitalist countries of western Europe, particularly Britain and France. These countries therefore took steps to stop the spread of communism wherever they saw it developing. Most Soviet politicians believed, however, that they were under threat from the West and that any measures they took were merely defensive, to protect themselves from western aggression. They pointed to a series of events in the period 1917–45 which showed that the West was out to destroy communism.

- In 1917 the Bolsheviks (later renamed Communists) took control of Russia, but they soon found themselves fighting a civil war to retain power. In 1919 the USA, Britain and France sent troops to help the Bolsheviks' opponents.
- In 1933 Adolf Hitler became chancellor in Germany. Hitler hated communism and considered the Slav people of the Soviet Union to be an inferior race. To protect his country in the late 1930s, Stalin tried to form an anti-Hitler alliance with France and Britain. But the two western countries dragged their feet and no alliance was formed. Stalin saw this as an indication of western support for Hitler because France and Britain wanted Hitler to destroy the Soviet Union. This view was reinforced when Britain's policy of appeasement resulted in Hitler acquiring parts of Czechoslovakia after the Munich Conference in September 1938. Czechoslovakia was on the Soviet border, but Stalin was not even invited to the conference.

- After Hitler invaded the Soviet Union in June 1941, the USA, Britain, France and the Soviet Union fought on the same side. Stalin urged his allies to launch a 'second front' in Europe to draw German troops out of the Soviet Union. The Allies were not ready to launch such an attack until June 1944 (D-Day), but Stalin believed that they were deliberately waiting for Germany to weaken the Soviet Union before they launched their attack.

However, the most significant reasons for the outbreak of the Cold War were the events at the end of the war and the different interpretations of why they were happening.

The Yalta Conference

In February 1945, Franklin Roosevelt of the USA, Joseph Stalin of the Soviet Union and Winston Churchill of Britain met at Yalta in the Soviet Union. The war in Europe was drawing to a conclusion and decisions had to be made about how Europe was to be organised after the war. It was decided that:

- Germany should be divided into 'zones of occupation', one controlled by the USSR, one by the USA, one by Britain and one by France. Since the German capital, Berlin, would be in the Soviet zone, it would also be divided into four similar sections.
- Once Germany was defeated, the Soviet Union would join the war against Japan.
- A United Nations Organisation would be set up to keep peace after the war.
- As east European countries were liberated from Nazi occupation, they would hold free elections to set up democratic governments.

The main area of dispute was Poland. Stalin wanted to keep the parts of Poland that he had won in the Nazi–Soviet Pact of 1939. He also wanted Poland expanded westwards by giving it parts of Germany. That would make Germany weaker and put a buffer zone between Germany and the Soviet Union. Germany had invaded the Soviet Union twice in 30 years, and Stalin wanted to make sure it did not happen again. He also wanted to make sure that Poland had a pro-Soviet government.

Stalin already had a government in exile (the Lublin Poles) ready to take over. But Roosevelt and Churchill supported another group, the strongly anti-communist 'London Poles'. These Poles had helped organise the Warsaw Uprising in August 1944, aiming to gain part of Poland before Stalin's Red Army took full control of the country. The uprising was defeated by the Nazis and nearly 300,000 Poles were killed. The Red Army was ordered not to help in the uprising. Stalin wanted to make sure that when his army cleared the Germans out of Poland, the Lublin Poles would have complete control. By January 1945 this had happened.

SOURCE B

Churchill, Roosevelt and Stalin in discussion at Yalta.

SOURCE C

I didn't say it was good, I said it was the best I could do.

President Roosevelt commenting on the Yalta Agreement to one of his advisers.

SOURCE D

So far there has been a worrying lack of progress made in the carrying out of the decisions we made in the conference, particularly those relating to Poland. I am frankly puzzled as to why this should be and must tell you that I do not fully understand the attitude of your government.

President Roosevelt writing to Stalin in April 1945.

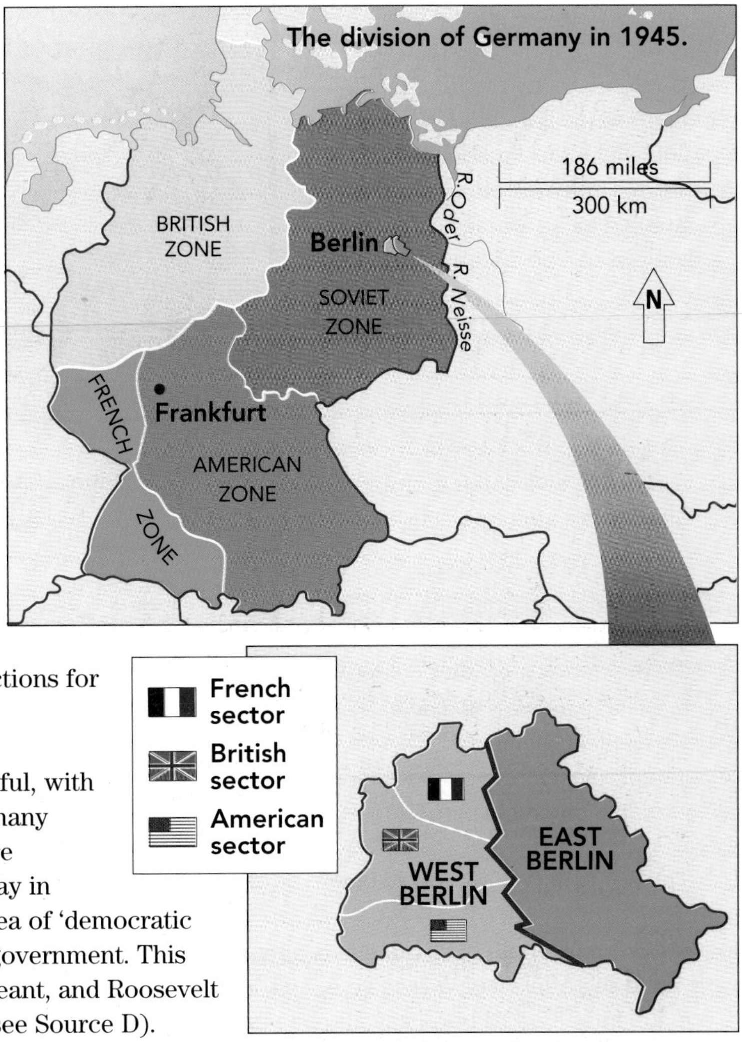

But Roosevelt and Churchill did not want Stalin to have a free hand in Poland. At Yalta they made him agree that some of the London Poles would be included in the government and that there would be free elections for a new government 'as soon as possible'.

The Yalta Conference appeared to be successful, with agreements on how eastern Europe and Germany would be organised. But in reality, things were different. The London Poles had hardly any say in their government. As for elections, Stalin's idea of 'democratic government' was an elected pro-communist government. This was not what Churchill and Roosevelt had meant, and Roosevelt wrote to Stalin expressing his unhappiness (see Source D).

The Potsdam Conference

Yalta had shown how difficult it was for the Allies to reach agreement. In July 1945 a second conference was held, at Potsdam in Germany. Here, divisions between the Soviet Union on one hand, and Britain and the USA on the other, were much more apparent.

By July 1945, Soviet troops had liberated the whole of eastern Europe from Nazi control. The USA and Britain had hoped that there would be free elections to set up democratic governments. Instead Soviet troops remained in the liberated countries.

In the USA, attitudes were beginning to harden. In April 1945, Franklin Roosevelt died and was replaced by Harry Truman. The new president was much less trusting of the Soviet Union than Roosevelt had been, and in his first month in office he had an angry exchange with the Soviet foreign minister, Molotov, in which he demanded that the Soviets carry out their obligations in the Yalta Agreement. In May, Truman claimed, 'We have to get tough with the Russians, they don't know how to behave.'

QUESTIONS

1 What are the main differences between communist and capitalist countries?

2 Why was there so much mistrust between East and West in 1945?

3 Why was it so difficult to reach a satisfactory agreement at the Yalta Conference?

Truman's tough stance was continued at the Potsdam Conference. By the time the conference got under way on 17 July 1945, the Americans had successfully tested an atomic bomb. One of Truman's first actions at Potsdam was to inform Stalin and Churchill that his country now had the bomb. He was confident that it would be years before the Soviet Union had one, so the USA could get tough with the Soviet Union.

SOURCE E

GERMANY
LOW
"IF WE DON'T LET HIM WORK, WHO'S GOING TO KEEP HIM?"

A cartoon from a British newspaper in July 1946. The foreign ministers of the wartime allies are arguing over what should be done to Germany now that the war is over.

The Potsdam Conference showed that Truman was not prepared to let Stalin have things all his own way. In July, Churchill lost a general election in Britain and was replaced by the Labour leader, Clement Attlee. Since Attlee was new and inexperienced, the conference was really a personal duel between Truman and Stalin.

The following points were agreed:

- Germany would be divided as agreed at Yalta, and the Allies would receive reparations.
- Poland's eastern border would be moved west to the rivers Oder and Neisse.
- The Nazi Party was banned and its leaders were to be tried as war criminals.
- Germans living in Poland, Hungary and Czechoslovakia would be sent back to Germany.

However, there were several major disagreements:

- The Soviet Union wanted to impose severe reparations on Germany to cripple it for years to come. Truman blocked this.
- The Soviet Union wanted to share in the occupation of Japan once it was defeated. Truman refused.
- Britain and the USA wanted a greater say in eastern Europe. They did not accept that Stalin had the right to set up pro-Soviet governments in these countries. Stalin said that this was what they had agreed at Yalta.

SOURCE F

From Stettin in the Baltic to Trieste in the Adriatic, an iron curtain has descended across the continent. Behind that line lie all the capitals of the ancient states of central and eastern Europe – Warsaw, Berlin, Prague, Vienna, Budapest, Bucharest and Sofia. All these famous cities and the populations around them lie in the Soviet sphere and all are subject to a very high and increasing measure of control from Moscow.

An extract from Churchill's speech at Fulton, Missouri, on 5 March 1946.

The Potsdam Conference had shown how divided the former wartime allies were. This division became even more apparent in the months after the conference. The development of the atomic bomb in the USA was a major source of worry to Stalin, who feared that the USA might use the threat of the bomb to prevent the spread of communism. He ordered his scientists to work flat out to develop a Soviet atomic bomb.

SOURCE G

Churchill making his speech at Fulton on 5 March 1946.

This further worried the USA, which saw an atomic bomb in the hands of the Soviet Union as a threat to world peace.

The Allies also fell out over arrangements in Germany. Britain and France accused the Soviet Union of taking too much in reparations from Germany, so as to prevent its recovery. They also wanted democratic elections in Germany, but Stalin blocked this.

The division between East and West was shown most clearly in March 1946 when Winston Churchill made his famous 'iron curtain' speech in the USA at Fulton, Missouri. President Truman had seen a copy of the speech before it was delivered and must have approved it. The speech (Source F) declared that Europe was being divided into two separate halves by Soviet policy. In the West were free, democratic states, but in the East, behind an 'iron curtain' were countries under the domination of communist parties subject to the Soviet Union. This was a clear statement of 'West versus East', and Stalin accused Churchill of trying to stir up a war against the Soviet Union.

How had the USSR gained control of eastern Europe by 1948?

It was a fact, however, that between 1945 and 1948 the Soviet Union made sure that every country in eastern Europe had a government that was both communist and sympathetic to the Soviet Union. As far as Stalin was concerned, this was a defensive measure aimed at creating a buffer zone between the Soviet Union and the West. The Soviet Union had been invaded from the west twice in the last 30 years; the establishment of communist governments in eastern Europe would make such an invasion more difficult.

Of course, as far as the West was concerned, and the USA in particular, the Soviet Union was not acting defensively. It was taking the first steps towards world domination. Here was clear proof that the western way of life was under threat. The spread of communism would have to be stopped.

SOURCE H

Mr Churchill now takes the stand of the warmongers and he is not alone. He has friends not only in Britain, but in the United States ... As a result of the German invasion, the Soviet Union's loss of life has been several times greater than that of Britain and the USA put together. And so what can be surprising about the fact that the Soviet Union, anxious for its future safety, is trying to see to it that governments loyal to the Soviet Union should exist in the countries through which the Germans made their invasion? How can anyone who has not taken leave of his senses describe these peaceful hopes of the Soviet Union as expansionist?

Stalin's response to Churchill's speech, 1946.

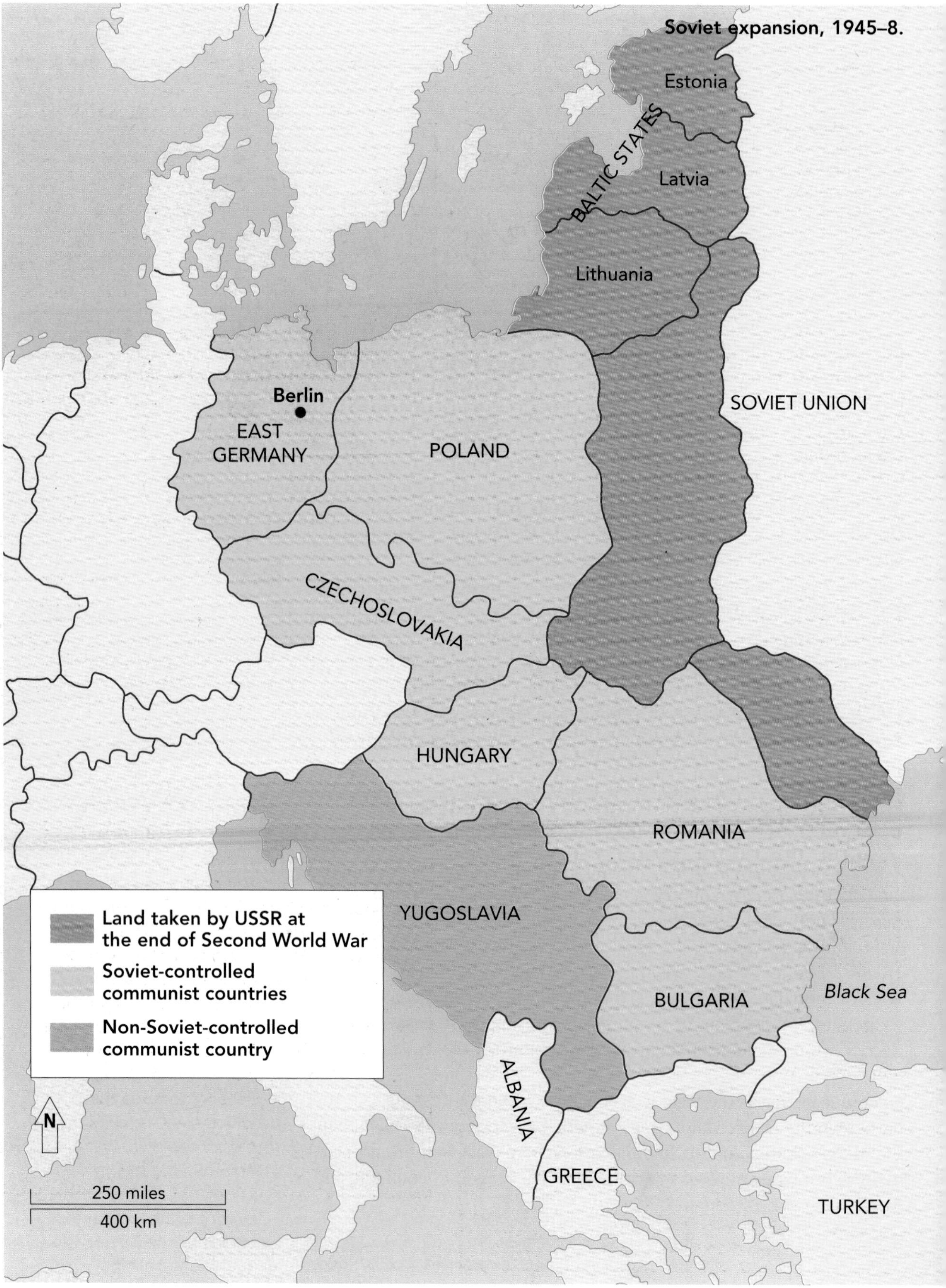
Soviet expansion, 1945–8.
Estonia
BALTIC STATES
Latvia
Lithuania
Berlin
EAST GERMANY
POLAND
SOVIET UNION
CZECHOSLOVAKIA
HUNGARY
ROMANIA
YUGOSLAVIA
BULGARIA
Black Sea
ALBANIA
GREECE
TURKEY
Land taken by USSR at the end of Second World War
Soviet-controlled communist countries
Non-Soviet-controlled communist country
N
250 miles
400 km

The Baltic States

At the end of the war, the Soviet Union extended its border some 500 kilometres west. It did this by formally annexing Latvia, Lithuania and Estonia, which it had occupied during the war with Finland in 1939–40. It also kept control of the eastern half of Poland, which it had occupied as part of the Nazi–Soviet agreement in 1939 (although the Germans had occupied this area from 1941 to 1945).

Poland

At the request of Britain and the USA at the end of June 1945, Stalin included a few London Poles in the new Polish government. In January 1947, however, fresh (rigged) elections saw the return of a totally communist government. The leader of the London Poles, Mikolaczyk, fled from Poland, fearing for his life.

Romania

After the expulsion of the Nazis, a coalition government dominated by communists was set up. In February 1945 the Soviet Union forced the king of Romania to appoint a communist prime minister. By the middle of the year, communists were in control, and in 1947 the monarchy was abolished.

Greece

Here the communists were not successful. They fought a civil war against royalists supported by Britain and the USA. Stalin stuck by his promise to the western allies not to provide support for the Greek communists, who were finally defeated in 1949.

Bulgaria

In late 1944 a communist-dominated coalition government was set up. In November 1945 the communists won rigged elections, and in 1946 they abolished the monarchy.

Czechoslovakia

Following the war, a coalition government ruled Czechoslovakia. From 1946 the communists were the largest party in the coalition. In 1948 the communists used the army to seize control. Many non-communists were arrested and the non-communist foreign secretary, Jan Masaryk, was murdered. Rigged elections were held in which the communists won a landslide victory. Other political parties were then banned.

East Germany

The Soviet Union controlled the eastern section of Germany after the war. In 1949 it became a separate communist state, the German Democratic Republic (East Germany).

Hungary

In November 1945 free elections were held and the non-communist Smallholders' Party won the most seats. In August 1947 fresh (rigged) elections were held and the communists won total control. All other political parties were then banned.

Yugoslavia

In Yugoslavia the communist resistance had fought bravely against the Germans, and in 1945 its leader, Marshal Tito, was elected president. At first, Tito and Stalin got on well, but relations deteriorated as it became clear that Tito did not intend to follow orders from Moscow. Yugoslavia was expelled from the Communist Information Bureau (Cominform), and economic sanctions were applied against it by other communist countries. Tito countered this by taking aid from the West – much to the annoyance of Stalin.

How did the USA react to Soviet expansion?

Not surprisingly, Truman was extremely concerned at the growth of Soviet influence in eastern Europe, but as most of the countries involved had been liberated by the Soviet Union and there were still Soviet troops in the area, there was little he could do.

In February 1947, however, Truman was informed by the British that they could no longer afford to station troops in Greece and Turkey. He knew that the withdrawal of British troops would almost certainly lead to the Soviet Union taking control of these two countries. He therefore paid for British troops to stay in the area and gave financial support to the two governments. This was the beginning of the American policy of 'containment' – preventing the further spread of communism. The policy was officially announced in a speech made by Truman on 12 March 1947. The views put forward in the speech have since become known as the 'Truman Doctrine' (Source I). In this speech, Truman let it be known that the USA was prepared to give help to any country under threat from communism.

The Marshall Plan

Truman did not intend to send soldiers to Europe to fight communism. Instead he would attack it at its roots. As he said in his 12 March speech, he believed that communism flourished where there was 'misery and want'. He was well aware that post-war Europe had plenty of misery and want. Governments were struggling to cope with the damage caused by the war and there was still rationing and shortages in many countries. On top of this, the USA was still owed almost $12 billion by European countries.

Truman therefore decided that the USA should use its wealth to provide economic aid to Europe. Restored economies in Europe would be less susceptible to communism and also provide greater trading opportunities for American companies. The plan was announced in a speech made by the American secretary of state, General George Marshall, in June 1947. He claimed that the American policy was not aimed at any country, but just at ending hunger and poverty. The Soviet Union was not fooled – at a conference of Cominform in September 1947, one delegate described the Marshall Plan as 'an American plan to enslave Europe'.

SOURCE I

The free peoples of the world look to us for support in maintaining their freedoms.

I believe that it must be the policy of the United States to support people who are resisting attempted subjugation by armed minorities or by any outside pressures. I believe that we must help free peoples to work out their own destiny in their own way.

Extracts from President Truman's speech on 12 March 1947.

A cartoonist's view of the Marshall Plan, drawn in 1947.

SOURCE J

NEIGHBOURS
"Come on, Sam! It's up to us again."

The countries of Europe, however, were keen to be enslaved, and between 1948 and 1952 the USA provided $13 billion to sixteen western countries. President Truman would have been perfectly happy to provide aid for east European countries too, and Poland and Czechoslovakia were keen to apply. But Stalin realised that with the money would come a commitment to 'western' ideas. He forbade any communist countries from receiving aid under the Marshall Plan.

In September 1947 the Soviet Union formed the Communist Information Bureau (Cominform) to strengthen ties between communist countries. The communist parties in western Europe (those in Italy and France were particularly strong) were ordered to try to wreck their countries' use of American aid by strikes, but they were unsuccessful. In January 1949, Stalin announced the formation of the Council for Mutual Economic Aid (Comecon) to rival the Marshall Plan. The communist countries, however, did not have surplus funds to provide financial assistance to each other.

What were the causes of the Berlin blockade?

Stalin's refusal to allow communist countries to apply for Marshall Aid had a significant effect on events in Germany. After the Second World War, Germany's economy was in ruins. The western powers did not want to restore Germany's military power, but the only way to end poverty and suffering in the country was to rebuild its industries and restore the economy. Therefore the western part of Germany was included in the Marshall Plan. Not surprisingly, Stalin refused to allow the Soviet zone to receive aid.

In 1947 the British and American zones of Germany had been combined to form 'Bizonia'. Britain and the USA then decided to introduce a new currency, the Deutschmark. Stalin was worried that a prosperous western Germany would be a threat to the Soviet Union's security. He wanted all the occupied zones to remain undeveloped. He was also concerned at the prospect of a wealthy western Germany beside a poor, Soviet-controlled eastern Germany.

SOURCE K

The Marshall Plan was seen in the Soviet Union as the Americans wanting to impose their influence over the countries to which they gave Marshall Aid. It was seen as an aggressive act on behalf of the Americans. This is why it was never accepted by our country.

Dimitri Sukhanov, a senior Soviet politician in 1947, commenting in 1988 on the Marshall Plan.

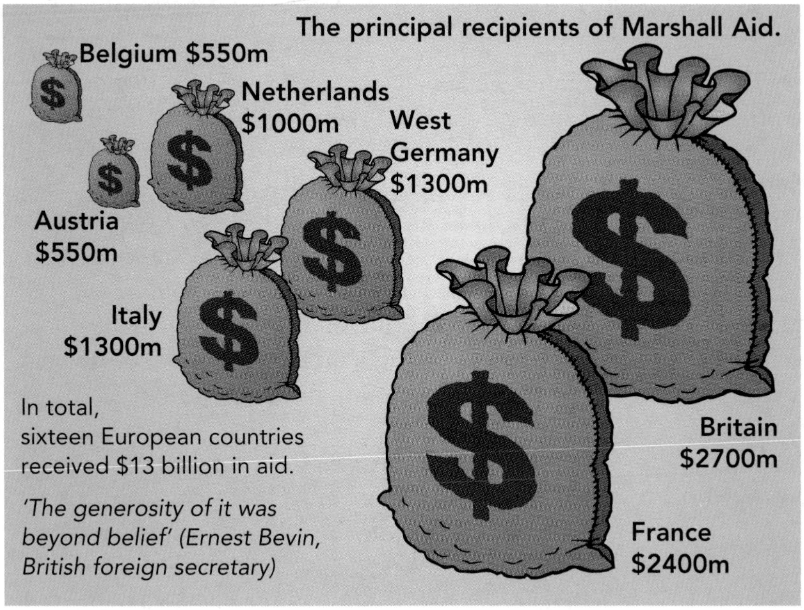
The principal recipients of Marshall Aid.
Belgium $550m
Netherlands $1000m
West Germany $1300m
Austria $550m
Italy $1300m
Britain $2700m
France $2400m
In total, sixteen European countries received $13 billion in aid.
'The generosity of it was beyond belief' (Ernest Bevin, British foreign secretary)

QUESTIONS

1 What was the purpose of
   a the Truman Doctrine
   b the Marshall Plan?
2 How were such plans viewed in the Soviet Union?
3 'There would not have been a Cold War if the USA had not introduced the Truman Doctrine and the Marshall Plan.' Do you agree?

SOURCE L

A painting by an American artist showing US planes landing supplies at Templehof Airport in West Berlin.

Stalin decided to try to stop the economic development of western Germany, by taking steps against West Berlin. Berlin was divided in the same way as Germany was, which meant that 2 million Germans in the British, American and French zones lived in the middle of the Soviet zone, but not under Soviet rule. On 24 June 1948, Stalin decided to blockade West Berlin by cutting off road and rail links. To break the blockade, the Allies would have to send tanks to smash through the road and rail blocks. Such action would be an act of war and Stalin doubted that the western powers would go that far. He thought that they were much more likely to abandon their zones and leave the whole of Berlin in Soviet hands.

But the British, French and Americans saw West Berlin as a test case. If they backed down, then Stalin would be encouraged to make other demands, elsewhere. So they decided to send supplies to West Berlin to keep it going. These would not be sent by road or rail, but would be flown from air bases in western Germany into three bases in West Berlin. This was a considerable task as it would require almost non-stop flights to move the enormous quantities of food, fuel and other necessities into West Berlin. What it meant, however, was that the ball was back in Stalin's court. To stop the supplies, he would have to shoot down planes that carried no military threat to the Soviet Union. This would show clearly that he was the aggressor. To further encourage him not to do so, the Americans stationed B-29 bombers in Britain, thus putting the Soviet Union within range of atomic bombs if war broke out.

Over the next eleven months, the three western allies made 275,000 trips to West Berlin and delivered over 2 million tons of supplies. The West had shown its commitment to West Berlin and Stalin's gamble had failed. On 12 May 1949 he called off the blockade.

The consequences of the blockade

Stalin's blockade of Berlin had been a test of the West's resolve and had been designed to win West Berlin for the Soviet Union. It was to have the opposite effect. The Allies stood firm, taking measures to strengthen their control of Germany and their opposition to the Soviet Union.

In May 1949 the British, American and French zones were formally united in the German Federal Republic (West Germany). In August 1949 the first elections were held and won by the Christian Democrats, led by Konrad Adenauer, a committed

SOURCE M

Aid being unloaded from American planes at Templehof Airport in June 1948.

opponent of communism. Part of this new country was West Berlin, where the three Allied zones also combined to form a West German oasis in the middle of East Germany, as the Soviet zone was renamed in October 1949.

Perhaps even more worrying for Stalin was the formation of the North Atlantic Treaty Organisation (NATO). This was a military alliance of the European powers plus Canada and the USA. It was a defensive alliance in which the members agreed to offer help if any of them was attacked. It was the first time the USA had signed a military alliance in peacetime and showed its commitment to containing communism, especially as it backed up the signing of the agreement by stationing troops in West Germany.

NATO was a direct challenge to the Soviet Union, although Stalin may have felt more confident in 1949 when his scientists informed him that they had successfully developed an atomic bomb. When NATO was expanded in 1955 to include West Germany, the Soviet Union responded by setting up its own military alliance, the Warsaw Pact.

The two alliances

- **NATO:** USA, Britain, Belgium, Canada, Denmark, France, Iceland, Italy, Luxembourg, Netherlands, Norway and Portugal. Greece and Turkey joined in 1952 and West Germany in 1955.
- **The Warsaw Pact:** Soviet Union, Albania (expelled 1968), Bulgaria, Czechoslovakia, East Germany, Hungary, Poland and Romania.

SOURCE N

Planes were taking off every thirty seconds, soldiers were loading trucks, the maintenance shops were a beehive of activity, and the mess halls and clubs were open. It was a 24-hour operation. The commanding officer stood in the control tower with his stop watch, checking the timing of the planes. To most people it seemed an impossible task to meet the needs of two million people by airlift. But except for water, Berlin was supplied with everything by air.

An American stationed at a base in the American zone of Germany describes the frenzied activity of the Berlin airlift.

The Story of 'Operation Little Vittles'

'Operation Vittles' was the unofficial name given to the Berlin airlift by the Americans. ('Vittles' is an American slang term for food.) There was also, however, an operation within the main airlift which some American pilots called 'Operation Little Vittles'.

This operation was the idea of Lieutenant Gail S. Halvorsen. He was so impressed by the friendliness of German children at Templehof airdrome (one of the bases at which American aid planes landed) that he made a promise to them that he would drop sweets for them on the next day. He made small parachutes out of scraps of cloth and used them to drop sweets to the children. As word spread of what he was doing, donations of thousands of pounds of sweets and scrap cloth came from all over the USA. By January 1949 more than 250,000 of the 'candy parachutes' had been dropped.

The Soviet Union tried to discredit what Halvorsen and the other pilots had done by running a story that excited children had badly damaged a cemetery near Templehof whilst chasing sweets dropped from American planes.

Who was more to blame for the start of the Cold War – the USA or the Soviet Union?

By 1955 Europe was divided between the communist countries behind the Iron Curtain and under Soviet control, and the capitalist countries of the West. Germany was also divided into two separate countries, and the two superpowers and their allies were arranged into separate military alliances, each of which had the option of turning any conflict into nuclear warfare. The Cold War was firmly under way and was to dominate world politics for the next 30 years.

Which of the two sides was most to blame is a question that would be answered differently in Moscow and Washington. The Soviet Union would claim that it had been invaded twice in the twentieth century and that the West had a history of anti-communism that made it vital for the Soviets to set up a pro-Soviet buffer zone in eastern Europe. The Americans would argue that the communists wanted world domination and that the only way to prevent western Europe (and ultimately the USA) coming under a system that they despised was to act in Europe to contain communism. The Berlin blockade showed what the Soviet Union would do if it were not checked.

Regardless of who was more to blame, there is no doubt that the major cause of the Cold War was that each 'side' was convinced of the correctness of its actions and fiercely distrustful of the other side. This was to be seen even more clearly in events outside Europe in Cuba and Vietnam.

QUESTIONS

1 Why did Stalin decide to blockade West Berlin?

2 **a** What options were open to the western allies to break the blockade?
b Why did they choose an airlift?

3 'Operation Little Vittles shows that the Americans were operating in the interests of the people of West Berlin and the Soviets were not.' Do you agree?

4 What were the consequences of the Berlin blockade?

Paper 1-type assessment: Causes of the Cold War

SOURCE A

THE BIRD WATCHER

A cartoon published in July 1948. The birds are carrying supplies into Berlin.

QUESTIONS

Section A Questions

1a Study Source A. Do you think this cartoon was published in Western Europe or in Eastern Europe? Support your answer by referring to details of the cartoon and your own knowledge. (6)

b Explain why the Soviet Union decided to gain control of Eastern Europe after the Second World War. (9)

Section B Questions

2a What was agreed at the Potsdam Conference in July 1945? (4)

b Explain why the Soviet Union was unhappy at the outcome of the Potsdam Conference. (6)

c 'The most important cause of the Cold War was the Soviet Union's fear of the West'. Do you agree with this statement? Explain your answer. (10)

How effectively did the USA contain the spread of communism?

Post-war events in Europe had led to bitter tension between the USA and the Soviet Union. The hostility between them was not confined to Europe. The Americans believed that it was their duty, and necessary to American security, to resist the expansion of communism wherever it occurred. During the 1960s this led them to the brink of nuclear war over the stationing of Soviet missiles on Cuba. It also resulted in American troops fighting a long and costly war in Vietnam.

The Cold War, 1949–61

The formation of NATO and the Warsaw Pact marked the beginning of a period in which relations between East and West were extremely tense. American fears were further increased when in 1949 China became a communist country under Mao Zedong. However, relations between communist China and the Soviet Union were not good because Mao felt that Stalin expected him to follow Soviet foreign policy. In 1960 relations deteriorated to the point where Soviet engineers and scientists in China were recalled to Moscow.

The arms race

As relations between the USA and the Soviet Union worsened, both sides began to develop their weapons so as to be able to 'outgun' their opponents. By 1949 both the USA and the Soviet Union had nuclear weapons. Then in 1952 the Americans developed a hydrogen bomb (H-bomb), which was capable of destroying Moscow. Within a year the Soviet Union had developed a similar bomb. In 1957 the Soviet Union devised a means of attaching nuclear warheads to rockets.

Soon both sides had intercontinental ballistic missiles (ICBMs), which could fire a nuclear warhead several thousand kilometres. By 1960 the missiles could be fired from nuclear submarines under the sea.

SOURCE A

Here in Asia we fight Europe's war with arms while diplomats there still fight it with words. If we lose the war with communism in Asia, the fall of Europe is inevitable. There is no substitute for victory.

General MacArthur commenting on the importance of the Korean War in 1951.

The arms race between the USA and the Soviet Union.

USA			USSR
ICBMs	450	76	ICBMs
Medium-range missiles	250	700	Medium-range missiles
Bombers	2260	1600	Bombers
Tanks	16,000	38,000	Tanks
Submarines Nuclear	32	12	Nuclear Submarines
Conventional	260	495	Conventional
Battleships and carriers	76	0	Battleships and carriers

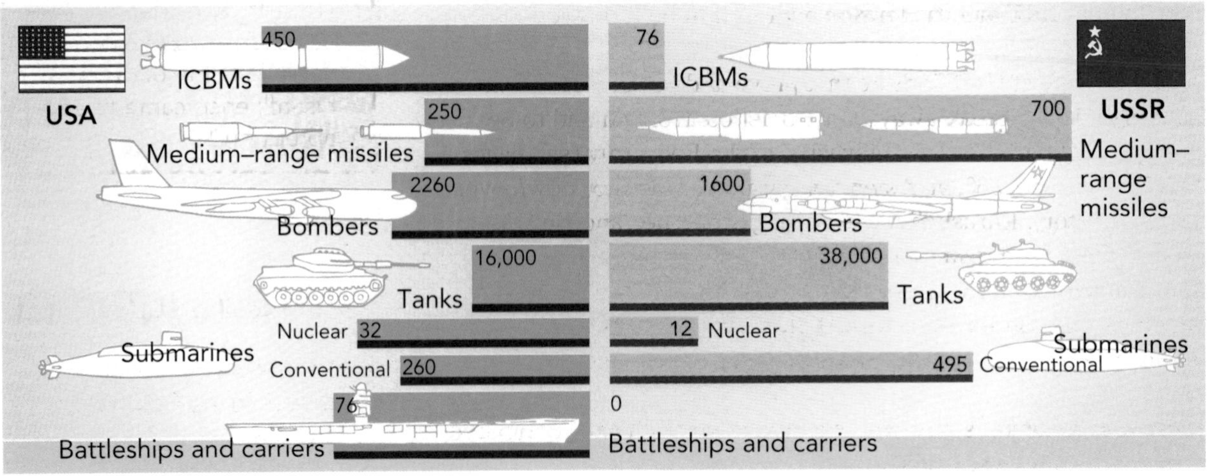

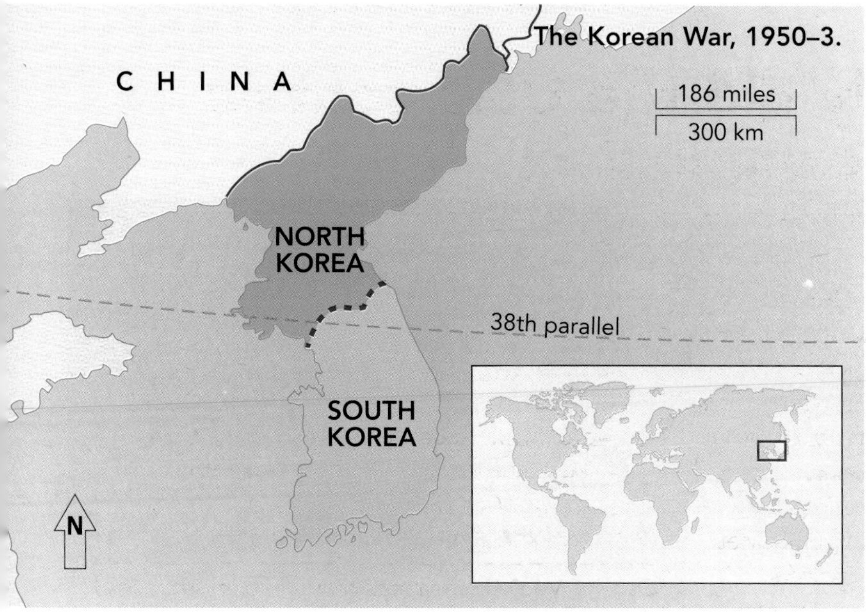

Although the two sides were building up nuclear stockpiles, they were careful to avoid direct confrontation and having to use their weapons. There were occasions, however, when conflict seemed near.

In 1950 troops from communist North Korea invaded South Korea, which was anti-communist. President Truman was convinced that the Soviet Union had told North Korea to invade, and he persuaded the United Nations to send a force under General MacArthur to help the South Koreans.

The American policy had stopped the spread of communism into South Korea, but at the cost of worsening relations between the USA and both China and the Soviet Union, and at the cost of thousands of American soldiers' lives.

Not surprisingly, relations between East and West were very strained after the Korean War, but when Stalin died in 1953 his successor, Nikita Khrushchev, appeared to want better relations. Summit talks were held in 1955 and the tension appeared to be lifting.

But there were still difficulties that prevented better relations. In 1956 Hungary tried to break away from Soviet control and had to be brought back into line by an invasion of the Red Army (see pages 246–7). Then, in 1960, an American spy plane was shot down over Soviet territory. Khrushchev was so angry that he cancelled the summit meeting due in that year. In 1961, after failing to persuade the Americans to withdraw from West Berlin, Khrushchev ordered the building of the Berlin Wall. West Berlin was now cut off from East Berlin. The only gap in the Iron Curtain had been closed.

These disagreements, however, paled into insignificance compared with the dispute over Cuba.

McCarthyism

Post-war America was intensely anti-communist. In 1947, ten Hollwood film producers were sent to gaol for refusing to tell the 'Un-American Activities Committee' whether they had ever been members of the Communist Party. In 1950 a law was passed banning communists from obtaining American passports.

A leading figure in the 'Red Scare' was Senator Joe McCarthy, who whipped up anti-communist feeling by claiming that he had a list of over 200 communists working in government departments. Although this was unlikely, anti-communist feeling was running so high that few politicians were prepared to stand up to him. Between 1950 and 1954 hundreds of Americans had their careers ruined as a result of accusations made in the communist 'witch hunt'.

Finally, in 1954 McCarthy's 'evidence' was exposed as nothing more than rumour and his influence came to an abrupt end.

QUESTION

What were the main events in the Cold War, 1949–61?

The USA and events in Cuba, 1959–62

Cuba

In 1898 the Americans helped the Cubans to win independence from Spain. From that time, the USA played a major part in Cuban affairs. The Americans built a huge naval base at Guantanamo and American companies invested heavily in Cuban industry. American companies had large stakes in most Cuban companies, particularly in mining and agriculture. In 1934 the Americans helped the Cuban military officer Fulgencio Batista to establish himself in power. His government became increasingly corrupt and repressive, and many Cubans saw him as a symbol of the American control of Cuba.

SOURCE B

Fidel Castro.

In 1959 Batista was overthrown by Fidel Castro. The new leader proposed reforms to improve the economy of Cuba and in particular to end corruption in government and the exploitation of the Cuban peasants and sugar mill workers. Castro began appointing communists to his government and signed a trade agreement with the Soviet Union in which Cuban sugar would be swapped for machinery, oil and economic aid.

Not surprisingly, the USA was extremely concerned to see an island that was only about 150 kilometres away from its southern coast adopting what looked like communist policies and establishing such friendly relations with the Soviet Union. It decided to take action to bring Castro into line. In the summer of 1960, the USA stopped buying Cuban sugar and later in the year it banned all trade with Cuba. Then, in January 1961, it broke off diplomatic relations with Cuba.

The Americans hoped that these measures would starve Castro into submission. But they seem to have pushed him closer to the Soviet Union. The Americans were aware that among the 'aid' that Castro was receiving from the Soviet Union were weapons. Consequently, in April 1961 the new American president, J. F. Kennedy, decided to support an invasion by the 'Cuban exiles'. These were a group of Cubans who had fled the country when Castro took over. They wanted a return to the days of Batista.

SOURCE C

What is the reason for all this silliness in Congress and in the American press about the Soviet presence in Cuba? The Soviet Union does not need to shift its weapons to any other country. Our nuclear rockets are so powerful that the Soviet Union has no need to search for sites beyond the boundaries of the Soviet Union.

A public statement made by Khrushchev in September 1962.

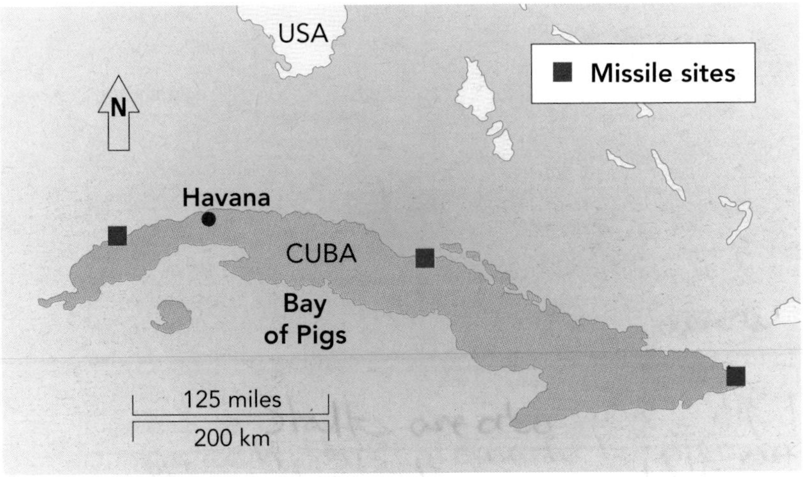

The Bay of Pigs.

The Bay of Pigs

The exiles received military training, weapons and transport from the American Central Intelligence Agency (CIA), and aimed to launch an attack on the coast of Cuba at the Bay of Pigs. They intended to establish a base for guerrilla activities against Castro and were confident that the Cuban people would support them. But the Bay of Pigs invasion was a disaster. A force of 1400 exiles landed in Cuba, but found themselves facing over 20,000 Cuban troops. There was no popular uprising to support the invasion, and those exiles who were not killed were quickly taken captive. Even though Kennedy was able to claim that there was no direct American government involvement in the invasion, Castro and Khrushchev knew that it had been planned by the CIA. Kennedy had been humiliated.

Consequences of the invasion

The Bay of Pigs invasion convinced Castro that he needed more support from the Soviet Union to defend himself against possible American attacks. In September 1961, Krushchev publicly announced that he would provide arms to Cuba. Within months Castro had an army with the latest military equipment, such as tanks and missiles, and large numbers of 'technicians' to help train his troops.

The USA was alarmed at what was happening in Cuba. In July 1961, Castro had nationalised all American industries and in December he had announced that he himself was a communist. Now he had a well-trained army with many of the most up-to-date modern weapons.

What the Americans were most concerned about was nuclear weapons. Khrushchev did not give Castro nuclear weapons, but his friendship with the Cuban leader meant that there was every chance that he might try to station nuclear weapons on the island. In September 1962, President Kennedy warned the Soviet Union that he would not allow Cuba to become a base for Soviet nuclear missiles. Khrushchev assured Kennedy that he had no intentions of doing so. In fact, however, he had decided as early as May that if weapons could be stationed on Cuba without detection, that was what he would do.

SOURCE D

- Spread false pictures of Castro looking fat sat at a table full of food beside two voluptuous women. The caption would say, 'My ration is different'.
- Prepare to blame Castro if the 1962 Mercury manned space flight carrying John Glenn crashed.
- Prepare a poisoned scuba diving suit as a gift for Castro.
- Blow up a US warship in Guantanamo Bay and blame Cuba.
- Start a terror campaign against Cuban exiles and blame it on Castro, e.g. sink a boatload of refugees on the way to Florida (real or simulated).

Ideas from the American Joint Chiefs of Staff in 1962 on how to discredit Castro. None of them was carried out.

QUESTIONS

1 Why were the Americans so concerned about what happened in Cuba?

2 Do you agree that the Bay of Pigs incident was a disaster for the USA?

SOURCE E

A photograph of the missile sites in Cuba with labels added by the American government.

SOURCE F

The 1930s taught us a clear lesson. Aggressive conduct, if allowed to go unchecked and unchallenged, ultimately leads to war. We will not prematurely or unnecessarily risk the costs of world-wide nuclear war in which the fruits of victory would be ashes in our mouths, but neither will we shrink from that risk at any time it must be faced.

President Kennedy broadcasting to the American people on 22 October 1962.

Missiles discovered

On 14 October 1962, an American U-2 spy plane flew over Cuba and took pictures of what looked like missile sites being built. Some were near completion and would be ready to fire missiles in just seven days. Even more worrying was the news that a fleet of Soviet ships was sailing to Cuba – presumably carrying more missiles for the new sites.

Kennedy was now in a very difficult position. He could not allow the Soviet Union to station nuclear weapons on Cuba, as that would place virtually the whole of the USA within range of nuclear missiles. But how could he stop it? Since Khrushchev denied that there were nuclear missiles on Cuba and thought that Kennedy was a weak leader, he would hardly respond to American demands to remove them. Other measures, such as invading Cuba or bombing the missile sites, would have dire consequences. At the very least, the Soviet Union would be likely to invade West Berlin. Much more likely would be the outbreak of a general war between the USA and the Soviet Union with the chance of nuclear weapons being used.

Kennedy and his advisers meet for thirteen days and nights from 16 October. Source G shows how difficult some of their discussions were. By 22 October, Kennedy had decided to place a blockade around Cuba to stop the Soviet fleet landing its missiles. The USA would also prepare troops ready for an invasion of the island, if necessary. That day, Kennedy broadcast the news of his planned blockade on American television (Source F) and called on Khrushchev to remove the missiles from Cuba.

The next day (23 October), Khrushchev replied that there were no nuclear missiles on Cuba and that the Soviet Union would ignore the blockade, which it called an act of piracy. The world now held its breath. Soviet ships were sailing towards an American blockade. If they ignored it, they would be fired on and war would be certain to follow.

SOURCE G

Tuesday 16 October
The group discusses whether the USA could be under threat from Cuba. President Kennedy seems to think that the threat is not really increased.

General Maxwell Taylor: I'd like to stress this last point, Mr President. We are very vulnerable to a conventional bombing attack in the Florida area.
Douglas Dillon: What if the planes carry a nuclear weapon?
The President: Well if they carry a nuclear weapon...
Rusk: We could just be utterly wrong – but we've never really believed that Khrushchev would start a nuclear war over Cuba.
Bundy: What is the impact on the balance of power of these missiles?
The President: What difference does it make? They've got enough to blow us up now anyway. This is a political struggle as much as military.

Thursday 18 October
The group discusses what it would be like to start a nuclear war.

Robert Kennedy: I think George Ball has a hell of a good point.
The President: What?
Robert Kennedy: I think it's the whole question of, you know, assuming that you do survive all this. What kind of country you are.
Ball: Yes, imagine having to live the rest of your life knowing what you have done.
Robert Kennedy: It's a hell of a burden to carry.

Friday 19 October
The military chiefs show that they support tough action.

General Le May: If we don't do anything to Cuba, then they're going to push on Berlin and push real hard because they have got us on the run ... This is almost as bad as the appeasement at Munich ... I just don't see any other solution except direct military action right now. A blockade would be considered by a lot of our friends and neutrals as being a pretty weak response to this. And I'm sure a lot of our own citizens would feel that way too.

Monday 22 October
The President discovers that American nuclear weapons could be fired without him knowing – and he does not like it!

The President: We may be attacking the Cubans and a reprisal may come. I don't want these nuclear weapons firing without our knowing it. Can we take care of it?
Nitze: The Chiefs will object to new orders because it will change their existing instructions. A Soviet nuclear attack requires the immediate execution of the European Defense Plan.
The President: What's the European Defense Plan?
Nitze: Nuclear war.
The President: No ... What we've got to do is to make sure that these fellows don't fire off weapons and put the United States under attack. I don't think we ought to accept the Chiefs' word on that one, Paul.

Unknown to the people involved in the discussions about Cuba, President Kennedy taped most of the talks. They provide some interesting insights into thinking at the time.

Who's who?

Political advisers: Robert Kennedy (the president's brother), Robert McNamara (Secretary of State for Defense), Paul Nitze (Assistant Secretary of State for Defense), Douglas Dillon (Treasury Secretary), Dean Rusk (Secretary of State), George Ball (Under Secretary of State), McGeorge Bundy (president's aide).

Military advisers: General Maxwell Taylor (Chairman, Joint Chiefs of Staff), General Curtis Le May (Air Force Chief of Staff).

SOURCE H

A cartoon published in the *Daily Express* in October 1962. President Kennedy and Khrushchev are seen as gunslingers waiting to see who will draw his gun first. Castro is seen riding on a donkey.

On 24 October 1962, a group of Soviet ships reached the American blockade. One oil tanker was allowed through without being searched. The other ships turned back. President Kennedy's brother, Robert, said that in the eyeball-to-eyeball confrontation 'Khrushchev just blinked'. Nuclear warfare had been avoided.

The Soviet ships had turned around, but the crisis was not over. The Soviet Union still had missiles on the island which had to be moved. Then, on 26 October, Khrushchev sent Kennedy a letter suggesting that, if the Americans lifted the blockade and promised not to invade Cuba, the nuclear weapons would be removed. This was excellent news for Kennedy and was the first time that the Soviet Union had admitted that it had nuclear weapons on Cuba. But before the USA could reply, things took a turn for the worse.

On 27 October, a second letter arrived from Khrushchev. It said that Soviet missiles on Cuba were no more of a threat to the USA than American missiles in Turkey were to the Soviet Union. Khrushchev said that he would remove the Cuban missiles if the USA removed its missiles in Turkey.

The Americans had considered removing the missiles in Turkey, but felt strongly that they could not be seen to do so because the Soviet Union had demanded it. Then on the same day a U-2 spy plane was shot down over Cuba. Some of Kennedy's advisers wanted him to take military action. Instead he decided to ignore Khrushchev's second letter and respond to the first. Kennedy sent a letter saying that he agreed to the terms set out in the letter of 26 October, but that if the missiles were not removed, an attack would follow.

On the same day, Robert Kennedy went to visit the Soviet ambassador in Washington and told him that the Americans would consider removing missiles in Turkey 'within a short time'. On 28 October, Khrushchev sent a message saying that the missiles on Cuba would be dismantled. The crisis was over.

Consequences of the crisis

Although Khrushchev had thought that Kennedy was a weak president, the American leader had emerged from the crisis as the victor – especially as the deal on the missiles in Turkey was kept

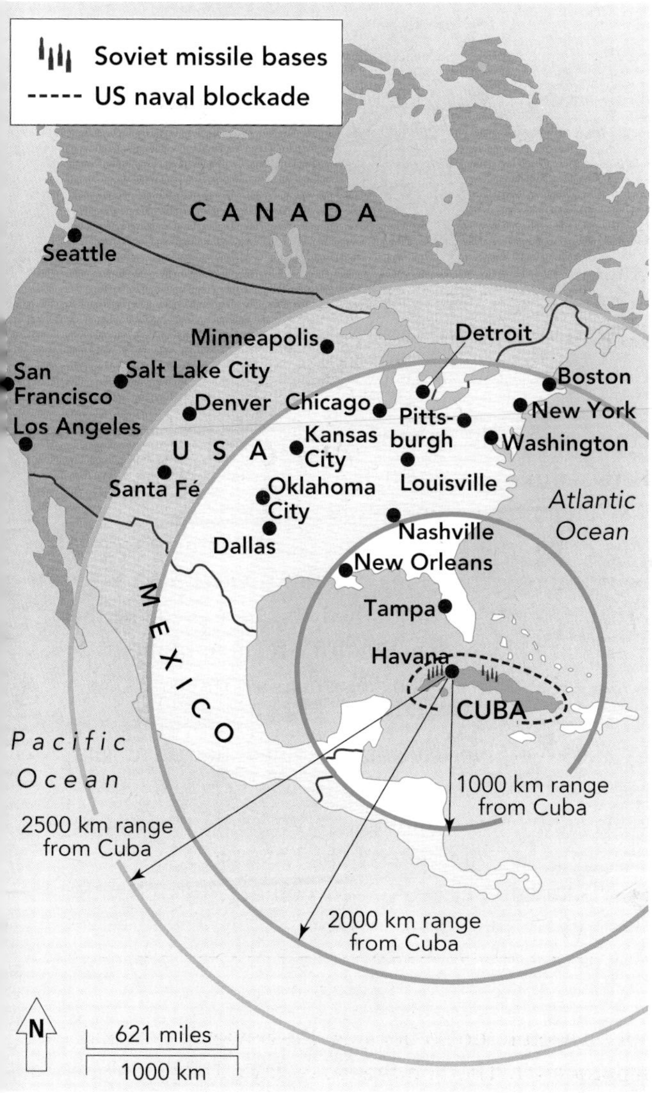

American cities that could be reached by missiles fired from Cuba.

quiet. Khrushchev claimed that the crisis was a victory for the Soviet Union and that the independence of communist Cuba had been guaranteed. In reality, some leading Soviet politicians were angry that their country had been forced to back down. This played a significant part in Khrushchev's dismissal in 1964.

The two sides had learned from the crisis that confrontation between them threatened world peace. So steps were taken to reduce the threat of nuclear war. A direct 'hot-line' phone link was set up between Washington and the Kremlin, and a Nuclear Test Ban Treaty was signed in 1963. Although the two sides had nearly gone to war, the crisis had helped to thaw the Cold War just a little.

SOURCE I

We sent the Americans a note saying that we agreed to remove our missiles and bombers on condition that the President gives us assurances that there would be no invasion of Cuba. Finally Kennedy gave in and agreed to make a statement giving us such an assurance. It was a great victory for us, a spectacular success without having to fire a single shot.

Extracts from Khrushchev's memoirs, written in the late 1960s.

The Cuban missile crisis – a summary

14 October	Soviet missile sites spotted.
16 October	President Kennedy informed.
22 October	Blockade set up. Kennedy broadcasts to nation.
23 October	Khrushchev calls blockade 'piracy'.
24 October	Soviet ships agree to turn round.
26 October	Khrushchev's first letter arrives.
27 October	Khrushchev's second letter arrives. US plane shot down. Kennedy responds to first letter. Robert Kennedy visits Soviet ambassador.
28 October	Khrushchev agrees to remove weapons.

QUESTIONS

1 How big a threat was the Cuban missile crisis to world peace?

2 What could a historian studying the Cuban missile crisis learn from Source G?

3 How reliable is Source I for a historian studying the consequences of the Cuban missile crisis?

American involvement in Vietnam

Why did the Americans fight in Vietnam?

Vietnam had been part of the French colonies until it was captured by the Japanese in 1941. After the Japanese defeat in the Second World War, the French tried to regain their old territory, but they were defeated by the Viet Minh, the armed forces of the Vietnamese independence movement. Vietnam was freed from French rule in 1954, but was divided into two separate countries. North Vietnam was run as a communist country and led by Ho Chi Minh. South Vietnam was anti-communist and led by Ngo Dinh Diem.

Diem's government in the south was hated by many of its people. He was a Catholic who ruled a largely Buddhist population in a corrupt and repressive way. Many Vietnamese peasants gave their support to the Vietcong, a group of communist guerrillas in South Vietnam who wanted to overthrow Diem. The Vietcong received supplies from the government in North Vietnam.

Diem's government, however, received aid from the Americans. They based their policy on the 'domino theory'. They believed that the Vietcong were trying to spread communism into South Vietnam. If the Vietcong were successful, the Americans believed that other countries in Asia would fall to communism like a row of dominoes. It was vital that the South Vietnamese government was supported, so Vietnam became part of the USA's Cold War containment policy.

How was help given?

Between 1954 and 1960, the USA sent equipment and 'military advisers' into South Vietnam. Meanwhile, the Vietcong and North Vietnam were being supplied by China and the Soviet Union. From 1961 President Kennedy began increasing the number of advisers in South Vietnam until there were more than 11,000 Americans in the country.

By 1963 the Americans had decided that Diem was too corrupt to support, and he was deposed and replaced by anti-communist army generals. Despite American aid, the Vietcong had managed to take over about 40 per cent of the countryside of South Vietnam by 1963.

War in Vietnam

1. 2 August 1964. North Vietnamese ships attack a US destroyer in the Gulf of Tonkin. US Congress passes the Tonkin Resolution giving President Johnson wide military powers.
2. 7 February 1965. Operation Rolling Thunder – bombing of targets in North Vietnam.
3. 14 November 1965. US Army fights North Vietnamese in La Drang Valley.
4. 22 January – 7 April 1968. Siege of Khe Sanh: 6000 American troops evacuated after 77 days.
5. Tet Offensive, 30 January – 26 February 1968. Vietcong attack Hue, Saigon and other towns.
6. 1 May – 29 June 1970. USA invades Cambodia.

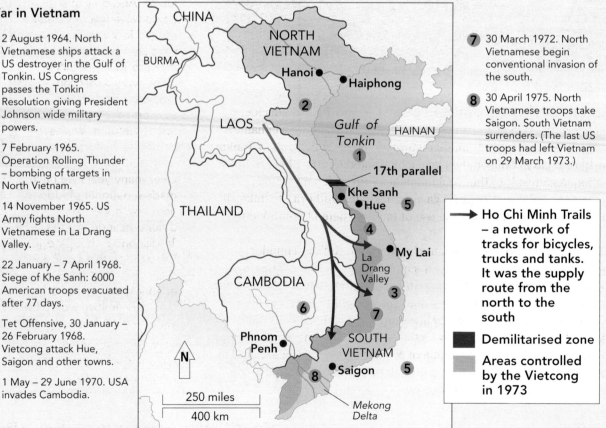

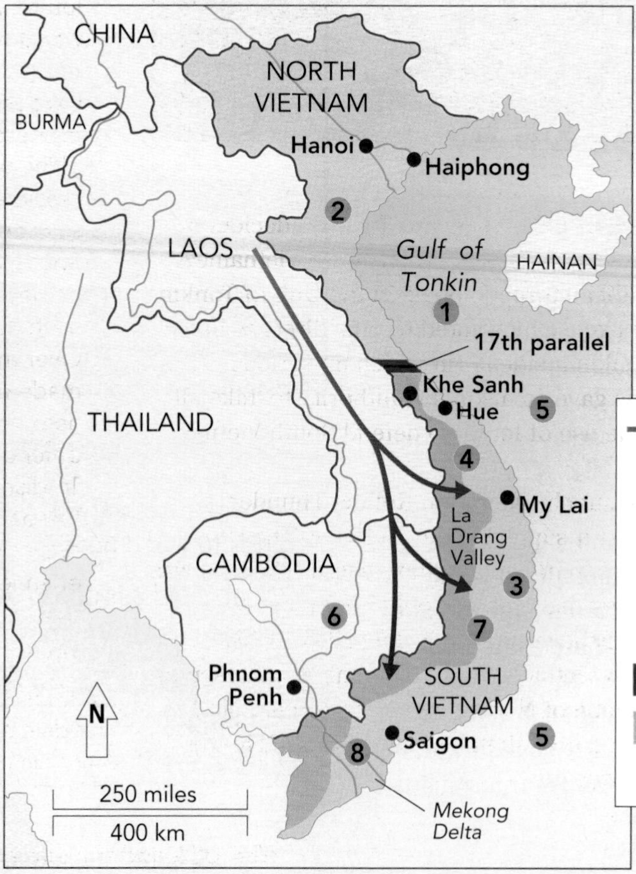

7. 30 March 1972. North Vietnamese begin conventional invasion of the south.
8. 30 April 1975. North Vietnamese troops take Saigon. South Vietnam surrenders. (The last US troops had left Vietnam on 29 March 1973.)

The domino theory.

SOURCE J

An aerial view of US bombing in North Vietnam.

SOURCE K

> We fight this war because we must fight if we are to live in a world where every country can shape its own future. And only in such a world will a future be safe. We are in Vietnam because we have a promise to keep. Since 1954 every American president has offered support to the people of South Vietnam. We have helped to build and we have helped to defend. Over many years we have made a national pledge to help South Vietnam defend its independence. To dishonour that pledge, to abandon this small and brave nation to its enemies, and to the terror that must follow, would be an unforgivable wrong.

President Johnson talking to the American people in 1965.

After Kennedy's assassination in 1963, President Johnson decided to increase American involvement in Vietnam. When North Vietnamese torpedo boats attacked American torpedo boats in the Gulf of Tonkin in 1964, it gave Johnson the excuse he wanted to take direct military action. As a result of the 'Tonkin incident' (in which no serious damage was done), Congress gave Johnson the authority to 'take all necessary steps, including the use of force' to defend South Vietnam.

Johnson's first move was to launch 'Operation Rolling Thunder' against North Vietnam, to stop it supplying the Vietcong. The USA bombed factories, supply lines, ports and military bases. The idea was for the bombing to be so heavy that troops would not be needed. However, the bombing was unsuccessful, so in July 1965 180,000 American troops were sent to Vietnam. Soon the number had risen to over half a million. The bombing of North Vietnam continued until more bombs had been dropped on it than had been dropped in the whole of the Second World War.

American difficulties

The American troops in Vietnam had vastly superior weapons to those used by the Vietcong. American soldiers had mortars, machine guns and rocket launchers and were supported by tanks, armoured vehicles and helicopters. Yet they could not win the war. Why was this?

The main reason for the American failure is that the way the war was fought gave an advantage to the Vietcong. The Americans could easily win any pitched battle, but the Vietcong avoided this and instead fought a guerrilla war. They came out of the jungle to carry out acts of sabotage and sudden ambushes, and then quickly returned into the jungle. As they had the support of most of the local population, they could easily be absorbed back into village life and the Americans could not tell the difference between ordinary peasants and Vietcong members.

The soldiers in Vietnam, who had an average age of just 19, found the war extremely frustrating. They might be victims of an ambush or a booby trap in which their comrades were killed or maimed. Yet when they went off in pursuit of the Vietcong who had attacked them, they were met by a wall of silence from villagers. Under these circumstances, soldiers sometimes lost control and carried out terrible atrocities. One of the most infamous of these occurred at My Lai in March 1968. A group of American soldiers landed by helicopter to search for Vietcong. When they could not find any, they rounded up the inhabitants of the village and massacred them all. The officer in charge, Lieutenant William Calley, was tried for the murder of 109 civilians. He was found guilty and sentenced to life imprisonment. But he was released after serving only three days on the instructions of President Nixon.

New tactics

The Americans adopted a variety of tactics to try to defeat the Vietcong guerrilla warfare.

- Strategic villages were set up. Whole villages were moved to new sites behind barbed wire. Careful control was kept on who entered and left the villages. Special aid was given to villagers to try to win their support.
- As the Vietcong could hide easily in the jungle,

SOURCE L

A Chinese poster showing the Vietnamese people resisting the Americans in South Vietnam.

QUESTIONS

1 Why did the Americans become involved in Vietnam?

2 Explain how American military involvement increased in the period 1954–65.

3 a What difficulties did the Americans have in Vietnam?

  b How did they attempt to overcome those difficulties?

An American soldier taking a member of the Vietcong prisoner.

SOURCE M

the Americans carried out a policy of defoliation. The leaves were removed from the trees by dropping Agent Orange (a strong chemical) from the air. The jungle was destroyed, but even today some areas are unfit for human habitation.

- Napalm, a type of petroleum jelly that burns fiercely and sticks to the skin, was dropped from aircraft to burn jungle or set fire to villages. Thousands of innocent villagers received terrible burns.

The new tactics did not work. The Vietcong continued to receive supplies from North Vietnam down a series of jungle tracks called the Ho Chi Minh Trails. Lorries, bikes and human backs carried millions of tons of supplies provided by North Vietnam and China. In the jungle, the Vietcong built an extensive network of tunnels where they had storehouses, workshops, kitchens and even hospitals. No amount of Agent Orange would destroy such a system.

The cost of the war in civilian lives was enormous. It has been estimated that 300,000 South Vietnamese civilians were killed in 1968. These deaths occurred in a war that the Americans were fighting to 'save the people from the evils of communism'. No wonder so many South Vietnamese hated the Americans and so many American soldiers began to wonder what they were doing in Vietnam.

SOURCE N

The problem with the American strategy was that, though the suffering of the enemy was great, it was not enough to make them concede. Throughout the war, the capacity of the North Vietnamese to absorb pain outstripped that of the Americans to inflict it. For the Americans, the war was a 'limited one' far from home. For the North Vietnamese it was total: they were fighting to defend their homeland.

A modern historian's view of the reasons why the Americans did not win the Vietnam War.

SOURCE O

We were sitting in this wretched little outpost one day when a sergeant of mine said to me, 'You know, Lieutenant. I don't see how we are ever going to win this.' And I said, 'Well, Sarge, I'm not supposed to say this to you as your officer – but I don't either!' So there was this sense, at least in my platoon and maybe in the whole company in general, that we just couldn't see what could be done to defeat these people.

A Marine Corps platoon commander remembering a conversation he had with one of his sergeants in Vietnam in 1966.

The Tet Offensive

Although the Vietcong largely stuck to guerrilla warfare, they did carry out some major offensives. One of these was the Tet Offensive of 1968, when communist troops attacked major South Vietnamese towns and American bases. They even carried out an attack on the American embassy in Saigon. At first the Americans were pushed into retreat, but they soon hit back and regained all the towns and bases that had been captured. By the end of the offensive, 50,000 communist troops had been killed. The Vietcong had hoped that the offensive would result in a revolution in South Vietnam, but it did not.

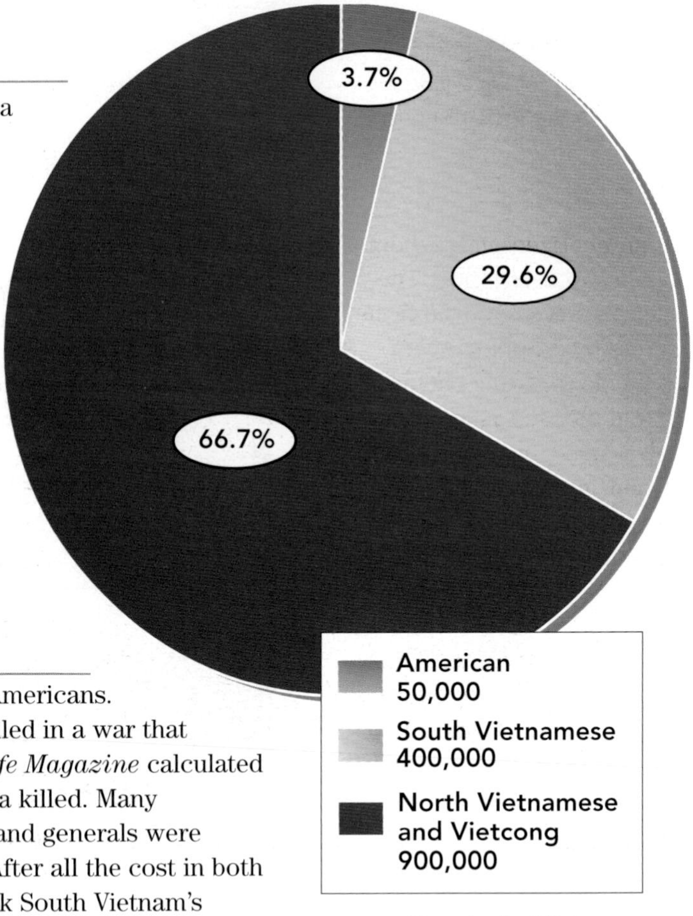

Deaths in Vietnam.

Time to get out

The offensive did have a major effect on the Americans. By 1968, 300 Americans a week were being killed in a war that was costing $30,000 million a year. In 1967, *Life Magazine* calculated that it cost $400,000 for each Vietcong guerrilla killed. Many Americans now realised that their politicians and generals were wrong when they said that victory was near. After all the cost in both money and lives, the Vietcong could still attack South Vietnam's capital, Saigon. The time had come to get out.

Protest at home

Most Americans supported their government's decision to send troops to Vietnam. They genuinely believed that there was a communist threat and that it was in the USA's interests to fight it. But as the war went on, attitudes changed. Vietnam was the first 'televised war'. Night after night, pictures could be seen of villages being napalmed, of civilian casualties and of American soldiers killed before they were out of their teens. Stories soon reached home of widespread drug addiction and indiscipline in the army. When the My Lai atrocity was reported in 1969, some Americans were shocked that their own troops could do such a thing.

The human costs of the Vietnam War.

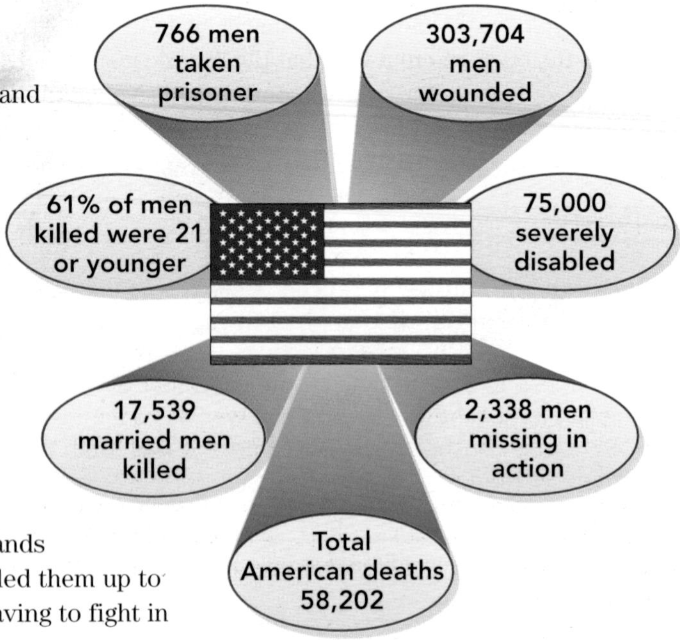

As more and more sons and brothers returned either in body bags or maimed for life, public opinion began to turn against the war. There were increasing numbers of demonstrations in American cities, and thousands of young men burned the 'draft cards' that called them up to fight in Vietnam. Some fled abroad to avoid having to fight in

SOURCE P

An American anti-war poster. It is based on a recruiting poster from the First World War. But on this occasion, Uncle Sam is wounded and wants to get out of the war.

a war of which they disapproved so much. President Johnson came under enormous criticism and across the USA students taunted him with chants of 'Hey, hey, LBJ, how many kids did you kill today?' Johnson decided to end the bombing of North Vietnam and not to stand for re-election in 1968. It was left to the next president, Richard Nixon, to find a way to get American troops out of Vietnam.

Vietnamisation

President Nixon had a difficult task in taking the USA out of the Vietnam War. He could not just say that the Americans had decided that it was all too much trouble and they were going to leave. Since 1965 American governments had been persuading people at home and abroad that the war was both just and vital to American interests. Thousands of Americans had died fighting for their country and it would be an insult to their memory merely to withdraw the troops and admit defeat.

But the American people had turned against the war and Nixon had promised that he would bring it to an end. His solution was to introduce a policy of 'Vietnamisation'. The Americans would give the war back to the South Vietnamese.

SOURCE Q

On 4 May 1970, 3000 students gathered at Kent State University to protest about the Vietnam War. At midday National Guardsmen fired tear gas to break up the demonstration. Some students threw the tear gas canisters back and hurled stones at the troops, who opened fire. Four students, none of whom was involved in the demonstration, were killed. President Nixon later called the student protestors 'bums'.

SOURCE R

I don't give a damn
For Uncle Sam
I ain't going
To Vietnam.

An anti-war protest chant from the late 1960s.

Obviously the South Vietnamese army was not strong enough to fight the war on its own, so the Americans would help build it up and would train and equip it. Then American troops could withdraw. While this policy was being put in place, peace talks would be held with North Vietnam to try to end the war.

QUESTIONS

1 Why did the Vietnam War become so unpopular in the USA?

2 a What was Vietnamisation?
  b What judgement does Source T make on this policy?

3 Do you think that the Vietnam War was one that the Americans could never win?

The communists triumph

The Americans slowly withdrew and at first the new policy appeared to be working well. Soon half the male population of South Vietnam was in the army and a major offensive by the North Vietnamese was successfully resisted. Then, in February 1973, a cease-fire was agreed with North Vietnam and the Vietcong. By the end of the year, all American troops had left Vietnam and the war appeared to be over.

The reality was something different, however. The Americans had suspected that the cease-fire might not last and had promised South Vietnam further support if fighting broke out again. They did not keep this promise. When the war restarted in 1974, the Americans sent supplies, but no troops.

During 1975 communist troops over-ran much of South Vietnam, and Saigon fell in April. Neighbouring Laos and Cambodia were also captured by communist forces. In 1976 North and South Vietnam were united in a single communist country under the rule of Ho Chi Minh. The American policy of containment in south-east Asia had failed.

SOURCE S

I saw the terrible destruction that was done to our country. I saw the villages and fields destroyed. Every time the Americans increased their destruction of our land, more and more young men and women would rally to our side to join us in our fight for freedom.

A member of the Vietcong explaining the effects of the American tactics in Vietnam.

SOURCE T

A British cartoon showing the problems facing President Nixon in 1969.

Paper 1–type assessment: US policy in Cuba and Vietnam

SOURCE A

'If this boy of yours *is* real, how come we gotta wind him up all the time?'

A British cartoon commenting on Nixon's policy of Vietnamisation in 1969.

QUESTIONS

Section A Questions

1a Study Source A. Explain the message of this cartoon. Support your answer by referring to details of the cartoon and your own knowledge. (6)

b Explain why the USA decided to go to war in Vietnam. (9)

Section B Questions

2a What happened in the 'Bay of Pigs Incident' in April 1961?(4)

b Explain why the Soviet Union wanted to station nuclear missiles in Cuba. (6)

c 'The most important outcome of the Cuban Missile Crisis was that President Kennedy's position as a world leader was improved'. Do you agree with this statement? Explain your answer. (10)

How secure was the USSR's control over eastern Europe 1948–c.1989?

By 1948 the Soviet Union had secured its western border by extending communism into a number of east European states. The task that lay ahead was to ensure that the communist system remained in place when it was challenged from within. In 1956 and 1968 Soviet military power ensured that communism survived in Hungary and Czechoslovakia, but in the 1980s the demand for change was so great that even the Soviet Union itself was swept away in the tide of reform.

Khrushchev and the countries of the Warsaw Pact

In 1953 Stalin died and was succeeded by Nikita Khrushchev. Would his treatment of the communist countries in the Warsaw Pact prove as tough as Stalin's had been?

Early signs of Khrushchev's approach were seen in East Germany in 1953 when workers demonstrated against working conditions and lack of political freedom. Khrushchev ordered the Soviet Red Army to 'restore order' and 21 workers were killed.

In 1956 there were demonstrations against food prices in Poland. The Polish government was unable to keep control and so, once again, Soviet troops were sent to restore order. But there were signs of a different approach too. Khrushchev appointed Vladislav Gomulka as the new leader of the Polish Communist Party. He had been imprisoned by Stalin and his appointment was very popular. Khrushchev also allowed some reforms that gave the Poles more freedom.

Then Khrushchev launched a bitter attack on Stalin's treatment of the Soviet Union's communist neighbours. He ended the dispute between the Soviet Union and Tito's communist Yugoslavia and told the Yugoslavian people that the Soviet Union believed in 'equality, non-interference, respect for sovereignty and national independence'.

But if the other communist countries hoped that under Khrushchev they would be allowed to have a much greater say in running their own affairs, they were soon to be disappointed.

Why was there opposition to Soviet control in Hungary in 1956?

During Stalin's years, Hungary had been ruled by Matyas Rakosi, a hard-line communist who ensured that the country remained loyal to the Soviet Union. His policies caused great resentment in Hungary:

- Soviet troops were stationed in Hungary to ensure loyalty, and a special secret police force (the AVO) carried out a terror campaign against anyone opposing government policy.
- Communist control extended to radio, newspapers and the arts. Strict censorship meant that Hungarians had no freedom of speech.
- In education, a communist 'eastern' history was taught to children. Hungary's historical links with the West were played down and its relations with eastern countries emphasised.
- Although the Hungarians were a deeply religious people, the Communist Party discouraged religious belief.

The Hungarian people heard the news of reform in Poland with great excitement. Perhaps this gave them an opportunity in their own country? Even within the Hungarian Communist Party there was opposition to Rakosi and he was forced to resign in July 1956. But his successor, Erno Gero, was not popular among the Hungarian people, who saw him as just another hard-line communist.

Soon Gero began to lose control. On 6 October 1956 thousands of Hungarians turned out to witness the state funeral of Laszlo Rajik. He was a communist leader who had wanted Hungary to break away from Soviet control. Stalin had him tried and executed. Now it was decided that he should be reburied and have a state funeral. This would allow the Hungarians to show proper respect. It also allowed them to voice their opposition to Moscow.

On 23 October there was rioting on the streets of the capital Budapest and fighting between demonstrators and the AVO. Khrushchev responded by appointing the reforming politician, Imre Nagy, as prime minister. But he also sent tanks into Budapest.

At first, Nagy appeared to be achieving reform with Soviet approval, and after just one week the Soviet tanks were withdrawn. Yet any hopes that Khrushchev had of Hungary 'settling down' were soon dashed. At the end of October, Nagy announced that one-party rule would end in Hungary, Soviet forces would be withdrawn from the country and Hungary would leave the Warsaw Pact.

How did the Soviet Union react?

These reforms were too much for Khrushchev. Although Nagy intended to keep Hungary as a communist country, there was no way that the Soviet Union would allow one of its 'satellite states' to leave the Warsaw Pact and threaten Soviet security. So, on 4 November, 200,000 Soviet troops, supported by 2500 tanks, arrived in Budapest. But unlike in Poland, the Hungarians fought against the Soviet troops. Nagy made an appeal to the United Nations for help, and radio messages begged for assistance from the West.

The western powers, however, did not send support. In 1956 Britain, the USA and France were squabbling over who should control the Suez Canal, and the Americans were not prepared to send troops into Hungary. Preventing the spread of communism was one thing, sending troops to fight in a country that was already communist was another.

SOURCE A

The Hungarian government immediately repudiates the Warsaw Treaty and declares Hungary's neutrality. It turns to the United Nations and requests the help of the great powers in defending the country's neutrality.

Prime Minister Nagy appealing to the United Nations for help against the invading forces.

SOURCE B

A member of the AVO murdered by demonstrators in October 1956.

QUESTIONS

1 How similar were the policies of Stalin and Khrushchev towards members of the Warsaw Pact?

2 Why did the Soviet Union invade Hungary?

SOURCE C

Hungarian rebels in the streets of Budapest in November 1956.

Although they fought with fierce determination, without military support from the West, the Hungarian rebels stood no chance against the Soviet Red Army. After two weeks of fierce fighting, up to 27,000 Hungarians are thought to have died, but Soviet control was restored. Nagy was dismissed and replaced by Janos Kadar. Nagy fled to the Yugoslavian embassy in Budapest. He was later captured and hanged in Moscow.

As Khrushchev had intended, the communist countries of eastern Europe had been taught a lesson, although communists around the world were horrified by the severity of the Soviet action. Anti-communist feeling in the West intensified. Although it had taken no action, the USA became even more determined to resist Soviet expansion in Europe. However, the people of Hungary were embittered by the lack of support from the West. The United Nations had been discredited. It had tried to call for a withdrawal of Soviet troops and to set up a Committee of Investigation, but these moves had been blocked by the Soviet Union.

Why was there opposition to Soviet control in Czechoslovakia in 1968?

By 1968 Khrushchev had been replaced as Soviet leader by Leonid Brezhnev. He continued the policy of firm Soviet control of satellite countries – as the Czechs were to find out in 1968.

- Czechoslovakia, like other communist countries, had no freedom of speech, and radio, television and newspapers were censored.
- All candidates in elections were members of the Communist Party. Many Czechs wanted the right to form their own parties, have more say in how their factories were run and not be subject to control by the Soviet Union.

SOURCE D

There is no stopping the wild onslaught of communism. Your turn will also come, once we perish. Save our souls! Save our souls! We implore you to help us in the name of justice and of freedom.

A broadcast from an unidentified radio station in Hungary on 4 November 1956.

- Czech industry was run for the benefit of the Soviet Union and few consumer goods were produced. So the standard of living for Czech citizens was low.

In the 1960s, protests against the low standard of living and lack of political freedom began to increase. In 1966 student demonstrations were broken up by the police and critics of the government were imprisoned.

By 1968 it was obvious that the Czech leadership was out of touch with the people. Consequently, in January, President Novotny was replaced by Jan Svoboda, and Alexander Dubcek became party secretary – effectively the ruler of Czechoslovakia.

Dubcek talked about providing 'socialism with a human face'. He wanted to raise people's living standards and give them more freedom. He introduced a number of reforms to reduce government control.

- He allowed public meetings and discussions, and relaxed censorship. It would no longer be a crime to criticise the government.
- Trade unions were given greater freedom and government control of industry was relaxed. Now managers and workers had a greater say in what they did.
- More foreign travel was allowed.

SOURCE E

Czech citizens attacking a Soviet tank in the streets of Prague in August 1968.

Dubcek's reforms became known as the 'Prague Spring' because they represented a thawing in the old repressive communist approach. But Dubcek was careful to reassure Brezhnev that Czechoslovakia had no intention of leaving the Warsaw Pact and that the changes he was making did not threaten the Soviet Union.

Brezhnev was not convinced. He disapproved of the increased liberties being given to the Czechs. Wouldn't people in other communist countries want them too? Anyway, Czechoslovakia was too important to lose to communism. It was the link between West Germany and the Soviet Union. It had to stay communist. Already Yugoslavia was independent and Romania was refusing to attend Warsaw Pact meetings. What if the three countries formed an alliance? Wouldn't that mean the end of the Warsaw Pact?

How did the Soviet Union react?

At first, Brezhnev tried to threaten Dubcek by having Warsaw Pact troops carry out army 'manoeuvres' in Czechoslovakia. Then in July 1968, Dubcek was warned that his reforms threatened the rule of the Communist Party in Czechoslovakia. Finally, when Dubcek invited Tito of Yugoslavia and Ceausescu of Romania to Czechoslovakia for talks, Brezhnev acted.

On 20 August 1968, Warsaw Pact forces entered Czechoslovakia and took control. Although there was some street fighting, there was none of the bloodshed that had been seen in Budapest in 1956. For some of the invading army, however, their hostile reception came as a shock. They had been told that the Czech government had invited them in to restore law and order. They expected to be greeted with enthusiasm, not contempt.

QUESTIONS

1 What were the consequences of the Soviet invasion in Hungary?

2 a What did Dubcek mean by 'socialism with a human face'?
  b Why did the Soviet Union oppose Dubcek's changes?

SOURCE F

A drawing on a wall in a Prague street in 1968, twenty years after the Soviet Union had liberated Czechoslovakia from Nazi rule.

One Czech student, Jan Palach, set fire to himself in Wenceslas Square as a protest against the invasion. His funeral became a focus for protest against the Soviet Union. In February 1969, thousands of Czechs took to the streets once more – this time to celebrate the Czech victory over the Soviet Union in the world ice hockey championships.

The Spring reversed

Dubcek was arrested, sent to Moscow and forced to agree to reverse his reforms. Then in 1969 he was forcibly removed from office and replaced by Gustav Husak. Shortly afterwards, over a thousand Czechs were detained in two days of arrests.

The Soviet Union had successfully clamped down on attempts to reform communist rule. In what became known as the Brezhnev Doctrine, the Soviet Union announced that it was the task of all Warsaw Pact countries to act together to resist an attempt by any member to abandon communism.

How similar were events in Hungary in 1956 and in Czechoslovakia in 1968?

Although there were obvious differences between the two events, in many ways they were very similar. The Hungarians had tried to break completely free from the Soviet Union, whereas the Czechs considered themselves to be loyal members of the Warsaw Pact. But as far as the Soviet Union was concerned, both 'uprisings' threatened the unity of the Warsaw Pact and therefore the security of the Soviet Union. They had to be stopped with force, before their influence spread to other communist countries. There was little difference in the eventual methods used to restore the control of the Moscow government.

Why was the Berlin Wall built in 1961?

As you read on pages 218–19, the city of Berlin was divided into four zones after the Second World War. By 1961 these had become West Berlin and East Berlin. The French, British and Americans controlled West Berlin, and their investment helped to create a wealthy city with all the consumer benefits that people in other western countries were enjoying. Soviet-controlled East Berlin, however, was not prosperous and was under strict communist control. Not surprisingly, many East Germans, particularly skilled craftsmen and professional people, crossed from East to West Berlin and on to West Germany. The Soviet Union had to find a way to stop this huge flood of refugees, which deprived East Germany of over two and a half million citizens between 1949 and 1961.

Of course, Berlin was also a pawn in the political game being played between the Soviet Union and the USA in the Cold War. The Soviet Union saw West Berlin as a capitalist boil in the middle of Soviet-controlled East Germany. It wanted the three western allies out of West Berlin. The USA, however, was determined to protect 'free' West Berlin from communism.

In June 1961, the Soviet leader, Khrushchev, met the new American president, J. F. Kennedy, in a summit meeting in Vienna. Khrushchev demanded that the western powers leave Berlin. Kennedy insisted that he would stand by Berlin. Both sides stepped up their spending on weapons and there seemed to be a threat of war over Berlin.

The wall goes up

Khrushchev, however, had a better solution than war. On 13 August 1961, Soviet troops put up barbed-wire barricades all around West Berlin. Later they were replaced with the more substantial 'Berlin Wall'. West Berlin was cut off from East Berlin and anyone trying to cross was shot. In all, 86 people are known to have died trying to cross the Berlin Wall between 1961 and 1989.

The building of the wall was extremely unpopular in Berlin. In places, East German troops had to clear protesters away from the wall. The border took no account of roads or even houses. Some roads simply came to an end as the wall crossed them, and some houses found that they had doorways in the East and back windows in the West. In several tenement blocks, East Berliners tried to cross to the West by throwing mattresses out of their windows and jumping on to them. Sometimes West Berliners caught them in fire blankets. Sometimes they fell to their deaths.

SOURCE G

The body of Peter Fechter, an eighteen-year-old bricklayer in East Berlin. On 17 August 1962 he tried to cross into West Berlin to join his sister. He was shot by border police as he climbed the barbed wire on the eastern side and fell back into the strip between East and West. He could be heard crying for help and shouting his sister's name as he slowly bled to death. Fechter was only 300 metres from the West Berlin border post, and as crowds grew on the western side to witness the awful spectacle, they begged the Americans to rescue him. But the soldiers were told by their officers not to intervene. An hour later, East German guards collected Fechter's body.

Yet the wall achieved its purpose. The flood of refugees to the West ended and the Soviet Union was able to develop East Berlin as it wanted. However, the wall did provide opponents of communism with a propaganda opportunity. If communism was such a great system, they asked, why did the Soviet Union have to build a wall to stop people running away?

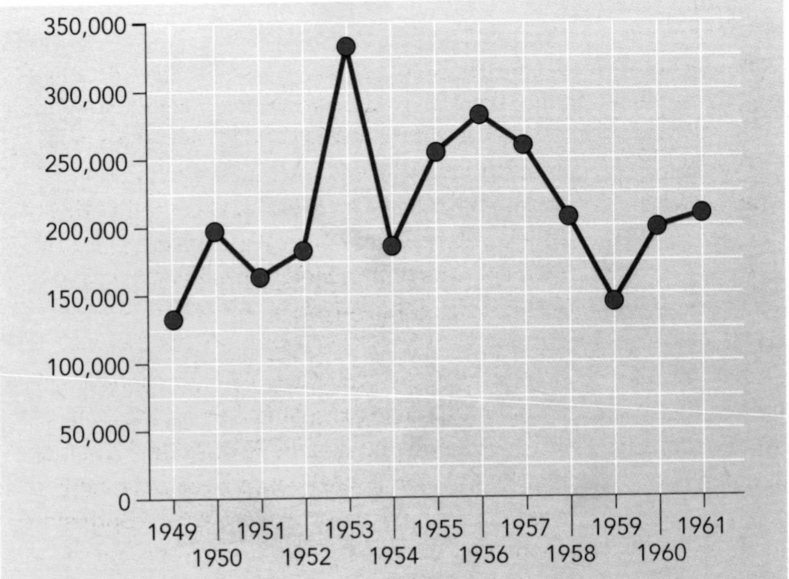

Refugees from East Berlin to West Berlin, 1949–61.

What was the significance of 'Solidarity' in Poland for the decline of Soviet influence in eastern Europe?

Soviet control was extremely unpopular in Poland. Many Poles were strong Catholics, who were fiercely proud of their country's history. They also remembered how the Red Army had failed to help the Poles in the Warsaw Rising of 1944, and claimed that Soviet troops had carried out atrocities in Poland equally as bad as those carried out by the Nazis.

In the period after 1949, there were many protests in Poland. In both 1956 and 1970, a series of strikes by Polish factory workers and farmers led to changes in the leadership of the country. During the 1970s, industry performed better in Poland than in most east European countries and there was a degree of prosperity within the country. Although they hated Soviet influence, many Poles seemed to have accepted that life under communism could be quite successful. In the late 1970s, however, the Polish economy went into recession and the standard of living fell. Polish workers began to form trade unions, and when the government announced increases in the price of food in July 1980, there was an outbreak of strikes.

The most influential of the newly formed trade unions was 'Solidarity'. This was a union of workers at the Gdansk shipyards, led by Lech Walesa. The union soon became a symbol of opposition to authoritarian communist government.

QUESTIONS

1 What were the similarities and differences in the Hungarian uprising and the Prague Spring?

2 Why was there so much opposition to Soviet control in Poland?

3 Why did the Polish government find it so difficult to deal with Solidarity?

Solidarity versus the government

In August 1980, Solidarity issued 21 demands calling for greater political and religious freedom. Its size was increasing all the time – by the end of 1980, Solidarity had over 9 million members.

The government was in a difficult position. Solidarity was a popular trade union and as many as a third of the members of the Polish Communist Party were in the union. Lech Walesa was a highly popular figure with enormous support in Poland. He was also becoming widely known across the world as the media in other countries watched events in Poland with interest.

SOURCE H

Lech Walesa addressing a Solidarity meeting.

Yet, although Walesa was careful not to provoke action that would offend the Soviet Union, the Polish government came under increasing pressure from Moscow to deal with Solidarity before it became too powerful and before its influence spread to other communist countries. The Soviet Union considered sending troops into Poland, as it had into Hungary and Czechoslovakia. But the Soviet government decided that Solidarity's support was too widespread to be dealt with by tanks.

Instead, in February 1981 a new prime minister, Wojciech Jaruzelski, was appointed. He was told to bring Solidarity into line. By this time, Solidarity was demanding a role in the government. Jaruzelski could not allow Solidarity to become a political party in opposition to the Communist Party. Yet the wave of strikes and protests was having a damaging effect on Poland's already fragile economy. Unemployment and inflation were rising and there were such food shortages that rationing had to be introduced in April 1981.

So, in December 1981, Jaruzelski declared martial law. This gave him special powers which he used to arrest Walesa and 10,000 other Solidarity members. Solidarity itself was declared illegal and meetings or demonstrations in its favour were banned. While Jaruzelski took these measures, Brezhnev sent the Red Army to carry out manoeuvres on the Polish border. It was a warning to the prime minister and the Polish people of what might happen if things were not settled to Moscow's liking.

SOURCE I

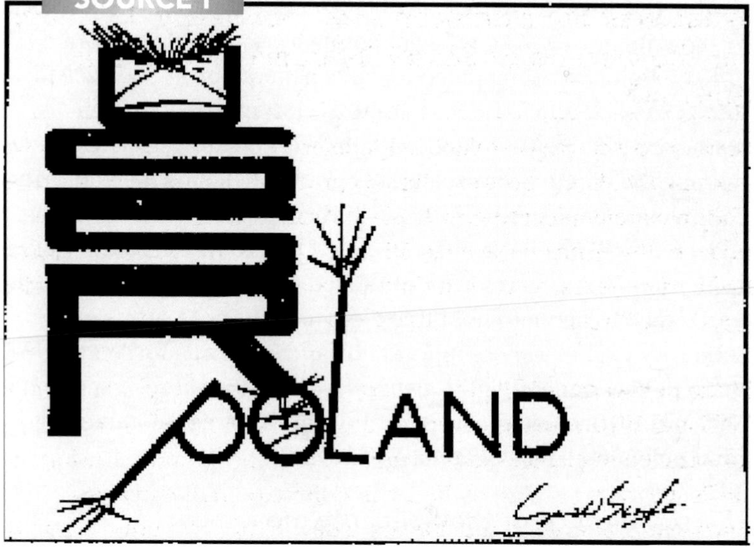

A cartoon in the *Sunday Times* in August 1980. The face of the Soviet Union is that of Leonid Brezhnev, the Soviet leader.

Having arrested the leaders of Solidarity, Jaruzelski now set up his own union, the Patriotic Movement for National Regeneration, and forced government workers to join it. But his tough measures did not work. Walesa's imprisonment merely added to his popularity both in Poland and abroad. Solidarity was not crushed and seemed to have even more support in other countries. Jaruzelski was forced to free Walesa in November 1982, and in 1983 Walesa was awarded the Nobel Peace Prize. He had become too powerful to be 'dealt with'.

Jaruzelski continued his campaign against Solidarity, but with little success. A sign of his desperation was that in 1983 he even turned on the Catholic Church, which had been criticising his government. In 1984 the Polish people were outraged to hear that a leading critic of the government, Father Jerzy Popielusko, had been beaten to death by secret police. Almost a quarter of a million Poles attended his funeral in what was really a protest against the government. In response to what was going on in the country, western nations introduced trade sanctions against Poland, which led to further economic problems.

SOURCE J

I was summoned three times to the Soviet Union. On the last occasion I was shown army manoeuvres all along the Polish border. The Soviet army leader, Marshal Ustinov, informed me that what was happening in Poland was intolerable.

General Jaruzelski describing the pressure put on him to deal with Solidarity in late 1981.

Although it was still technically banned, Solidarity once more began to show its power. When the government tried to impose price rises in 1986, Solidarity threatened to call a general strike. Jaruzelski was forced to back down. He was also forced to witness foreign politicians coming to Poland for talks with Lech Walesa, as if he were running the country. Jaruzelski was gradually losing his authority. Following the reforms of Mikhail Gorbachev in the Soviet Union, economic reforms were introduced in Poland. In 1987 Jaruzelski held a referendum on his reforms, but failed to win support. In 1989 he was forced to agree to hold free elections. In those elections Solidarity won massive support and Jaruzelski was forced to give a share in government. Shortly afterwards Jaruzelski resigned and in 1990 Walesa became president of Poland's first non-communist government since the Second World War.

SOURCE K

Mikhail Gorbachev.

The significance of the Solidarity movement

Solidarity had begun life as a trade union aiming to improve conditions for workers in the shipyards. But it had quickly become a mouthpiece for opposition to oppressive communism in Poland. Its greatest significance is that it became so powerful that the Polish government and the Soviet Union were unable to stamp it out. The days of 1956 and 1968, when opposition could be dealt with by Soviet tanks, were in the past. What Solidarity showed people in communist countries was that, if they stood together against oppression, it was very difficult for the authorities to deal with them. This was to prove a very vital lesson in the dramatic events of 1989.

How far was Gorbachev responsible for the collapse of Soviet control over eastern Europe?

The Soviet Union in crisis

In 1985 Mikhail Gorbachev became leader of the Soviet Union. Although it was one of the two great 'superpowers' in the world, the Soviet Union and communism were in crisis.

- Communism was based on a belief in equality and fairness. It had become obvious, however, that there was great corruption in the Soviet system. Party members often lived in luxury and had access to goods that the workers could only dream of.
- The people of the Soviet Union no longer had faith in their government. They did not believe the promises made by politicians and bitterly resented the lack of good-quality consumer goods available in the country, when the West seemed to be getting richer.
- Industry and agriculture were not performing efficiently. Many goods produced in Soviet factories were of such poor quality that they did not work properly. Despite its huge agricultural areas, the Soviet Union had to import millions of tons of grain.
- The Soviet Union's role as head of the Warsaw Pact meant that it was spending huge sums on weapons while many of its citizens lived in poverty. Since 1979 thousands of Soviet troops had been

fighting a war to protect the communist government in Afghanistan. It was estimated that this war alone was costing $8 billion a year.

Gorbachev's solutions

- Gorbachev proposed that the Soviet economy should be improved by a process of 'perestroika' (restructuring) to include some of the practices that made capitalism successful.
- There should be more 'glasnost' (openness) to restore faith in the government and end corruption. Soviet citizens should be more aware of the reasons for government actions. Dissidents (people who criticised the government) should no longer be persecuted.
- There should be a cutback in the money spent on arms and defence. The Soviet Union should pull out of Afghanistan and negotiate arms reductions with the USA. It should also stop spending huge sums interfering in other countries' affairs. The Brezhnev Doctrine should be dropped.

SOURCE L

A cartoon from a British newspaper in January 1990 showing the communist hammer and sickle in tears.

Gorbachev wasted little time in putting his plans into action. In February 1986 the leading Soviet dissident, Andrei Sakharov, was released from prison, and in 1987 reforms were introduced to allow market forces, with buying and selling for individual profit, to be part of the country's economic system. In the same year, a disarmament treaty was signed with the USA, and two years later, further cuts in nuclear weapons were introduced. In December 1988 Gorbachev announced at the United Nations that the Brezhnev Doctrine was no longer part of Soviet policy. From now on, communist governments in eastern Europe had to be responsible for their own policies and could not expect support from the Soviet Red Army.

Reactions to Gorbachev's policies

Hard-line communists were horrified by what Gorbachev was doing. They accused him of betraying communism and threatening the security of the Soviet Union. Introducing market forces into the economy went against the principles of communism. Glasnost and freeing dissidents were bound to stir up trouble and raise the expectations of Soviet citizens when there was little chance of providing them with what they wanted. And the decision to abandon the Brehznev Doctrine and withdraw support from other communist countries was highly dangerous. How was the Soviet Union to be defended if countries in the Warsaw Pact chose to abandon communism?

As it was, this was exactly what happened. In an extraordinary summer in 1989, one by one the communist governments came to an end in Europe.

The break-up of the Soviet Union

By the end of 1989, Gorbachev was in a difficult position. He was a great hero in the eyes of the world. In October he was awarded the Nobel Peace Prize and in December he and the American president, George Bush, met to announce the end of the Cold War.

N
Iron Curtain
2 Poland
In June, Solidarity won free elections, and by the end of the year it had formed the government. In December, Lech Walesa became president.
3 East Germany
In September, thousands of East Germans escaped to Austria and West Germany. In November, the Berlin Wall was pulled down. Free elections were held in March 1990, and East and West Germany were reunited in October 1990.
1 Hungary
In May, the government dismantled the border with non-communist Austria. There was now a hole in the Iron Curtain. In December, free elections were announced for 1990.
Berlin
Warsaw
SOVIET UNION
EAST GERMANY
POLAND
WEST GERMANY
Prague
CZECHOSLOVAKIA
AUSTRIA
Budapest
HUNGARY
ROMANIA
4 Czechoslovakia
In November, mass demonstrations led to the opening of the border with the West. In December, the communist government resigned.
Bucharest
Belgrade
YUGOSLAVIA
BULGARIA
Sofia
ITALY
5 Romania
In December, there was a revolution and the communist dictator, Ceauşescu, and his wife were executed.
ALBANIA
GREECE
300 miles
480 km
6 Bulgaria
In November, Todor Zhirkov, the communist leader since 1954, resigned. A non-communist government was elected in April 1990.

The fall of communist Europe, 1989.

But inside the Soviet Union, Gorbachev was extremely unpopular. The hard-liners hated what he had done and blamed his policies for the fall of communism in eastern Europe. At the same time he was unpopular with liberals in the Soviet Union. His economic reforms did not work because the task was too big to be done quickly. Corruption and inefficiency ran so deep that people were either unable or unwilling to make the changes he required. Many managers, for example, saw his drive for efficiency as a threat to their positions. So they simply made sure that the reforms were not introduced.

SOURCE M

'My life's work has been accomplished,' Mr Gorbachev said last Thursday. Not quite. He did not set out to abolish the Soviet Union, nor the Communist Party. These events happened in spite of his resistance and because, in the long run, the entire Soviet system was heading for disaster. Mr Gorbachev's career is proof not of the impact that one man can make on history, but of how powerful historical forces sweep aside the efforts of one man to resist them.

From an article in an English newspaper on 15 December 1991, shortly before Mikhail Gorbachev's resignation.

However, Gorbachev had taken the lid off a box that could not be closed. The people of the Soviet Union had been promised reforms and resented the fact that they were not getting them. Certainly government was more open, but that merely allowed people to see more of the problems – and the greater freedom to criticise the government just led to more discontent. There were also those, such as Boris Yeltsin, the ex-mayor of Moscow, who criticised Gorbachev for his failure to introduce reforms to make the Soviet Union even more democratic.

The fall of Gorbachev

Following the fall of communism in eastern Europe and the failure of his domestic reforms, Gorbachev's position in the Soviet Union came under great pressure. In February 1990, 250,000 people demonstrated against communism in Moscow, and in the annual May Day parade in Red Square, Gorbachev was heckled by demonstrators. In August 1991 there was an attempt to overthrow Gorbachev, after which he had little authority.

Under pressure from Boris Yeltsin, Gorbachev signed a decree suspending the activities of the Communist Party. Then, in December 1991, the Soviet Union was formally disbanded. A new Commonwealth of Independent States was formed, in which each of the twelve member states was considered to have equal authority. The Russian-dominated Soviet Union was gone. So was its leader. In the same month, Gorbachev resigned.

QUESTIONS

1 Why was communism in crisis in 1985?
2 What solutions did Mikhail Gorbachev propose?
3 Explain the meaning of Source L.
4 Why did the Soviet Union break up?
5 Source M says that Gorbachev lost office because he could not resist historical forces. Do you agree?

SOURCE N

What was my reaction the other night? I'll tell you. I'm a tough old retired colonel, but I had tears in my eyes. The right to choose is priceless. At some point it's worth more than life itself. To see people standing on the wall, where once they would have been shot, I could hardly take it in.

The views of Gail S. Halvorsen, the pilot who organised the 'Little Vittles' campaign in 1948, talking of how he felt when the Berlin Wall came down in 1989.

Paper 1-type assessment: Soviet control over Eastern Europe

SOURCE A

A drawing on the wall of a Prague street in 1968.

QUESTIONS

Section A Questions

1a Study Source A. Do you think the cartoonist supported or opposed the Soviet invasion of Czechoslovakia in 1968? Support your answer by referring to details of the cartoon and your own knowledge. (6)

b Explain why the Soviet Union invaded Czechoslovakia in 1968. (9)

Section B Questions

2a What policies were followed by the government of Matyas Rakosi in Hungary up to 1956? (4)

b Explain why the West did not come to the aid of Hungary in 1956. (6)

c 'The most important reason for the collapse of Soviet control in eastern Europe in 1989 was the weakness of the Soviet economy'. Do you agree with this statement? Explain your answer. (10)

Glossary

anarchy political and social disorder
Anschluss union of Germany and Austria
anti-Semitic anti-Jewish
appeasement policy of making concessions in order to satisfy an aggressor e.g. Britain tried to avoid war by making concessions to Hitler
armistice agreement to stop fighting so that peace terms can be discussed
Aryan according to the Nazis, the 'master race': the pure, white, Caucasian race

Black Thursday the day the Wall Street Crash started in the USA, Thursday 24 October, 1929
Blitzkrieg German for 'lightning war', meaning a surprise attack
Bolshevik Russian revolutionary party led by Lenin: the name (meaning 'majority') refers to the 1903 split in the Social Democratic Party (see also 'Mensheviks')
Bonus Marchers First World War veterans who set up camp around Washington in 1932 demanding a 'bonus' payment promised by the government

capitalism economic system with limited government intervention, based on privately-owned business and the creation of profit
Cheka Lenin's secret police
coalition government formed by more than one political party
Cold War post-1945 conflict between communist East and capitalist West
collectivisation pooling of land in Russia which peasants worked together
communism system of government in which property is publicly owned, based on the theories of Karl Marx and intended to bring about a fairer society
concordat agreement between the Nazis and the Catholic church
Congress the parliament of the USA, consisting of two 'houses', the Senate and the House of Representatives
conscientious objectors men who refused to fight because of their anti-war beliefs
conscription compulsory military service

demilitarisation the removal of military forces from an area
democracy system of government whereby leaders are voted in to office by the people
desertion leaving the army without permission
dictatorship government by a ruler with complete power
disarmament reduction of armed forces
Duma Russian parliament

Enabling Law law giving Hitler the power to make laws without the Reichstag

fascism system of extreme right-wing, nationalistic views opposing democracy and free speech
Final Solution Nazi term for the policy of putting Jews to death
Five-Year Plans economic plans setting targets for all industrial factories and workers in the Soviet Union
Freikorps semi-official right-wing bands of soldiers in Germany after the First World War
Führer German for 'leader' and the title given to Hitler

Gestapo Nazi police force
Glasnost Russian term for 'openness': one of Gorbachev's policies for liberalising communist rule over the Soviet Union
Great Depression the economic slump following the Wall Street Crash in the USA, 1929
Great Purges when Stalin ordered thousands of his opponents to be killed or tried and imprisoned

Holocaust mass murder of Jews between 1941 and 1945

humanitarian for the benefit of the human race
hyperinflation period of rapid price rises

international arbitration the peaceful settlement of disputes by specially appointed international representatives
iron curtain imaginary boundary separating the capitalist West from the communist East

Kristallnacht German for 'the night of the broken glass' – the event of 9 November 1938 when Nazis attacked Jews and their property
Ku Klux Klan extremist, racist group that terrorised the black community, foreigners, Catholics and homosexuals in southern USA
kulaks wealthy peasants in the Soviet Union

Lebensraum German for 'living space', as when Hitler tried to gain more territory in Eastern Europe
Luftwaffe German airforce

mandate system system after the First World War by which colonies of the defeated powers were given by the League of Nations to the victorious powers to administer
Marshall Plan US provision of economic aid to European countries, announced in 1947, to prevent the spread of communism
Martial Law suspension of ordinary law in favour of military government
Mensheviks Russian revolutionary party (meaning 'minority') formed after the 1903 split of the Social Democratic Party (see also 'Bolsheviks')
militarism army discipline extended to political parties and everyday life
munitions military weapons

nationalism strong patriotic feeling leading to a sense of superiority over other nations
NATO North Atlantic Treaty Organisation: military alliance formed in 1949 of the European powers plus Canada and the USA
New Deal President Roosevelt's programme of legislation to cope with the effects of the Depression
NKVD Stalin's secret police in the Soviet Union

October Manifesto the Tsar's promise during the 1905 Revolution to give Russians a constitutional monarchy and an elected parliament

perestroika Russian for 'restructuring': one of Gorbachev's policies for liberalising communist rule over the USSR
plebiscite a referendum, when all electors can vote on an important public issue
Politburo the Cabinet of the Soviet Union
Prague Spring reforms in Czechoslovakia in 1968 before Warsaw Pact forces took control of the country
prohibition to ban something, such as the banning of the manufacture, sale and transport of alcohol in the USA after 1920
propaganda information that is presented in a way intended to influence how people think
puppet state state entirely controlled by another country
putsch attempt to gain political power by force

Red Army army created by Trotsky to defeat the Whites in the Russian Civil War, 1918-20
Red Guards unofficial military force which helped the Bolsheviks in the run-up to the November Revolution of 1917
Red Scare period of anti-communist propaganda and persecution in the USA
redistribution taking money from the rich to distribute to those most in need
Reichstag German parliament
reparations payments made by Germany to compensate countries after the First World War
republic state which does not have a monarch
russification Stalin's programme to undermine the cultures of ethnic minorities in order to unify the different national groups of the Soviet Union

sanctions measures taken against a country, such as stopping trade, in protest against the country's political actions

segregation policy of keeping black and white people separate

sharecroppers agricultural workers in southern USA who received a proportion of the crop instead of cash

slump economic depression resulting in a huge rise in unemployment

Solidarity powerful Polish trade union which spearheaded opposition to the country's communist government

soviets councils of workers and soldiers in Russia

Spartacists communist group in Germany after the First World War

Suffragettes women who campaigned for votes for women

Suffragists members of the National Union of Women's Suffrage Societies, a moderate body using peaceful means to campaign for votes for women

Supreme Court highest court in the USA

totalitarian regime form of government that allows no opposition

Truman Doctrine President Truman's pledge to help any country under threat from communism

Tsar/Tsarina Russia's absolute monarch and his wife

universal suffrage votes for all adult men and women

Untermenschen derogatory term meaning 'inferior peoples' applied by the Nazis to Jews, Eastern Europeans and black people

Vietcong South Vietnamese communist guerrillas

vietnamisation policy of withdrawing American troops from Vietnam while preparing the South Vietnamese army to fight on its own

Wall Street Crash the sudden collapse of the US stock market in October 1929

Warsaw Pact military alliance of the communist countries of Europe, established in 1955 in response to NATO

welfare state system of measures designed to ensure a basic minimum standard of living for all

Whites anti-communist forces in the Russian Civil War

Zemstvos local councils in pre-revolutionary Russia

Index